CHILTON'S
REPAIR & TUNE-UP GUIDE
DATSUN F10·310 NISSAN STANZA 1976-82

F10 1976-78
310 1979-82
Stanza 1982

Managing Editor KERRY A. FREEMAN, S.A.E.
Senior Editor RICHARD J. RIVELE, S.A.E.

President WILLIAM A. BARBOUR
Executive Vice President JAMES A. MIADES
Vice President and General Manager JOHN P. KUSHNERICK

CHILTON BOOK COMPANY
Radnor, Pennsylvania
19089

SAFETY NOTICE
Proper service and repair procedures are vital to the safe, reliable operation of all motor vehicles, as well as the personal safety of those performing repairs. This book outlines procedures for servicing and repairing vehicles using safe, effective methods. The procedures contain many NOTES, CAUTIONS and WARNINGS which should be followed along with standard safety procedures to eliminate the possibility of personal injury or improper service which could damage the vehicle or compromise its safety.

It is important to note that repair procedures and techniques, tools and parts for servicing motor vehicles, as well as the skill and experience of the individual performing the work vary widely. It is not possible to anticipate all of the conceivable ways or conditions under which vehicles may be serviced, or to provide cautions as to all of the possible hazards that may result. Standard and accepted safety precautions and equipment should be used when handling toxic or flammable fluids, and safety goggles or other protection should be used during cutting, grinding, chiseling, prying, or any other process that can cause material removal or projectiles.

Some procedures require the use of tools specially designed for a specific purpose. Before substituting another tool or procedure, you must be completely satisfied that neither your personal safety, nor the performance of the vehicle will be endangered.

Although information in this guide is based on industry sources and is as complete as possible at the time of publication, the possibility exists that the manufacturer made later changes which could not be included here. While striving for total accuracy, Chilton Book Company cannot assume responsibility for any errors, changes, or omissions that may occur in the compilation of this data.

PART NUMBERS
Part numbers listed in this reference are not recommendations by Chilton for any product by brand name. They are references that can be used with interchange manuals and aftermarket supplier catalogs to locate each brand supplier's discrete part number.

ACKNOWLEDGMENTS
The Chilton Book Company thanks the Nissan Motor Corporation in U.S.A., Gardena, California 90247, and Marsh Pontiac-Datsun, Ardmore, Pennsylvania, for their assistance in the preparation of this book.

Copyright © 1982 by Chilton Book Company
All Rights Reserved
Published in Radnor, Pa. by Chilton Book Company
and simultaneously in Canada
by VNR Publishers, 1410 Birchmount Road,
Scarborough, Ontario M1P 2E7

Manufactured in the United States of America
1234567890   1098765432

Chilton's Repair & Tune-Up Guide: Datsun F10, 310 and Nissan Stanza 1976–82
ISBN 0-8019-7196-9 pbk.
Library of Congress Catalog Card No. 81-70238

CONTENTS

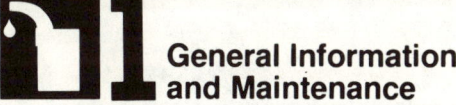
1 General Information and Maintenance
- 1 How to Use this Book
- 1 Tools and Equipment
- 4 Routine Maintenance and Lubrication

2 Tune-Up
- 18 Tune-Up Procedures
- 19 Tune-Up Specifications

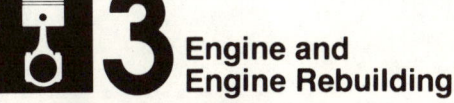
3 Engine and Engine Rebuilding
- 32 Engine Electrical System
- 38 Engine Service and Specifications
- 58 Engine Rebuilding

4 Emission Controls and Fuel System
- 80 Emission Control System and Service
- 95 Fuel System Service

5 Chassis Electrical
- 109 Accessory Service
- 113 Instrument Panel Service
- 116 Lights, Fuses and Flashers

90 Chilton's Fuel Economy and Tune-Up Tips

6 Clutch and Transmission
- 118 Manual Transmission
- 121 Clutch
- 126 Automatic Transmission

7 Suspension and Steering
- 128 Front Suspension
- 135 Rear Suspension
- 138 Steering

8 Brakes
- 148 Front Brakes
- 150 Rear Brakes
- 155 Brake Specifications

9 Body
- 160 Repairing Scratches and Small Dents
- 164 Repairing Rust
- 170 Body Care

10 Troubleshooting
- 175 Problem Diagnosis

207 Appendix
211 Index

Quick Reference Specifications For Your Vehicle

Fill in this chart with the most commonly used specifications for your vehicle. Specifications can be found in Chapters 1 through 3 or on the tune-up decal under the hood of the vehicle.

 ## Tune-Up

Firing Order_____

Spark Plugs:

    Type_____

    Gap (in.)_____

Point Gap (in.)_____

Dwell Angle (°)_____

Ignition Timing (°)_____

    Vacuum (Connected/Disconnected)_____

Valve Clearance (in.)

    Intake_____   Exhaust_____

Capacities

Engine Oil (qts)

    With Filter Change_____

    Without Filter Change_____

Cooling System (qts)_____

Manual Transmission (pts)_____

    Type_____

Automatic Transmission (pts)_____

    Type_____

Front Differential (pts)_____

    Type_____

Rear Differential (pts)_____

    Type_____

Transfer Case (pts)_____

    Type_____

FREQUENTLY REPLACED PARTS

Use these spaces to record the part numbers of frequently replaced parts.

PCV VALVE   **OIL FILTER**   **AIR FILTER**

Manufacturer_____   Manufacturer_____   Manufacturer_____

Part No._____   Part No._____   Part No._____

General Information and Maintenance

HOW TO USE THIS BOOK

This book is structured in ten easy to follow chapters, using as little mechanic's jargon as possible and highlighting important procedures with scores of illustrations. Everything from engine rebuilding to replacing your radiator cap is covered. Of course, even the best mechanic won't attempt a repair without the proper tools. That's why operations like rebuilding your transmission or differential assembly are not included here—they require a range of special tools which are too expensive to be useful to the average shade-tree mechanic.

Before tangling with any repairs, read through the entire section and make sure you have the time, tools and replacement parts necessary. This will save you the frustration of hoofing it down to the bus stop Monday morning because you forgot a widget or a what-cha-ma-call-it while making repairs Sunday afternoon.

Each section begins with a brief description of the particular system and a smattering of the theory behind it. When repairs involve a high level of technical know-how, we tell you how to remove the part and replace it with a new or overhauled unit. In this way you can shave dollars off your regular labor costs.

A few basic mechanic's rules should be mentioned here. First, whenever the left side of the vehicle is referred to, it means the driver's side of the car. The right side is the passenger's side. Second, most screws and nuts and bolts are removed by turning them counterclockwise and tightened by turning clockwise. Never crawl under a car supported only by a floor or bumper jack . . . use support stands! Never smoke or position an exposed flame near a battery or any part of the fuel system. Common sense is your best safeguard against injury.

TOOLS AND EQUIPMENT

The following list contains the basic tools needed to perform most of the procedures described in this guide. Your Datsun is built with metric screws and bolts; if you don't already have a set of metric wrenches—buy them. Standard wrenches are either too loose or too tight a fit on metric fasteners.

1. Metric sockets, also a $^{13}/_{18}$ in. spark plug socket. If possible, buy various length socket drive extensions. One break in this department is that the metric sockets available in the US will all fit the ratchet handles and extensions you may already have (¼, ⅜, and ½ in. drive);

2 GENERAL INFORMATION AND MAINTENANCE

2. Set of metric combination (one end open and one box) wrenches;
3. Spark plug wire gauge;
4. Flat feeler gauge for breaker points and valve lash checking;
5. Slot and phillips heads screwdrivers;
6. Timing light, preferably a DC battery hook-up type;
7. Dwell/tachometer;
8. Oil can filler spout;
9. Oil filter strap wrench. Makes removal of a tight filter much simpler. Never use to install filter;
10. Pair of channel lock pliers. Always handy to have;
11. Two sturdy jackstands—cinder blocks, bricks, and other makeshift supports are just not safe.

In addition to these basic tools, there are several other tools and gauges you may find useful. These include:
1. A compression gauge. The screw-in type is slower to use but eliminates the possibility of a faulty reading due to escaping pressure;
2. A manifold vacuum gauge;
3. A test light;
4. An induction meter. This is used for determining whether or not there is current in a wire. These are handy for use if a wire is broken somewhere in a wiring harness.

As a final note, you will probably find a torque wrench necessary for all but the most basic work. The beam type models are perfectly adequate, although the newer click type are more precise.

NOTE: *Datsun special tools referred to in this guide are available through Kent-Moore Corporation, 29784 Little Mack, Roseville, Michigan 48066. For Canada, contact Kent-Moore of Canada, Ltd., 2395 Cawthra Mississauga, Ontario, Canada L5A 3P2.*

SERVICING YOUR CAR SAFELY

It is virtually impossible to anticipate all of the hazards involved with automotive maintenance and service, but care and common sense will prevent most accidents.

The rules of safety for mechanics range from "don't smoke around gasoline," to "use the proper tool for the job." The trick to avoiding injuries is to develop safe work habits and take every possible precaution.

Dos

• Do keep a fire extinguisher and first aid kit within easy reach.
• Do wear safety glasses or goggles when cutting, drilling, grinding or prying, even if you have 20–20 vision. If you wear glasses for the sake of vision, they should be made of hardened glass that can serve also as safety glasses, or wear safety goggles over your regular glasses.
• Do shield your eyes whenever you work around the battery. Batteries contain sulphuric acid. In case of contact with the eyes or skin, flush the area with water or a mixture of water and baking soda and get medical attention immediately.
• Do use safety stands for any undercar service. Jacks are for raising vehicles; safety stands are for making sure the vehicle stays raised until you want to come down. Whenever the car is raised, block the wheels remaining on the ground and set the parking brake.
• Do use adequate ventilation when working with any chemicals or hazardous materials. Like carbon monoxide, the asbestos dust resulting from brake lining wear can be poisonous in sufficient quantities.
• Do disconnect the negative battery cable when working on the electrical system. The secondary ignition system can contain up to 40,000 volts.
• Do follow manufacturer's directions whenever working with potentially hazardous materials. Both brake fluid and antifreeze are poisonous if taken internally.
• Do properly maintain your tools. Loose hammerheads, mushroomed punches and chisels, frayed or poorly grounded electrical cords, excessively worn screwdrivers, spread wrenches (open end), cracked sockets, slipping ratchets, or faulty droplight sockets can cause accidents.
• Do use the proper size and type of tool for the job being done.

Always use jackstands or ramps when working under your car

GENERAL INFORMATION AND MAINTENANCE

• Do when possible, pull on a wrench handle rather than push on it, and adjust your stance to prevent a fall.

• Do be sure that adjustable wrenches are tightly closed on the nut or bolt and pulled so that the face is on the side of the fixed jaw.

• Do select a wrench or socket that fits the nut or bolt. The wrench or socket should sit straight, not cocked.

• Do strike squarely with a hammer; avoid glancing blows.

• Do set the parking brake and block the drive wheels if the work requires the engine running.

Don'ts

• Don't run an engine in a garage or anywhere else without proper ventilation—EVER! Carbon monoxide is poisonous; it takes a long time to leave the human body and you can build up a deadly supply of it in your system by simply breathing in a little every day. You may not realize you are slowly poisoning yourself. Always use power vents, windows, fans or open the garage doors.

• Don't work around moving parts while wearing a necktie or other loose clothing. Short sleeves are much safer than long, loose sleeves; hard-toed shoes with neoprene soles protect your toes and give a better grip on slippery surfaces. Jewelry such as watches, fancy belt buckles, beads or body adornment of any kind is not safe working around a car. Long hair should be hidden under a hat or cap.

• Don't use pockets for toolboxes. A fall or bump can drive a screwdriver deep into your body. Even a wiping cloth hanging from the back pocket can wrap around a spinning shaft or fan.

• Don't smoke when working around gasoline, cleaning solvent or other flammable material.

• Don't smoke when working around the battery. When the battery is being charged, it gives off explosive hydrogen gas.

• Don't use gasoline to wash your hands; there are excellent soaps available. Gasoline may contain lead, and lead can enter the body through a cut, accumulating in the body until you are very ill. Gasoline also removes all the natural oils from the skin so that bone dry hands will suck up oil and grease.

• Don't service the air conditioning system unless you are equipped with the necessary tools and training. The refrigerant, R-12, is extremely cold when compressed, and when released into the air will instantly freeze any surface it contacts, including your eyes. Although the refrigerant is normally non-toxic, R-12 becomes a deadly poisonous gas in the presence of an open flame. One good whiff of the vapors from burning refrigerant can be fatal.

SERIAL NUMBER IDENTIFICATION

Chassis

The chassis serial number is stamped into the firewall. The model designation, such as 310, precedes the serial number. The chassis number is also located on a dashboard plate which is visible through the windshield.

Vehicle Identification Plate

The vehicle identification plate is attached to the firewall. This plate gives the vehicle model, engine displacement in cc, SAE horsepower rating, wheelbase, engine number, and chassis number.

Engine

The engine number is stamped on the right side top edge of the cylinder block on all models. The engine serial number is preceded by the engine model code.

Engine ID number

Transmission

The transmission/transaxle number is stamped on the front upper face of the transmission case.

4 GENERAL INFORMATION AND MAINTENANCE

Locations of various identification plates

Transmission ID number

Air filter replacement

ROUTINE MAINTENANCE

Air Cleaner

All Datsuns covered in this guide are equipped with a disposable paper cartridge air cleaner element. At every tuneup, or sooner if the car is operated in a dusty area, undo the wing nut, remove the housing top, and withdraw the element. Check the element. Replace the filter if it is extremely dirty. Loose dust can sometimes be removed by striking the filter against a hard surface several times or by blowing through it with compressed air. The filter should be replaced every 24,000 miles. Before installing either the original or a replacement filter, wipe out the inside of the air cleaner housing with a clean rag or paper towel. Install the paper air cleaner filter, seat the top cover on the bottom housing, and tighten the wing nut.

NOTE: *Some flat, cartridge type air cleaner elements have the word "UP" printed on them. Be sure the side with "UP" on it faces up.*

Air Induction Valve Filter

This filter is located in the air cleaner of late model Datsuns, both fuel injected and carburetor models. To replace it, remove the screws and remove the valve filter case. Install the new filter, paying attention to which direction the valve is facing so that exhaust gases will not flow backwards through the system.

GENERAL INFORMATION AND MAINTENANCE

Air induction valve filter replacement

Positive Crankcase Ventilation Valve

This valve feeds crankcase blow-by gases into the intake manifold to be burned with the normal air/fuel mixture. The PCV valve should be replaced every 24,000 miles. Make sure that all PCV connections are tight. Check that the connecting hoses are clear and not clogged. Replace any brittle or broken hoses.

To replace the valve, which is located in the intake manifold directly below the carburetor:

1. Squeeze the hose clamp with pliers and remove the hose.
2. Using a wrench, unscrew the PCV valve and remove the valve.
3. Disconnect the ventilation hoses and flush with solvent.
4. Install the new PCV valve and replace the hoses and clamp.

1. Seal type oil level gauge
2. Baffle plate
3. Flame arrester
4. Filter
5. P.C.V. valve
6. Steel net
7. Baffle plate

Typical PCV system

Fuel Evaporative Emissions System

Check the evaporation control system every 12,000 miles. Check the fuel and vapor lines for proper connections and correct routing as well as condition. Replace damaged or deteriorated parts as necessary.

A carbon filled canister stores fuel vapors until the engine is started and the vapors are drawn into the combustion chambers and burned.

To check the operation of the carbon canister purge control valve, disconnect the rubber hose between the canister control valve and the T-fitting, at the T-fitting. Apply vacuum to the hose leading to the control valve. The vacuum condition should be maintained indefinitely. If the control valve leaks, remove the top cover of the valve and check for a dislocated or cracked diaphragm. If the diaphragm is damaged, a repair kit containing a

1. Cover
2. Diaphragm
3. Retainer
4. Diaphragm spring

Typical vapor canister

Canister filter replacement

GENERAL INFORMATION AND MAINTENANCE

new diaphragm, retainer, and spring is available and should be installed.

The carbon canister has an air filter in the bottom of the canister. The filter element should be checked once a year or every 12,000 miles; more frequently if the car is operated in dusty areas. Replace the filter by pulling it out of the bottom of the canister and installing a new one.

Heat Control Valve

The heat control valve, or Early Fuel Evaporative System, is a thermostatically operated valve in the exhaust manifold. It closes when the engine is warming up to direct hot exhaust gases to the intake manifold, in order to pre-heat the incoming air/fuel mixture. If it sticks shut, the result will be frequent stalling during warmup, especially in cold or damp weather. If it sticks open, the result will be a rough idle after the engine is warm.

The heat control valve should be checked for free operation every six months or 6,000 miles. Simply give the counterweight a twirl (engine cold) to make sure that no binding exists. If the valve sticks, apply a heat control solvent to the ends of the shaft. This type of solvent is available in auto parts stores. Sometimes lightly rapping the end of the shaft with a hammer (engine hot) will break it loose. If this fails, the components will have to be removed from the car for repair.

NOTE: *The 1980 and later engines do not use the heat control valve. Instead, these engines warm the fuel mixture by a coolant passage under the carburetor. No maintenance is required.*

Belts

TENSION CHECKING, ADJUSTING AND REPLACEMENT

Check the belts driving the fan, air pump, air conditioning compressor, and the alternator for cracks, fraying, wear, and tension every 6,000 miles. It is recommended that the belts be replaced every 24 months or 24,000 miles. Belt deflection at the midpoint of the longest span between pulleys should not be more than $7/16$ of an inch with 22 lbs of pressure applied to the belt.

To adjust the tension on all components except the air conditioning compressor, power steering pump, and some late model air pumps, loosen the pivot and mounting bolts of the component which the belt is driving, then, using a wooden lever, pry the component toward or away from the engine until the proper tension is achieved.

CAUTION: *An overtight belt will wear out the pulley bearings on the assorted components.*

Tighten the component mounting bolts securely. If a new belt is installed, recheck the tension after driving about 1,000 miles.

NOTE: *The replacement of the inner belt on multi-belted engines may require the removal of the outer belts.*

Belt tension adjustments for the factory installed air conditioning compressor and power steering pump are made at the idler pulley. The idler pulley is the smallest of the three pulleys. At the top of the slotted bracket holding the idler pulley there is a bolt which is used to either raise or lower the pulley. To free the bolt for adjustment, it is necessary to loosen the lock nut in the face of the idler pulley. After adjusting the belt tension,

EXHAUST GAS FLOWS:
◀ VALVE CLOSED
◀■■ VALVE OPENED

1. Intake manifold
2. Stove gasket
3. Manifold stove
4. Heat shield plate
5. Snap ring
6. Counterweight
7. Key
8. Stopper pin
9. Screw
10. Thermostat spring
11. Heat control valve
12. Control valve shaft
13. Exhaust manifold
14. Cap
15. Bushing
16. Coil spring

Heat riser used on earlier models with A series engines

GENERAL INFORMATION AND MAINTENANCE

How to Spot Worn V-Belts

V-Belts are vital to efficient engine operation—they drive the fan, water pump and other accessories. They require little maintenance (occasional tightening) but they will not last forever. Slipping or failure of the V-belt will lead to overheating. If your V-belt looks like any of these, it should be replaced.

Cracking or weathering

This belt has deep cracks, which cause it to flex. Too much flexing leads to heat build-up and premature failure. These cracks can be caused by using the belt on a pulley that is too small. Notched belts are available for small diameter pulleys.

Softening (grease and oil)

Oil and grease on a belt can cause the belt's rubber compounds to soften and separate from the reinforcing cords that hold the belt together. The belt will first slip, then finally fail altogether.

Glazing

Glazing is caused by a belt that is slipping. A slipping belt can cause a run-down battery, erratic power steering, overheating or poor accessory performance. The more the belt slips, the more glazing will be built up on the surface of the belt. The more the belt is glazed, the more it will slip. If the glazing is light, tighten the belt.

Worn cover

The cover of this belt is worn off and is peeling away. The reinforcing cords will begin to wear and the belt will shortly break. When the belt cover wears in spots or has a rough jagged appearance, check the pulley grooves for roughness.

Separation

This belt is on the verge of breaking and leaving you stranded. The layers of the belt are separating and the reinforcing cords are exposed. It's just a matter of time before it breaks completely.

8 GENERAL INFORMATION AND MAINTENANCE

tighten the lock nut in the face of the idler pulley.

NOTE: *1980 and later California models come equipped with special fan belts which, if loose, generate friction heat by slipping and shrink, taking up the slack.*

The optional air conditioning drive belt is adjusted in a similar fashion.

Cooling System

Your Datsun's internal combustion engine generates power by the controlled explosion of a mixture of gasoline and air in the combustion chamber of each cylinder. The piston of each cylinder is at the top of its upward travel when the explosion occurs and subsequently is forced downward, creating mechanical power. But not all of the force of the ignited fuel mixture is expended in forcing the piston down; some is released as heat, and the job of the cooling system is to effectively remove that heat from the engine before it raises the cylinder head and block temperature too greatly.

To drain the cooling system, allow the engine to cool down BEFORE ATTEMPTING TO REMOVE THE RADIATOR CAP. Then turn the cap until it hisses. Wait until all pressure is off the cap before removing it completely. To avoid burns and scalding, always handle a warm radiator cap with a heavy rag. After the radiator cap is off, drain the radiator by loosening the petcock or plug at the bottom of the radiator. See "Coolant" section under "Fluid Level Checks" in this chapter for refilling procedures.

Air Conditioning

This book contains no repair or maintenance procedures for the air conditioning system. It is recommended that any such repairs be left to the experts, whose personnel are well aware of the hazards and who have the proper equipment.

CAUTION: *The compressed refrigerant used in the air conditioning system expands into the atmosphere at a temperature of −21.7° F or lower. This will freeze any surface, including your eyes, that it contacts. In addition, the refrigerant decomposes into a poisonous gas in the presence of flame. Do not open or disconnect any part of the air conditioning system.*

SIGHT GLASS CHECK

You can safely make a few simple checks to determine if your air conditioning system needs service. The tests work best if the temperature is warm (about 70° F).

NOTE: *If your vehicle is equipped with an after-market air conditioner, the following system check may not apply. You should contact the manufacturer of the unit for instructions on systems checks.*

1. Place the automatic transmission in Park or the manual transmission in Neutral. Set the parking brake.
2. Run the engine at a fast idle (about 1,500 rpm) either with the help of a friend, or by temporarily readjusting the idle speed screw.
3. Set the controls for maximum cold with the blower on high.
4. Locate the sight glass in one of the system lines. Usually it is on the left alongside the top of the radiator.
5. If you see bubbles, the system must be recharged. Very likely there is a leak at some point.
6. If there are no bubbles, there is either no refrigerant at all or the system is fully charged. Feel the two hoses going to the belt-driven compressor. If they are both at the same temperature, the system is empty and must be recharged.
7. If one hose (high-pressure) is warm and the other (low-pressure) is cold, the system may be all right. However, you are probably making these tests because you think there is something wrong, so proceed to the next step.
8. Have an assistant in the car turn the fan control on and off to operate the compressor clutch. Watch the sight glass.
9. If bubbles appear when the clutch is disengaged and disappear when it is engaged, the system is properly charged.
10. If the refrigerant takes more than 45 seconds to bubble when the clutch is disengaged, the system is overcharged. This usually causes poor cooling at low speeds.

CAUTION: *If it is determined that the system has a leak, it should be corrected as soon as possible. Leaks may allow moisture to enter and cause a very expensive rust problem.*

NOTE: *Exercise the air conditioner for a few minutes, every two weeks or so, during the cold months. This avoids the possibility of the compressor seals drying out from lack of lubrication.*

GENERAL INFORMATION AND MAINTENANCE

How to Spot Bad Hoses

Both the upper and lower radiator hoses are called upon to perform difficult jobs in an inhospitable environment. They are subject to nearly 18 psi at under hood temperatures often over 280°F., and must circulate nearly 7500 gallons of coolant an hour—3 good reasons to have good hoses.

Swollen hose

A good test for any hose is to feel it for soft or spongy spots. Frequently these will appear as swollen areas of the hose. The most likely cause is oil soaking. This hose could burst at any time, when hot or under pressure.

Cracked hose

Cracked hoses can usually be seen but feel the hoses to be sure they have not hardened; a prime cause of cracking. This hose has cracked down to the reinforcing cords and could split at any of the cracks.

Frayed hose end (due to weak clamp)

Weakened clamps frequently are the cause of hose and cooling system failure. The connection between the pipe and hose has deteriorated enough to allow coolant to escape when the engine is hot.

Debris in cooling system

Debris, rust and scale in the cooling system can cause the inside of a hose to weaken. This can usually be felt on the outside of the hose as soft or thinner areas.

10 GENERAL INFORMATION AND MAINTENANCE

Hoses

HOSE REPLACEMENT

Remove the radiator cap and drain the radiator into a clean pan if you are going to reuse the old coolant. Remove the hose clamps and remove the hose by either cutting it off or twisting it to break its seal on the radiator and engine coolant inlets. When installing the new hose, do not overtighten the hose clamps or you might cut the hose. Refill the radiator with coolant, run the engine with the radiator cap on and then recheck the coolant level.

Fluid Level Checks

ENGINE OIL

The best time to check the engine oil is before operating the engine or after it has been sitting for at least 10 minutes in order to gain an accurate reading. This will allow the oil to drain back in the crankcase. To check the engine oil level, make sure that the vehicle is resting on a level surface, remove the oil dipstick, wipe it clean and reinsert the stick firmly for an accurate reading. The oil dipstick has two marks to indicate high and low oil level. If the oil is at or below the "low level" mark on the dipstick, oil should be added as necessary. The oil level should be maintained in the safety margin, neither going above the "high level" mark or below the "low level" mark.

Oil dipstick markings

TRANSMISSION

Manual

Check the level of the lubricant in the transmission every 3,000 miles. The lubricant level should be even with the bottom of the filler hole. Hold in on the filler plug when unscrewing it. When you are sure that all of the threads of the plug are free of the transmission case, move the plug away from the case

Manual transaxle fill plug location

slightly. If lubricant begins to flow out of the transmission, then you know it is full. If not, add SAE90 gear oil as necessary. It is recommended that the transmission lubricant be changed every 24,000 miles.

Automatic

Check the level of the automatic transmission fluid every 2,000 miles. There is a dipstick at the right rear of the engine under the hood. It has a scale on each side, one for COLD and the other for HOT. The transmission is considered hot after 15 miles of highway driving.

Park the car on a level surface with the engine running. If the transmission is not hot, shift into Drive, Low, then Neutral or Park. Set the handbrake and block the wheels.

Remove the dipstick, wipe it clean, then reinsert it firmly. Remove the dipstick and check the fluid level on the appropriate scale. The level should be at the "Full" mark.

If the level is below the "Full" mark, add Type A or DEXRON® type automatic transmission fluid as necessary, with the engine running, through the dipstick tube. Do not overfill, as this may cause the transmission to malfunction and damage itself.

Automatic transaxle dipstick

BRAKE AND CLUTCH MASTER CYLINDER

Check the levels of brake fluid in the brake and clutch master cylinder reservoirs every

GENERAL INFORMATION AND MAINTENANCE 11

Typical brake master cylinder reservoir

Typical clutch master cylinder

3,000 miles. The fluid level should be maintained to a level not below the bottom line on the reservoirs and not above the top line. Any sudden decrease in the level in either of the three reservoirs (two for the brakes and one for the clutch) indicates a probable leak in that particular system and the possibility of a leak should be checked out.

COOLANT

Check the coolant level every time you change the oil. Check for loose connections and signs of deterioration of the coolant hoses. Maintain the coolant level 3 in. below the level of the filler neck when the engine is cold. Add a mixture of 70% to 50% water and 30% to 50% ethylene glycol antifreeze as necessary. Never remove the radiator cap when the vehicle is hot or overheated. Wait until it has cooled. Place a thick cloth over the radiator cap to shield yourself from the heat and turn the radiator cap *slightly* until the sound of escaping pressure can be heard. *Do not turn any more.* Allow the pressure to release gradually. When no more pressure can be heard escaping, then remove the cap with the heavy cloth *cautiously*. Never add cold water to an overheated engine while the engine is not running. Run the engine until it reaches normal operating temperature after filling the radiator to make sure that the thermostat has opened and all air is bled from the system.

REAR AXLE

Check the rear axle lubricant every 6,000 miles. Remove the filler plug in the axle housing. The lubricant should be up to the bottom of the filler hole with the vehicle resting on a level surface. Add SAE90 gear oil as necessary to bring the lubricant up to the proper level.

STEERING GEAR

Check the level of the lubricant in the steering gear every 12,000 miles. If the level is low, check for leakage. An oily film is not considered a leak; solid grease must be present. Change the lubricant every 36,000 miles. Use steering gear lubricant. The lubricant is added and checked through the filler plug hole in the top of the steering gear.

POWER STEERING RESERVOIR

Some models are equipped with power steering.

Check the oil level in the reservoir by checking the side of the dipstick marked "HOT" after running the vehicle, or the side marked "COLD" when the car has not been used. In each case, fluid should reach the appropriate full line. Check the fluid level often. When refilling, use DEXRON® ATF. The unit holds approximately 1½ qts. See chapter 8, "Suspension and Steering" for system bleeding procedures.

BATTERY

The battery is located in the engine compartment. Routinely check the battery electrolyte level and specific gravity. A few minutes occasionally spent monitoring battery condition is worth saving hours of frustration when your car won't start due to a dead battery. Only distilled water should be used to top up the battery, as tap water, in many areas, contains harmful minerals. Two tools which will

Always check the gasket in the radiator cap when checking coolant level

GENERAL INFORMATION AND MAINTENANCE

Make sure the battery electrolite is at the bottom of the filler holes

facilitate battery maintenance are a hydrometer and a squeeze bulb filler. These are cheap and widely available at automotive parts stores, hardware stores, etc. The specific gravity of the electrolyte should be between 1.27 and 1.20. Keep the top of the battery clean, as a film of dirt can sometimes completely discharge a battery. A solution of baking soda and water may be used to clean the top surface, but be careful to flush this off with clear water and that none of the solution enters the filler holes. Clean the battery posts and clamps with a wire brush to eliminate corrosion deposits. Special clamp and terminal cleaning brushes are available for just this purpose. Lightly coat the posts and clamps with petroleum jelly or chassis grease after cleaning them.

Periodically clean the battery terminals and posts

Tires

Check the air pressure in your tires every few weeks. Make sure that the tires are cool, as you will get a false reading when the tires are heated because air pressure increases with temperature. A decal tells you the proper tire pressure for the standard equipment tires.

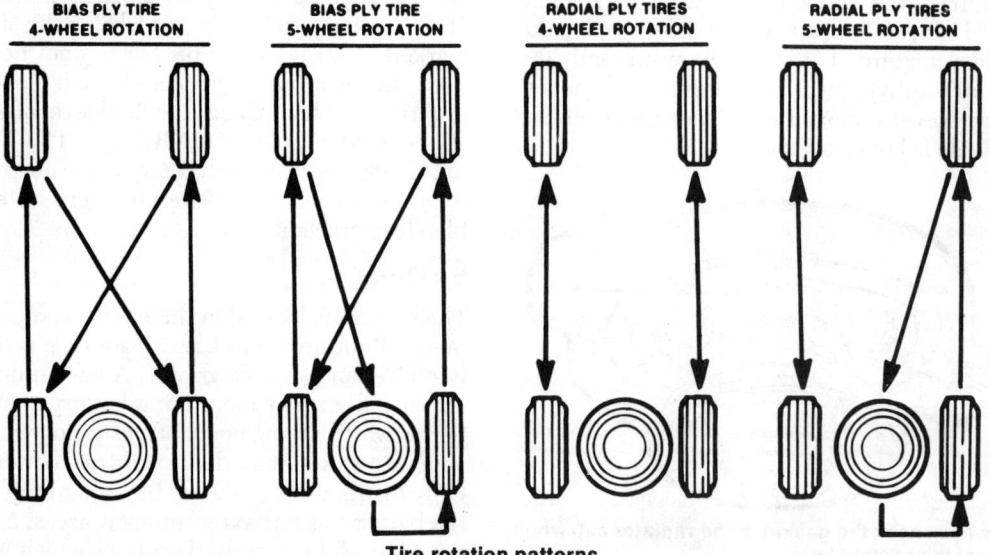

Tire rotation patterns

GENERAL INFORMATION AND MAINTENANCE

Capacities

Year	Model	Engine Crankcase with Filter (qts)	Transaxle (pts) 4-sp	Transaxle (pts) 5-sp	Auto. Total	Fuel Tank (gal)	Cooling System (qts)
1976–78	F10	3.6	4.9	4.9	—	10.6①	7.0
1979–81	310	3.4	4.9	4.9	—	13.25	6.25
1982	310	4.12	4.9	5.75	12.75	13.25	6.50
	Stanza	4.12	—	5.75	12.75	14.25	6.4

① Wagon: 9.1

Naturally, when you replace tires you will want to get the correct tire pressures for the new ones from the dealer or manufacturer. It pays to buy a tire pressure gauge to keep in the car, since those at service stations are usually inaccurate or broken.

While you are checking the tire pressure, take a look at the tread. The tread should be wearing evenly across the tire. Excessive wear in the center of the tread could indicate overinflation. Excessive wear on the outer edges could indicate underinflation. An irregular wear pattern is usually a sign of incorrect front wheel alignment or wheel balance. A front end that is out of alignment will usually pull the car to one side of a flat road when the steering wheel is released. Incorrect wheel balance will produce vibration in the steering wheel, while unbalanced rear wheels will result in floor or trunk vibration.

Rotating the tires every 6,000 miles or so will result in increased tread life. Use the correct pattern for your tire switching. Most automotive experts agree that radial tires are better all around performers, giving longer wear and better handling. An added benefit which you should consider when purchasing tires is that radials have less rolling resistance and can give up to a 10% increase in fuel economy over a bias-ply tire.

Tires of different construction should never be mixed. Always replace tires in sets of four or five when switching tire types and never substitute a belted tire for a bias-ply, a radial for a belted tire, etc. An occasional pressure check and periodic rotation could make your tires last much longer than a neglected set and maintain the safety margin which was designed into them.

Fuel Filter

The fuel filter on all models is a disposable plastic unit. It's located on the right inner fender. The filter should be replaced at least every 24,000 miles. A dirty filter will starve the engine and cause poor running.

REPLACEMENT

1. Locate fuel filter on right-side of the engine compartment.
2. Disconnect the inlet and outlet hoses from the fuel filter. Make certain that the inlet hose (bottom) doesn't fall below the fuel tank level or the gasoline will drain out.
3. Pry the fuel filter from its clip and replace the assembly.
4. Replace the inlet and outlet lines; secure the hose clamps to prevent leaks.
5. Start the engine and check for leaks.

LUBRICATION

Oil and Fuel Recommendations

Your Datsun is designed to operate on lead-free fuel. The octane ratings are listed on the inside of the fuel filler door, but these need only be checked when traveling outside of the United States. Should you find the gasoline available, say in Mexico, to be of too low an octane, mix enough Premium to raise the octane level. No benefit will be derived from running a higher octane gasoline than that recommended.

Oil must be selected with regard to the anticipated temperatures during the period before the next oil change. Using the chart, se-

14 GENERAL INFORMATION AND MAINTENANCE

Typical fuel filter location

Oil Viscosity Selection Chart

	Anticipated Temperature Range	SAE Viscosity
Multi-grade	Above 32°F	10W—40 10W—50 20W—40 20W—50 10W—30
	May be used as low as −10°F	10W—30 10W—40
	Consistently below 10°F	5W—20 5W—30
Single-grade	Above 32°F	30
	Temperature between +32°F and −10°F	10W

lect the oil viscosity for the lowest expected temperature and you will be assured of easy cold starting and sufficient engine protection. The oil you pour into your Datsun engine should have the designation "SE or SE/SF" marked on the top of its container.

Oil Changes

The mileage figures given in your owner's manual are the Datsun recommended intervals for oil and filter changes assuming average driving. If your Datsun is being used under dusty, polluted, or off-road conditions, change the oil and filter sooner than specified. The same thing goes for cars driven in stop-and-go traffic or only for short distances.

Always drain the oil after the engine has been running long enough to bring it to operating temperature. Hot oil will flow easier and more contaminants will be removed along

GENERAL INFORMATION AND MAINTENANCE

with the oil than if it were drained cold. You will need a large capacity drain pan, which you can purchase at any store which sells automotive parts. Another necessity is containers for the used oil. You will find that plastic bottles, such as those used for bleach or fabric softener, make excellent storage jugs. One ecologically desirable solution to the used oil disposal problem is to find a cooperative gas station owner who will allow you to dump your used oil into his tank. Another is to keep the oil for use around the house as a preservative on fences, railroad tie borders, etc.

Datsun recommends changing both the oil and filter during the first oil change and the filter every other oil change thereafter. For the small price of an oil filter, it's cheap insurance to replace the filter at every oil change. One of the larger filter manufacturers points out in its advertisements that not changing the filter leaves one quart of dirty oil in the engine. This claim is true and should be kept in mind when changing your oil.

CHANGING YOUR ENGINE OIL

1. Run the engine until it reaches normal operating temperature.
2. Jack up the front of the car and support it on safety stands if necessary to gain access to the filter.
3. Slide a drain pan of at least 6 quarts capacity under the oil pan.
4. Loosen the drain plug. Turn the plug out by hand. By keeping an inward pressure on the plug as you unscrew it, oil won't escape past the threads and you can remove it without being burned by hot oil.
5. Allow the oil to drain completely and then install the drain plug. Don't overtighten the plug, or you'll be buying a new pan or a trick replacement plug for buggered threads.
6. Using a strap wrench, remove the oil filter. Keep in mind that it's holding about one quart of dirty, hot oil.

Apply a light coat of oil to the filter gasket before installation

7. Empty the old filter into the drain pan and dispose of the filter.
8. Using a clean rag, wipe off the filter adapter on the engine block. Be sure that the rag doesn't leave any lint which could clog an oil passage.
9. Coat the rubber gasket on the filter with fresh oil. Spin it onto the engine *by hand;* when the gasket touches the adapter surface give it another ½–¾ turn. No more, or you'll squash the gasket and it will leak.
10. Refill the engine with the correct amount of fresh oil. See the "Capacities" chart.
11. Crank the engine over several times and then start it. If the oil pressure "idiot light" doesn't go out or the pressure gauge shows zero, shut the engine down and find out what's wrong.
12. If the oil pressure is OK and there are no leaks, shut the engine off and lower the car.

Transmission

MANUAL

Change the transmission lubricant in your manual transmission every 36,000 miles as follows:

1. Park the car on a level surface and apply the parking brake. Jack up the car and support it on stands.

Removing the oil filter with a strap wrench

Manual transaxle drain plug

2. Remove the oil filler plug (the upper one).
3. Place a drain pan under the drain plug in the transmission bottom pan.
4. Slowly remove the drain plug keeping an upward pressure on it until you can quickly pull it out.
5. Allow all of the old gear oil to drain and then replace the plug. Don't overtighten it.
6. Fill the transmission with SAE 90 gear oil. Refill with the quantity shown in the "Capacities" chart. An oil suction gun or squeeze bulb filler are handy for this chore and can be used for the rear axle, too.
7. Replace the filler plug and lower the car.

AUTOMATIC

The transmission fluid in an automatic transmission should be changed every 24,000 miles of normal driving or every 12,000 miles of driving under abnormal or severe conditions. The fluid should be drained immediately after the vehicle has been driven, but before it has had the chance to cool. Follow the procedure given below:
1. Drain the automatic transmission fluid from the transmission into a large drain pan, by removing the transmission drain plug.
2. Pour the same amount of Dexron® II automatic transmission fluid, which was drained from the oil pan, in through the filler pipe. Make sure that the funnel, container, hose, or any other item used to assist in filling the transmission is clean.
3. Start the engine. Do NOT race it. Allow the engine to idle for a few minutes.
4. Place the selector lever in Park and apply the parking brake. With the transmission fluid at operating temperatures, check the fluid level; add fluid to bring the level to the "FULL" mark on the dip-stick.

Chassis Greasing

Datsun doesn't install lubrication fittings in lube points on the steering linkage or suspension. You can buy metric threaded fittings to grease these points or use a pointed, rubber tip end on your grease gun. Lubricate all joints equipped with a plug every 24,000 miles. Replace the plugs after lubrication.

PUSHING AND TOWING

All cars sold outside of California, with manual transmission, and Canadian cars with manual transmissions can be pushed started. Cars with automatic transmissions may not be push started. Check to make sure that the bumpers of both vehicles are aligned so neither will be damaged. Be sure that all electrical system components are turned off (headlights, heater blower, etc.). Turn on the ignition switch. Place the shift lever in third or fourth gear and push in the clutch pedal. At about 15 mph, signal the driver of the pushing vehicle to fall back, depress the accelerator pedal and release the clutch pedal slowly. The engine should start.

The manufacturer advises against trying to tow-start your Datsun for fear of ramming the tow-vehicle when the engine starts.

Both manual and automatic Datsuns may be towed for short distances and at speeds no more than 20 mph. If the car must be towed a great distance, it should be done with the drive wheels off the ground.

JUMP STARTING

Jump starting is the favored method of starting a car with a dead battery. Make sure that the cables are properly connected, negative-to-negative and positive-to-positive, or you stand a chance of damaging the electrical systems of both cars.

JACKING

Never use the tire changing jack for anything other than that. If you intend to use this tool to perform your own maintenance, a good scissors or small hydraulic jack and two sturdy jackstands would be a wise purchase. Always chock the wheels when changing a tire or working beneath the car. It cannot be overemphasized, CLIMBING UNDER A CAR SUPPORTED BY JUST THE JACK IS EXTREMELY DANGEROUS.

GENERAL INFORMATION AND MAINTENANCE

JUMP STARTING A DEAD BATTERY

The chemical reaction in a battery produces explosive hydrogen gas. This is the safe way to jump start a dead battery, reducing the chances of an accidental spark that could cause an explosion.

Jump Starting Precautions

1. Be sure both batteries are of the same voltage.
2. Be sure both batteries are of the same polarity (have the same grounded terminal).
3. Be sure the vehicles are not touching.
4. Be sure the vent cap holes are not obstructed.
5. Do not smoke or allow sparks around the battery.
6. In cold weather, check for frozen electrolyte in the battery.
7. Do not allow electrolyte on your skin or clothing.
8. Be sure the electrolyte is not frozen.

Jump Starting Procedure

1. Determine voltages of the two batteries; they must be the same.
2. Bring the starting vehicle close (they must not touch) so that the batteries can be reached easily.
3. Turn off all accessories and both engines. Put both cars in Neutral or Park and set the handbrake.
4. Cover the cell caps with a rag—do not cover terminals.
5. If the terminals on the run-down battery are heavily corroded, clean them.
6. Identify the positive and negative posts on both batteries and connect the cables in the order shown.
7. Start the engine of the starting vehicle and run it at fast idle. Try to start the car with the dead battery. Crank it for no more than 10 seconds at a time and let it cool off for 20 seconds in between tries.
8. If it doesn't start in 3 tries, there is something else wrong.
9. Disconnect the cables in the reverse order.
10. Replace the cell covers and dispose of the rags.

Make certain vehicles do not touch

This hook-up for negative ground cars only

Tune-Up

TUNE-UP PROCEDURES

The following procedures are specific ones for your Datsun. To help you should the car need more than a regular tune-up. See Chapter 10, "Troubleshooting," for engine troubleshooting procedures.

The following procedures will show you exactly how to tune your Datsun. For 1976–79 models, Datsun recommends a tune-up, including distributor points (unless equipped with electronic ignition), and spark plugs every 12,000 miles.

In 1980, Datsun began using a new, more durable spark plug in all models sold in the United States. Datsun recommends that the new plugs be replaced every 30,000 miles or 24 months, which ever comes first. Certain 1980 Canadian Datsuns still use the conventional 12 month, 12,000 mile spark plugs. All United States 1980 and later models have electronic ignition systems, so there are no breaker points and condenser to replace.

Even though the manufacturer suggests a 30,000 mile, 24 month spark plug replacement span for 1980 and later U.S.A. models, it would be wise to remove the plugs and inspect them every 12,000 miles.

If you're experiencing some specific problem with your engine, turn to Chapter 10, "Troubleshooting," and follow the programmed format until you pinpoint the trouble. If you're just doing a tune-up to restore your Datsun's pep and economy, proceed with the following steps.

It might be noted that the tune-up is a good time to take a look around the engine compartment for problems in the making, such as oil and fuel leaks, deteriorating radiator or heater hoses, loose and/or frayed fan belts, etc.

Spark Plugs

A typical spark plug consists of a metal shell surrounding a ceramic insulator. A metal electrode extends downward through the center of the insulator and protrudes a small distance. Located at the end of the plug and attached to the side of the outer metal shell is the side electrode. The side electrode bends in at a 90 degree angle so that its tip is even with, and parallel to, the tip of the center electrode. The distance between these two electrodes (measured in thousandths of an inch) is called the spark plug gap. The spark plug in no way produces a spark but merely provides a gap across which the current can arc. The coil produces anywhere from 20,000 to 40,000 volts, which travels to the distributor where it is distributed through the spark plug wire to the spark plugs. The current

Tune-Up Specifications

When analyzing compression test results, look for uniformity among cylinders, rather than specific pressures.

Year	Model	Spark Plug Type	Spark Plug Gap (in.)	Distributor Point Dwell (deg)	Distributor Point Gap (in.)	Ignition Timing (deg) MT	Ignition Timing (deg) AT	Fuel Pump Pressure (psi)	Idle Speed (rpm) MT	Idle Speed (rpm) AT ①	Valve Clearance (in.) In	Valve Clearance (in.) Ex
1976	F10 49s.	BP-5ES	.031–.035	49–55	.018–.022	10B	—	3.8	700	—	.014 Hot	.014 Hot
	F10 Calif.	BP-5ES	.031–.035	Electronic	②	10B	—	3.8	700	—	.014 Hot	.014 Hot
1977	F10 49s.	BP-5ES	.039–.043	49–55	.018–.022	10B	—	3.8	700	—	.014 Hot	.014 Hot
	F10 Calif.	BP-5ES	.039–.043	Electronic	②	10B	—	3.8	700	—	.014 Hot	.014 Hot
1978	F10	BP-5ES	.039–.043	Electronic	②	10B	—	3.8	700	—	.014 Hot	.014 Hot
1979	310	BP-5ES ④	.039–.043	Electronic	②	10B ③	—	3.8	700	—	.014 Hot	.014 Hot
1980	310	BP-5ES ④	.039–.043	Electronic	②	8B	—	3.8	750	—	.014 Hot	.014 Hot
1981	310	BP-5ES-11 ④	.039–.043	Electronic	②	5B	—	3.8	750	—	.014 Hot	.014 Hot
1982	310	BP-5ES-11 ④	.039–.043	Electronic	②	2A ⑤	2A ⑤	3.8	750	750 ⑥	.011 Hot	.011 Hot
	Stanza	⑦	.039–.043	Electronic	②	0	0	3.8	650	—	.012 Hot	.012 Hot

① In Drive
② Reluctor gap: (1976–78) .008–.016; (1979–82) .012–.020
③ Calif.: 5B
④ Canada: BPR-5ES; gap .031–.035
⑤ Canada: 4A
⑥ Canada: AT 650
⑦ Intake: BPR-6-ES-11
 Exhaust: BPR-5ES-11

TUNE-UP

passes along the center electrode and jumps the gap to the side electrode, and, in so doing, ignites the air/fuel mixture in the combustion chamber.

Spark plug life and efficiency depend upon the condition of the engine and the temperatures to which the plug is exposed. Combustion chamber temperatures are affected by many factors such as compression ratio of the engine, air/fuel mixtures, exhaust emission equipment, and the type of driving you do. Spark plugs are designed and classified by number according to the heat range at which they will operate most efficiently.

HEAT RANGE

While spark plug heat range has always seemed to be somewhat of a mystical subject for many people, in reality, the entire subject is quite simple. Basically, it boils down to this; the amount of heat the plug absorbs is determined by the length of the lower insulator. The longer the insulator (or the farther it extends into the engine), the hotter the plug will operate; the shorter the insulator the cooler it will operate. A plug that absorbs little heat and remains too cool will quickly accumulate deposits of oil and carbon since it is not hot enough to burn them off. This leads to plug fouling and consequently to misfiring. A plug that absorbs too much heat will have no deposits, but, due to the excessive heat, the electrodes will burn away quickly and in some instances, preignition may result. Preignition takes place when plug tips get so hot that they glow sufficiently to ignite the fuel/air mixture before the actual spark occurs. This early ignition will usually cause a pinging during low speeds and heavy loads. In severe cases, the heat may become high enough to start the fuel/air mixture burning throughout the combustion chamber rather than just to the front of the plug as in normal operation. At this time, the piston is rising in the cylinder making its compression stroke. The burning mass is compressed and an explosion results, forcing the piston back down in the cylinder while it is still trying to go up. Obviously, something must go, and it does—pistons are often damaged.

The general rule of thumb for choosing the correct heat range when picking a spark plug is: if most of your driving is long distance, high speed travel, use a colder plug; if most of your driving is stop and go, use a hotter plug. Factory-installed plugs are, of course, compromise plugs, since the factory has no way of knowing what sort of driving you do. It should be noted that most people never have occasion to change their plugs from the factory-recommended heat range.

REMOVAL AND INSTALLATION

NOTE: *The stanza has two spark plugs in each cylinder. All eight plugs should be replaced at every tune-up for maximum fuel efficiency and power. Unplug and remove each spark plug one at a time from the high tension harness to avoid confusing the wiring.*

1. Grasp the spark plug boot and pull it straight out. Don't pull on the wire. If the boot(s) are cracked, replace them.
2. Place the spark plug socket firmly on the plug. Turn the spark plug out of the cylinder head in a counterclockwise direction.

NOTE: *The Datsun cylinder head is aluminum, which is easily stripped. Remove plugs only when the engine is cold.*

If removal is difficult, loosen the plug only slightly and drip penetrating oil onto the threads. Allow the oil time enough to work and then unscrew the plug. Proceeding in this

Spark plug heat ranges

Spark plug wire removal

TUNE-UP 21

Spark plug removal

Spark plug gap adjustment

manner will prevent damaging the threads in the cylinder head. Be sure to keep the socket straight to avoid breaking the ceramic insulator.

3. Continue and remove the remaining spark plugs.

4. Inspect the plugs using the "Color Insert" section illustrations and then clean or discard them according to condition.

New spark plugs come pre-gapped, but double check the setting or reset them if you desire a different gap. The recommended spark plug gap is listed in the "Tune-Up Specifications" chart. Use a spark plug wire gauge for checking the gap. The wire should pass through the electrode with just a slight drag. Never attempt to adjust the plug gap with a flat-bladed feeler gauge; a false reading will result. Using the electrode bending tool on the end of the gauge, bend the side electrode to adjust the gap. Never attempt to adjust the center electrode. Lightly oil the threads of the replacement plug and install it hand-tight. It is a good practice to use a torque wrench to tighten the spark plugs on any car and especially on the Datsun, since the head is aluminum. Torque the spark plugs to 14–22 ft. lbs. Install the ignition wire boots firmly on the spark plugs.

CHECKING AND REPLACING SPARK PLUG CABLES

Visually inspect the spark plug cables for burns, cuts, or breaks in the insulation. Check the spark plug boots and the nipples on the distributor cap and coil. Replace any damaged wiring. If no physical damage is obvious, the wires can be checked with an ohmmeter for excessive resistance. Remove the distributor cap and leave the wires connected to the cap. Connect one lead of the ohmmeter to the corresponding electrode inside the cap and the other lead to the spark plug terminal (remove it from the spark plug for the test). Replace any wire which shows over 50,000 ohms. Generally speaking, however, resistance should not run over 35,000 ohms and 50,000 ohms should be considered the outer limits of acceptability. Test the coil wire by connecting the ohmmeter between the center contact in the cap and either of the primary terminals at the coil. If the total resistance of the coil and cable is more than 25,000 ohms, remove the cable from the coil and check the resistance of the cable alone. If the resistance is higher than 15,000 ohms, replace the cable. It should be remembered that wire resistance is a function of length, and that the longer the cable, the greater the resistance. Thus, if the cables on your car are longer than the factory originals, resistance will be higher and quite possibly outside of these limits.

Checking plug wire resistance with an ohmmeter

When installing a new set of spark plug cables, replace the cables one at a time so there will be no mixup. Start by replacing the longest cable first. Install the boot firmly over the spark plug. Route the wire exactly the same as the original. Insert the nipple firmly into the tower on the distributor cap. Repeat the process for each cable.

TUNE-UP

Breaker Points and Condenser

NOTE: *Certain 1976–1977 and virtually all 1978 and later Datsuns are equipped with electronic, breakerless ignition systems. See the following section for maintenance procedures.*

INSPECTION OF THE POINTS

1. Disconnect the high-tension wire from the top of the distributor and the coil.
2. Remove the distributor cap by prying off the spring clips on the sides of the cap.
3. Remove the rotor from the distributor shaft by pulling it straight up. Examine the condition of the rotor. If it is cracked or the metal tip is excessively worn or burned, it should be replaced. Clean the tip with fine emery paper.
4. Pry open the contacts of the points with a screwdriver and check the condition of the contacts. If they are excessively worn, burned or pitted, they should be replaced.
5. If the points are in good condition, adjust them and replace the rotor and the distributor cap. If the points need to be replaced, follow the replacement procedure given below.

REPLACEMENT OF THE BREAKER POINTS AND CONDENSER

1. Remove the coil high-tension wire from the top of the distributor cap. Remove the distributor cap and place it out of the way. Remove the rotor from the distributor shaft by pulling up.
2. Remove the condenser from the distributor body.
3. Remove the points assembly attaching screws and then remove the points. A magnetic screwdriver or one with a holding mechanism will come in handy here, so that you don't drop a screw into the distributor and have to remove the entire distributor to retrieve it. After the points are removed, wipe off the cam and apply new cam lubricant. If you don't, the points will wear out in a few thousand miles.
4. Slip the new set of points onto the locating dowel and install the screws that hold the assembly onto the plate. Don't tighten them all the way yet, since you'll only have to loosen them to set the point gap.
5. Install the new condenser and attach the condenser lead to the points.
6. Set the point gap and dwell (see the following sections).

ADJUSTMENT OF THE BREAKER POINTS WITH A FEELER GAUGE

1. If the contact points of the assembly are not parallel, bend the stationary contact so that they make contact across the entire surface of the contacts. Bend only the stationary bracket part of the point assembly; not the movable contact.
2. Turn the engine until the rubbing block of the points is on one of the high points of the distributor cam. You can do this by either turning the ignition switch to the start position and releasing it quickly ("bumping" the engine) or by using a wrench on the bolt which holds the crankshaft pulley to the crankshaft.
3. Place the correct size feeler gauge between the contacts (see the Tune-Up Chart). Make sure that it is parallel with the contact surfaces.
4. With your free hand, insert a screwdriver into the eccentric adjusting screw, then twist the screwdriver to either increase or decrease the gap to the proper setting.

Adjusting point gap

5. Tighten the adjustment lockscrew and recheck the contact gap to make sure that it didn't change when the lockscrew was tightened.
6. Replace the rotor and distributor cap, and the high-tension wire which connects the top of the distributor and the coil. Make sure that the rotor is firmly seated all the way onto the distributor shaft and that the tab of the rotor is aligned with notch in the shaft. Align the tab in the base of the distributor cap with the notch in the distributor body. Make sure that the cap is firmly seated on the distributor and that the retainer clips are in place. Make sure that the end of the high-tension wire is firmly placed in the top of the distributor and the coil.

TUNE-UP 23

1. Cap
2. Rotor
3. Condenser
4. Ground wire
5. Lead wire
6. Breaker points
7. Breaker plate
8. Cam assembly
9. Governor spring
10. Governor weight
11. Thrust washer
12. Shaft assembly
13. Vacuum control assembly
14. Terminal assembly
15. Clamp
16. Retaining plate
17. Gear set

Point type distributor

Dwell Angle

The dwell angle or cam angle is the number of degrees that the distributor cam rotates while the points are closed. There is an inverse relationship between dwell angle and point gap. Increasing the point gap will decrease the dwell angle and vice versa. Check-

TUNE-UP

ing the dwell angle with a meter is a far more accurate method of measuring point opening than the feeler gauge method.

After setting the point gap to specification with a feeler gauge as described above, check the dwell angle with a meter. Attach the dwell meter according to the manufacturer's instruction sheet. The negative lead is grounded and the positive lead is connected to the primary wire terminal which runs from the coil to the distributor. Start the engine, let it idle and reach operating temperature, and observe the dwell on the meter. The reading should fall within the allowable range. If it does not, the gap will have to be reset or the breaker points will have to be replaced.

ADJUSTMENT OF THE BREAKER POINTS WITH A DWELL METER

1. Adjust the points with a feeler gauge as previously described.
2. Connect the dwell meter to the ignition circuit as according to the manufacturer's instructions. One lead of the meter is connected to a ground and the other lead is connected to the distributor post on the coil. An adapter is usually provided for this purpose.
3. If the dwell meter has a set line on it, adjust the meter to zero the indicator.
4. Start the engine.

NOTE: *Be careful when working on any vehicle while the engine is running. Make sure that the transmission is in Neutral and that the parking brake is applied. Keep hands, clothing, tools and the wires of the test instruments clear of the rotating fan blades.*

5. Observe the reading on the dwell meter. If the reading is within the specified range, turn off the engine and remove the dwell meter.

NOTE: *If the meter does not have a scale for 4 cylinder engines, multiply the 8 cylinder reading by two.*

6. If the reading is above the specified range, the breaker point gap is too small. If the reading is below the specified range, the gap is too large. In either case, the engine must be stopped and the gap adjusted in the manner previously covered.

After making the adjustment, start the engine and check the reading on the dwell meter. When the correct reading is obtained, disconnect the dwell meter.

7. Check the adjustment of the ignition timing.

Electronic Ignition

The electronic ignition system differs from the conventional breaker points system in form only; its function is exactly the same—to supply a spark to the spark plugs at precisely the right moment to ignite the compressed gas in the cylinders and create mechanical movement.

Located in the distributor, in addition to the normal rotor cap, is a spoked rotor (reluctor) which fits on the distributor shaft where the breaker points cam is found on nonelectronic ignitions. The rotor (reluctor) revolves with the top rotor cap and, as it passes a pickup coil inside the distributor body, breaks a high flux phase which occurs while the space between the reluctor spokes passes the pickup coil. This allows current to flow to the pickup coil. Primary ignition current is then cut off by the electronic ignition unit, allowing the magnetic field in the ignition coil to collapse, creating the spark which the distributor passes on to the spark plug.

The 1979–82 IC ignition system uses a ring type pickup coil which surrounds the reluctor instead of the single post type pickup coil on earlier models.

The dual spark plug ignition system used on the 1982 stanza uses two ignition coils and each cylinder has two spark plugs which fire simultaneously. In this manner the engine is able to consume large quantities of recirculated exhaust gas which would cause a single spark plug cylinder to misfire and idle roughly.

Because no points or condenser are used, and because dwell is determined by the electronic unit, no adjustments are necessary. Ignition timing is checked in the usual way, but unless the distributor is disturbed it is not likely to ever change very much.

Service consists of inspection of the distributor cap, rotor, and ignition wires, replacing when necessary. These parts can be expected to last for at least 40,000 miles. In addition, the reluctor air gap should be checked periodically.

1. The distributor cap is held on by two clips. Release them with a screwdriver and lift the cap straight up and off, with the wires attached. Inspect the cap for cracks, carbon tracks, or a worn center contact. Replace it if necessary, transferring the wires one at a time from the old cap to the new.
2. Pull the ignition rotor (not the spoked reluctor) straight up to remove. Replace it if

TUNE-UP

Stanza distributor

its contacts are worn, burned, or pitted. Do not file the contacts. To replace, press it firmly onto the shaft. It only goes on one way, so be sure it is fully seated.

3. Before replacing the ignition rotor, check the reluctor air gap. *Use a non-magnetic feeler gauge.* Rotate the engine until a reluctor spoke is aligned with the pick-up coil (either bump the engine around with the starter, or turn it with a wrench on the crankshaft pulley bolt). The gap should measure 0.008–0.016 in. through 1978, or 0.012–0.020 in. for 1979–82. Adjustment, if necessary, is made by loosening the pickup coil mounting screws and shifting the coil either closer to or farther from the reluctor. On 1979–82

models, center the pickup coil (ring) around the reluctor. Tighten the screws and recheck the gap.

4. Inspect the wires for cracks or brittleness. Replace them one at a time to prevent crosswiring, carefully pressing the replacement wires into place. The cores of electronic wires are more susceptible to breakage than those of standard wires, so treat them gently.

TROUBLESHOOTING

1976–78

The main differences between the 1976–77 and 1978 systems are: (1) the 1976–77 system uses an external ballast resistor located next

TUNE-UP

F10 and 310 electronic ignition distributor

to the ignition coil, and (2) the earlier system uses a wiring harness with individual eyelet connectors to the electronic unit, while the later system uses a multiple plug connector. You will need an accurate voltmeter and ohmmeter for these tests, which must be performed in the order given.

1. Check all connections for corrosion, looseness, breaks, etc., and correct if necessary. Clean and gap the spark plugs.

2a. Disconnect the harness (connector or plug) from the electronic unit. Turn the ignition switch On. Set the voltmeter to the DC 50v range. Connect the positive (+) voltmeter lead to the black/white wire terminal, and the negative (−) lead to the black wire terminal. Battery voltage should be obtained. If not, check the black/white and black wires for continuity; check the battery terminals for corrosion; check the battery state of charge.

2b. Next, connect the voltmeter + lead to the blue wire and the − lead to the black wire. Battery voltage should be obtained. If not, check the blue wire for continuity; check the ignition coil terminals for corrosion or looseness; check the coil for continuity. On 1976–77 models, also check the external ballast resistor.

3. Disconnect the distributor harness wires from the ignition coil ballast resistor on 1976–77 models, leaving the ballast resistor-to-coil wires attached. On 1978 models, disconnect the ignition coil wires. Connect the leads of an ohmmeter to the ballast resistor outside terminals (at each end) for 1976–77, and to the two coil terminals for 1978. Resistance on the F10 should be 0 ohms with the ohmmeter in the X1 range.

4. Disconnect the harness from the electronic control unit. Connect an ohmmeter to

the red and the green wire terminals. Resistance should be 720 ohms. If far more or far less, replace the distributor pick-up coil.

5. Disconnect the anti-dieseling solenoid connector (see Chapter 4). Connect a voltmeter to the red and green terminals of the electronic control harness. When the starter is cranked, the needle should deflect slightly. If not, replace the distributor pick-up coil.

6. Reconnect the ignition coil and the electronic control unit. Leave the antidieseling solenoid wire disconnected. Unplug the high tension lead (coil to distributor) from the distributor and hold it 1/8–1/4 in. from the cylinder head with a pair of insulated pliers and a heavy glove. When the engine is cranked, a spark should be observed. If not, check the lead, and replace if necessary. If still no spark, replace the electronic control unit.

7. Reconnect all wires.

1976–77: connect the voltmeter + lead to the blue electronic control harness connector and the − lead to the black wire. The harness should be attached to the control unit.

1978: connect the voltmeter + lead to the − terminal of the ignition coil and the − lead to ground.

As soon as the ignition switch is turned On, the meter should indicate battery voltage. If not, replace the electronic control unit.

1979–82, Except Stanza

1. Make a check of the power supply circuit. Turn the ignition OFF. Disconnect the connector from the top of the IC unit. Turn the ignition ON. Measure the voltage at each terminal of the connector in turn by touching the probe of the positive lead of the voltmeter to one of the terminals, and touching the probe of the negative lead of the voltmeter to a ground, such as the engine. In each case, battery voltage should be indicated. If not, check all wiring, the ignition switch, and all connectors for breaks, corrosion, discontinuity, etc. and repair as necessary.

2. Check the primary windings of the ignition coil. Turn the ignition OFF. Disconnect the harness connector from the negative coil terminal. Use an ohmmeter to measure the resistance between the positive and negative coil terminals. If resistance is 0.84–1.02 ohms the coil is OK. Replace if far from this range.

If the power supply, circuits, wiring, and coil are in good shape, check the IC unit and pick-up coil, as follows:

3. Turn the ignition OFF. Remove the distributor cap and ignition rotor. Use an ohmmeter to measure the resistance between the two terminals of the pick-up coil, where they attach to the IC unit. Measure the resistance by reversing the polarity of the probes. If approximately 400 ohms are indicated, the pick-up coil is OK, but the IC unit is bad and must be replaced. If other than 400 ohms are measured, go to the next Step.

4. Be certain the two pin connector on the IC unit is secure. Turn the ignition ON. Measure the voltage at the ignition coil negative terminal. Turn the ignition OFF.

CAUTION: *Remove the tester probe from the coil negative terminal before switching the ignition OFF, to prevent burning out the tester.*

If zero voltage is indicated, the IC unit is bad and must be replaced. If battery voltage is indicated, proceed.

5. Remove the IC unit from the distributor:

   a. Disconnect the battery ground (negative) cable.

   b. Remove the distributor cap and ignition rotor.

   c. Disconnect the harness connector at the top of the IC unit.

   d. Remove the two screws securing the IC unit to the distributor.

   e. Disconnect the two pick-up coil wires from the IC unit.

CAUTION: *Pull the connectors free with a pair of needlenosed pliers. Do not pull on the wires to detach the connectors.*

   f. Remove the IC unit.

6. Measure the resistance between the terminals of the pick-up coil. It should be approximately 400 ohms. If so, the pick-up coil is OK, and the IC unit is bad. If not approximately 400 ohms, the pick-up coil is bad and must be replaced.

7. With a new pick-up coil installed, install the IC unit. Check for a spark at one of the spark plugs (see Step 4.1 in the Troubleshooting Section at the end of this Chapter). If a good spark is obtained, the IC unit is OK. If not, replace the IC unit.

Stanza

Complete step 1, under 1979–82, above. Complete step 2, under 1979–82, above: the resistance should be between 1.04–1.27 ohms. If not, replace ignition coil(s).

NOTE: *The manufacturer does not give a complete system of tests for the Stanza.*

TUNE-UP

Therefore, before attempting anything else, try this spark performance test:

1. Turn the ignition switch to the "OFF" position.
2. Disconnect the anti-dieseling solenoid valve connector to cut off the fuel supply to the engine.
3. Disconnect the high tension cable from the distributor. Hold the cable with insulated pliers to avoid getting shocked. Position the wire about a ¼ of an inch from the engine block and have an assistant turn over the engine using the starter. A spark should jump from the cable to the engine block. If not, there is probably something amiss with the ignition system. Further testing should be left to your Datsun dealer.

Ignition Timing

CAUTION: *When performing this or any other operation with the engine running, be very careful of the alternator belt and pulleys. Make sure that your timing light wires don't interfere with the belt.*

Ignition timing is an important part of the tune-up. It is always adjusted after the points are gapped (dwell angle changed), since altering the dwell affects the timing. Three basic types of timing lights are available, the neon, the DC, and the AC powered. Of the three the DC light is the most frequently used by professional tuners. The bright flash put out by the DC light makes the timing marks stand out on even the brightest of days. Another advantage of the DC light is that you don't need to be near an electrical outlet. Neon lights are available for a few dollars, but their weak flash makes it necessary to use them in a fairly dark work area. One neon light lead is attached to the spark plug and the other to the plug wire. The DC light attaches to the spark plug and the wire with an adapter and two clips attach to the battery posts for power. The AC unit is similar, except that the power cable is plugged into a house outlet.

Ignition timing is the measurement, in degrees of crankshaft rotation, of the point at which the spark plugs fire in each of the cylinders. It is measured in degrees before or after Top Dead Center (TDC) of the compression stroke. Ignition timing is controlled by turning the distributor body in the engine.

Ideally, the air/fuel mixture in the cylinder will be ignited by the spark plug just as the piston passes TDC of the compression stroke. If this happens, the piston will be beginning its downward motion of the power stroke just as the piston passes TDC of the compression stroke. If this happens, the piston will be beginning its downward motion of the power stroke just as the compressed and ignited air/fuel mixture starts to expand. The expansion of the air/fuel mixture then forces the piston down on the power stroke and turns the crankshaft.

Because it takes a fraction of a second for the spark plug to ignite the mixture in the cylinder, the spark plug must fire a little before the piston reaches TDC. Otherwise, the mixture will not be completely ignited as the piston passes TDC and the full power of the explosion will not be used by the engine.

The timing measurement is given in degrees of crankshaft rotation before or after the piston reaches TDC (ATDC) (BTDC). If the setting for the ignition timing is 5° BTDC, the spark plug must fire 5° before each piston reaches TDC. This only holds true, however, when the engine is at idle speed.

As the engine speed increases, the pistons go faster. The spark plugs have to ignite the fuel even sooner if it is to be completely ignited when the piston reaches TDC. To do this, the distributor has a means to advance the timing of the spark as the engine speed increases. This is accomplished by centrifugal weights within the distributor and a vacuum diaphragm, mounted on the side of the distributor. It is necessary to disconnect the vacuum line from the diaphragm when the ignition timing is being set.

The timing is best checked with a timing light. This device is connected in series with the No. 1 spark plug. The current which fires the spark plug also causes the timing light to flash.

The timing marks are located at the front crankshaft pulley and consist of a notch on the crankshaft pulley and a scale of degrees of crankshaft rotation attached to the front cover.

When the engine is running, the timing light is aimed at the marks on the flywheel pulley and the pointer.

IGNITION TIMING ADJUSTMENT

NOTE: *Datsun does not give ignition timing adjustments for 1980 and later California Datsuns. The procedure has been discontinued.*

TUNE-UP

1. Set the dwell to the proper specification.
2. Locate the timing marks on the crankshaft pulley and the front of the engine.
3. Clean off the timing marks so that you can see them.
4. Use chalk or white paint to color the mark on the crankshaft pulley and the mark on the scale which will indicate the correct timing when aligned with the notch on the crankshaft pulley.
5. Attach a tachometer to the engine.
6. Attach a timing light to the engine, according to the manufacturer's instructions.
7. Leave the vacuum line connected to the distributor vacuum diaphragm on all 1976–79 models.
8. Check to make sure that all of the wires clear the fan and then start the engine. Allow the engine to reach normal operating temperature.
9. Adjust the idle to the correct setting.
10. Aim the timing light at the timing marks. If the marks that you put on the pulley and the engine are aligned when the light flashes, the timing is correct. Turn off the engine and remove the tachometer and the timing light. If the marks are not in alignment, proceed with the following steps.
11. Turn off the engine.
12. Loosen the distributor lockbolt just enough so that the distributor can be turned with a little effort.
13. Start the engine. Keep the wires of the timing light clear of the fan.
14. With the timing light aimed at the pulley and the marks on the engine, turn the distributor in the direction of rotor rotation to retard the spark, and in the opposite direction of rotor rotation to advance the spark. Align the marks on the pulley and the engine with the flashes of the timing light. Tighten the hold-down bolt.

Valve Lash

Valve adjustment determines how far the valves enter the cylinder and how long they stay open and closed.

If the valve clearance is too large, part of the lift of the camshaft will be used in removing the excessive clearance. Consequently, the valve will not be opening as far as it should. This condition has two effects: the valve train components will emit a tapping sound as they take up the excessive clearance and the engine will perform poorly because the valves don't open fully and allow the proper amount of gases to flow into and out of the engine.

If the valve clearance is too small, the intake valves and the exhaust valves will open

A series
Valve adjustment—

310 E series
Valve adjustment—

Typical valve adjustment with a feeler gauge

CA20 valve sequence

too far and they will not fully seat on the cylinder head when they close. When a valve seats intself on the cylinder head, it does two things: it seals the combustion chamber so that none of the gases in the cylinder escape and it cools itself by transferring some of the heat it absorbs from the combustion in the cylinder to the cylinder head and to the engine's cooling system. If the valve clearance is too small, the engine will run poorly because of the gases escaping from the combustion chamber. The valves will also become overheated and will warp, since they cannot transfer heat unless they are touching the valve seat in the cylinder head.

NOTE: *While all valve adjustments must be made as accurately as possible, it is better to have the valve adjustment slightly loose than slightly tight, as a burned valve may result from overly tight adjustments.*

VALVE ADJUSTMENT

1. Run the engine until it reaches normal operating temperature. Oil temperature, not water temperature, is critical to valve adjustment. With this in mind, make sure the engine is fully warmed up since this is the only way to make sure the parts have reached their full expansion. Generally speaking, this takes around fifteen minutes. After the engine has reached normal operating temperature, shut it off.
2. Purchase a new valve cover gasket before removing the valve cover. The new silicone gasket sealers are just as good or better if you can't find a gasket.
3. Note the location of any hoses or wires which may interfere with valve cover removal, disconnect them and move them aside. Then, remove the bolts which hold the valve cover in place.
4. After the valve cover has been removed, the next step is to get the number one piston at TDC on the compression stroke. There are at least two ways to do it; you can bump the engine over with the starter or turn it over by using a wrench on the front pulley attaching bolt. The easiest way to find TDC is to turn the engine over slowly with a wrench (after first removing no. 1 plug) until the piston is at the top of its stroke and the TDC timing mark on the crankshaft pulley is in alignment with the timing mark pointer. At this point, the valves for no. 1 should be closed.

NOTE: *Make sure both valves are closed with the valve springs up as high as they will go. An easy way to find the compression stroke is to remove the distributor cap and see toward which spark plug lead the rotor is pointing. If the rotor points to number one spark plug lead, number one cylinder is on its compression stroke. When the rotor points to number two spark plug lead, number two cylinder is on its compression stroke, etc.*

5. With no. 1 piston at TDC of the compression stroke, check the clearance on valves Nos. 1, 2, 3 and 5 on F10 and 310 through 1981. On 1983 310, check 1, 4, 6 and 7. On Stanza check 1, 2, 3 and 6 (counting from the front to the rear).
6. To adjust the clearance, loosen the locknut with a wrench and turn the adjuster with a screwdriver while holding the locknut. The correct size feeler gauge should pass with a slight drag between the rocker arm and the valve stem.
7. Turn the crankshaft one full revolution to position the no. 4 piston at TDC of the compression stroke. Adjust valves nos. 4, 6, 7 and 8 on F10 and 1978–81 310. On 1982 310 check 2, 3, 5 and 8. On Stanza check 4, 5, 7 and 8 in the same manner as the first four.
8. Replace the valve cover.

Carburetor

IDLE SPEED AND MIXTURE ADJUSTMENT

NOTE: *1980 and later model Datsuns require a CO Meter to adjust their mixture ratios, therefore, no procedures concerning this adjustment are given. Also, many California model Datsuns have a plug over their mixture control screw. It is suggested that in both of these cases, mixture adjustment be left to a qualified technician.*

1. Start the engine and allow it to run until it reaches normal operating temperature.
2. Allow the engine idle speed to stabilize by running the engine at idle for at least two minutes.
3. If you have not done so already, check and adjust the ignition timing to the proper setting.
4. Shut off the engine and connect a tachometer.
5. Disconnect and plug the air hose between the three way connector and the check valve, if equipped. On 1980–82 models, disconnect the air induction hose and plug the pipe. With the transmission in Neutral, check

1. Throttle adjusting screw
2. Idle adjusting screw
3. Idle limiter cap
4. Stopper

Carburetor adjusting screws

the idle speed on the tachometer. If the reading is correct, continue on to Step 6 for 1976–79 Datsuns. For 1980–82 and certain California models, proceed to step 8 below if the idle is correct. If the idle is not correct, for all models, turn the idle speed adjusting screw clockwise with a screwdriver to increase idle speed or counterclockwise to decrease it.

6. With the automatic transmission in Drive (wheels blocked and parking brake on) or the manual transmission in Neutral, turn the mixture screw out until the engine rpm starts to drop due to an overly rich mixture.

7. Turn the screw until just before the rpm starts to drop due to an overly lean mixture. Turn the mixture screw in until the idle speed drops 35–45 rpm. If the mixture limiter cap will not allow this adjustment, remove it, make the adjustment, and re-install it. Go on to step 18 for all 1976–79 models.

8. Install the air hose. If the engine speed increases, reduce it with the idle speed screw.

Engine and Engine Rebuilding

ENGINE ELECTRICAL
Distributor
REMOVAL

1. Unfasten the reatining clips and lift the distributor cap straight up. It will be easier to install the distributor if the wiring is not disconnected from the cap. If the wires must be removed from the cap mark their positions to aid in installation.
2. Disconnect the distributor wiring harness.
3. Disconnect the vacuum lines.
4. Note the position of the rotor in relation to the base. Scribe a mark on the base of the distributor and on the engine block to facilitate reinstallation. Align the marks with the direction the metal tip of the rotor is pointing.
5. Remove the bolt(s) which holds the distributor to the engine.
6. Lift the distributor assembly from the engine.

INSTALLATION

1. Insert the distributor shaft and assembly into the engine. Line up the mark on the distributor and the one on the engine with the metal tip of the rotor. Make sure that the vacuum advance diaphragm is pointed in the same direction as it was pointed originally. This will be done automatically if the marks on the engine and the distributor are lined up with the rotor.
2. Install the distributor hold-down bolt and clamp. Leave the screw loose enough so that you can move the distributor with heavy hand pressure.
3. Connect the primary wire to the coil. Install the distributor cap on the distributor housing. Secure the distributor cap with the spring clips.
4. Install the spark plug wires if removed. Make sure that the wires are pressed all the way into the top of the distributor cap and firmly onto the spark plug.
5. Adjust the point dwell and set the ignition timing.

NOTE: *If the crankshaft has been turned or the engine disturbed in any manner (i.e. disassembled and rebuilt) while the distributor was removed, or if the marks were not drawn, it will be necessary to initially time the engine. Follow the procedure given below.*

INSTALLATION—ENGINE DISTURBED

1. It is necessary to place the No. 1 cylinder in the firing position to correctly install the distributor. To locate this position, the ignition timing marks on the crankshaft front pulley are used.

ENGINE AND ENGINE REBUILDING 33

2. Remove the No. 1 cylinder spark plug. Turn the crankshaft until the piston in the No. 1 cylinder is moving up on the compression stroke. This can be determined by placing your thumb over the spark plug hole and feeling the air being forced out of the cylinder. Stop turning the crankshaft when the timing marks that are used to time the engine are aligned.

3. Oil the distributor housing lightly where the distributor bears on the cylinder block.

4. Install the distributor so that the rotor, which is mounted on the shaft, points toward the No. 1 spark plug terminal tower position when the cap is installed. Of course you won't be able to see the direction in which the rotor is pointing if the cap is on the distributor. Lay the cap on the top of the distributor and make a mark on the side of the distributor housing just below the No. 1 spark plug terminal. Make sure that the rotor points toward that mark when you install the distributor.

5. When the distributor shaft has reached the bottom of the hole, move the rotor back and forth slightly until the driving lug on the end of the shaft enters the slots cut in the end of the oil pump shaft and the distributor assembly slides down into place.

6. When the distributor is correctly installed, the breaker points should be in such a position that they are just ready to break contact with each other. This is accomplished by rotating the distributor body after it has been installed in the engine. Once again, line up the marks that you made before the distributor was removed from the engine.

7. Install the distributor hold-down bolt.

8. Install the spark plug into the No. 1 spark plug hole and continue from Step 3 of the preceding distributor installation procedure.

Firing Order

To avoid confusion, replace the spark plug wires one at a time.

A series engine
Firing order—1,3,4,2

E15 engine
Firing order—1,3,4,2

CA20 engine

Alternator

ALTERNATOR PRECAUTIONS

To prevent damage to the alternator and regulator, the following precautionary measures must be taken when working with the electrical system.

1. Never reverse battery connections.
2. Booster batteries for starting must be connected properly. Make sure that the positive cable of the booster battery is connected to the positive terminal of the battery that is getting the boost. This applies to both negative and ground cables.
3. Disconnect the battery cables before using a fast charger; the charger has a tendency to force current through the diodes in the opposite direction for which they are designed. This burns out the diodes.
4. Never use a fast charger as a booster for starting the vehicle.

34 ENGINE AND ENGINE REBUILDING

1. Pulley assembly
2. Front cover
3. Front bearing
4. Rotor
5. Rear bearing
6. Stator
7. Rear cover
8. Brush assembly
9. Diode set plate assembly
10. Diode cover
11. Through-bolt

F10 alternator

1. Pulley assembly
2. Front cover
3. Front bearing
4. Rotor
5. Rear bearing
6. Stator
7. Diode (Set plate) assembly
8. Brush assembly
9. IC voltage regulator
10. Rear cover
11. Through bolt

Integral regulator type alternator

ENGINE AND ENGINE REBUILDING

1. Feeler gauge
2. Screw
3. Phillips screwdriver
4. Upper contact

Adjusting the point gap

1. Wrench
2. Phillips screwdriver
3. Adjusting screw
4. Locknut

Adjusting the regulated voltage

5. Never disconnect the voltage regulator while the engine is running.
6. Do not ground the alternator output terminal.
7. Do not operate the alternator on an open circuit with the field energized.
8. Do not attempt to polarize an alternator.

REMOVAL AND INSTALLATION

1. Disconnect the negative battery terminal.
2. Disconnect the two lead wires and connector from the alternator.
3. Loosen the drive belt adjusting bolt and remove the belt.
4. Unscrew the alternator attaching bolts and remove the alternator from the vehicle.
5. Install the alternator in the reverse order of removal.

Regulator

REMOVAL AND INSTALLATION

NOTE: *1978–82 models are equipped with integral regulator alternators. Since the regulator is part of the alternator, no adjustments are possible or necessary.*

1. Disconnect the negative battery terminal.
2. Disconnect the electrical lead connector of the regulator.
3. Remove the two mounting screws and remove the regulator from the vehicle.
4. Install the regulator in the reverse order of removal.

ADJUSTMENT

1. Adjust the voltage regulator core gap by loosening the screw which is used to secure the contact set on the yoke, and move the contact up or down as necessary. Retighten the screw. The gap should be 0.024–0.039 in.
2. Adjust the point gap of the voltage regulator coil by loosening the screw used to secure the upper contact and move the upper contact up or down. The point gap is 0.014–0.018 in.
3. The core gap and point gap on the charge relay coil is or are adjusted in the same

Alternator and Regulator Specifications

Model	Year	Alternator Identification Number	Rated Output @ 5000 RPM	Output @ 2500 RPM (not less than)	Brush Length (in.)	Brush Spring Tension (oz.)	Regulated Voltage
F-10	1976–77	LT150-26	50	37.5	0.295	9.0–12.2	14.3–15.3
	1978	LR150-36①	50	40	0.295	8.99–12.7	14.3–15.3
		LR160-46①②	60	45	0.295	8.99–12.17	14.4–15.0
310	1979–80	LR160-46①	60	40	0.295	8.99–12.17	14.4–15.0
310 U.S.A.	1981–82	LR160-125①	50	35	0.295	8.99–12.17	14.4–15.0
310 Canada	1981–82	LR150-99①	50	35	0.295	8.99–12.17	14.4–15.0
Stanza	1982	LR160-104①	60	40	0.295	8.99–12.17	14.4–15.1

① Uses integral voltage regulator ② With air conditioning

36 ENGINE AND ENGINE REBUILDING

manner as previously outlined for the voltage regulator coil. The core gap is to be set at 0.032–0.039 in. and the point gap adjusted to 0.016–0.024 in.

4. The regulated voltage is adjusted by loosening the locknut and turning the adjusting screw clockwise to increase, or counterclockwise to decrease the regulated voltage. The voltage should be between 14.3–15.3 volts at 68°F.

Starter

Datsun began using a gear reduction starter in some 1978 Canadian and United States models. The differences between the gear reduction and conventional starters are: the gear reduction starter has a set of ratio reduction gears while the conventional starter does not; the brushes on the gear reduction starter are located on a plate behind the starter drive housing, while the conventional starter's brushes are located in its rear cover. The extra gears on the gear reduction starter make the starter pinion gear turn at about half the speed of the starter, giving the starter twice the turning power of a conventional starter.

REMOVAL AND INSTALLATION

1. Disconnect the negative battery cable from the battery.
2. Disconnect the starter wiring at the starter, taking note of the positions for correct reinstallation.
3. Remove the bolts attaching the starter to the engine and remove the starter from the vehicle.
4. Install the starter in the reverse order of removal.

BRUSH REPLACEMENT

Non-Reduction Gear Type

1. With the starter out of the vehicle, remove the bolts holding the solenoid to the top of the starter and remove the solenoid.

1. Magnetic switch assembly
2. Dust cover (Adjusting washer)
3. Torsion spring
4. Shift lever
5. Dust cover
6. Thrust washer
7. E-ring
8. Rear cover metal
9. Through bolt
10. Rear cover
11. Brush holder
12. Brush (−)
13. Brush spring
14. Brush (+)
15. Yoke
16. Field coil
17. Armature
18. Center bracket
19. Pinion assembly
20. Dust cover
21. Pinion stopper
22. Stopper clip
23. Gear case
24. Gear case metal

Non-reduction gear starter

ENGINE AND ENGINE REBUILDING

1. Magnetic switch assembly
2. Dust cover (Adjusting washer)
3. Torsion spring
4. Shift lever
5. Through bolt
6. Rear cover
7. O-ring
8. Yoke
9. Field coil
10. Brush
11. Armature
12. Center bearing
13. Brush spring
14. Brush holder
15. Dust cover
16. Center housing
17. Reduction gear
18. Pinion gear
19. Packing
20. Gear case

Reduction gear starter

2. To remove the brushes, remove the two thru-bolts, and the two rear cover attaching screws and remove the rear cover.
3. Disconnect the electrical leads and remove the brushes.
4. Install the brushes in the reverse order of removal.

Reduction Gear Type

1. Remove the starter. Remove the solenoid.
2. Remove the through bolts and the rear cover. The rear cover can be pried off with a screwdriver, but be careful not to damage the O-ring.
3. Remove the starter housing, armature, and brush holder from the center housing. They can be removed as an assembly.
4. Remove the positive side brush from its holder. The positive brush is insulated from the brush holder, and its lead wire is connected to the field coil.
5. Carefully lift the negative brush from the commutator and remove it from the holder.
6. Installation is the reverse.

STARTER DRIVE REPLACEMENT

Non-Reduction Gear Type

1. With the starter motor removed from the vehicle, remove the solenoid from the starter.
2. Remove the two thru-bolts and separate the gear case from the yoke housing.
3. Remove the pinion stopper clip and the pinion stopper.
4. Slide the starter drive off the armature shaft.
5. Install the starter drive and reassemble the starter in the reverse order of removal.

Reduction Gear Type

1. Remove the starter.
2. Remove the solenoid and the shift lever.
3. Remove the bolts securing the center housing to the front cover and separate the parts.
4. Remove the gears and starter drive.
5. Installation is the reverse.

38 ENGINE AND ENGINE REBUILDING

Pinion stopper removal

BATTERY

Refer to Chapter One for details on battery maintenance.

REMOVAL AND INSTALLATION

1. Disconnect the negative (ground) cable from the terminal, and then the positive cable. Special pullers are available to remove the cable clamps.
   NOTE: *To avoid sparks, always disconnect the ground cable first, and connect it last*
2. Remove the battery hold-down clamp.
3. Remove the battery, being careful not to spill the acid.
   NOTE: *Spilled acid can be neutralized with a baking soda/water solution. If you somehow get acid into your eyes, flush it out with lots of water and get to a doctor.*
4. Clean the battery posts thoroughly before reinstalling, or when installing a new battery.
5. Clean the cable clamps, using a wire brush, both inside and out.
6. Install the battery and the hold-down clamp or strap. Connect the positive, and then the negative cable. Do not hammer them in place. The terminals should be coated lightly (externally) with grease to prevent corrosion. There are also felt washers impregnated with an anti-corrosion substance which are slipped over the battery posts before installing the cables; these are available in auto parts stores.
   CAUTION: *Make absolutely sure that the battery is connected properly before you turn on the ignition switch. Reversed polarity can burn out your alternator and regulator within a matter of seconds.*

ENGINE MECHANICAL

Removal and Installation

The engine and transmission must be removed as a single unit.

1. Mark the location of the hinges on the hood and then remove the hood.
2. Disconnect the battery cables and remove the battery.
3. Drain the coolant from the radiator and remove the radiator and radiator hoses.
4. Remove the air cleaner and all attendant hoses and lines.
5. Disconnect the following:
   a. Ignition coil ground wire and high tension lead
   b. Wires to the distributor at the block connector
   c. Carburetor throttle linkage
   d. Fusible links
   e. Engine harness connectors
   f. Fuel line to the carburetor and the fuel return hose
   g. Heater hoses and all vacuum hoses
   h. Air pump hoses
   NOTE: *On models with air conditioning, it is necessary to remove the compressor and the condenser from their mounts. DO NOT ATTEMPT TO UNFASTEN ANY OF THE AIR CONDITIONER HOSES. See chapter one for additional warnings.*
6. Remove the slave cylinder from the clutch housing.
7. Unhook the speedometer cable from the transmission and remove the shift linkage from the transmission.

F10 engine harness connector

F10, 310 slave cylinder

ENGINE AND ENGINE REBUILDING

Battery and Starter Specifications
All cars use 12 volt, negative ground electrical systems

Year	Model	Battery Amp Hour Capacity	Lock Test Amps	Lock Test Volts	Lock Test Torque (ft. lbs.)	Starter No Load Test Amps	Starter No Load Test Volts	Starter No Load Test RPM	Brush Spring Tension (oz)	Min Brush Length (in)
All	F10	60	Not Recommended			60	12	7,000	49–64	0.47
All	310	60	Not Recommended			60 100 RG	11.5 11	7,000 3,900	50–64 56–70	0.47 0.43
1982	Stanza	60 U.S.A. 65 Canada	Not Recommended			60 U.S.A. 100 Canada (U.S. option)	11.5 U.S.A. 11.0 Canada	7,000 U.S.A., 3,900 Canada	4.0–4.9 U.S.A. 3.5–4.4 Canada	0.43

RG: Reduction Gear type starter

ENGINE AND ENGINE REBUILDING

General Engine Specifications

Year	Model	Type (model)	Engine Displacement Cu In. (cc)	Carburetor Type	Horsepower (SAE) @ rpm	Torque @ rpm (ft. lbs.)	Bore x Stroke (in.)	Compression Ratio	Normal Oil Pressure (psi)
1976–78	F10	OHV 4 (A14)	85.2 (1397)	Dual throat downdraft	80 @ 6,000	83 @ 3,600	2.99 x 3.03	8.5:1	43–50
1979–80	310	OHV 4 (A14)	85.2 (1397)	Dual throat downdraft	65 @ 5,600	75 @ 3,600	2.99 x 3.03	8.9:1	43–50
1981	310	OHV 4 (A15)	90.8 (1488)	Dual throat downdraft	N.A.	N.A.	2.992 x 3.228	8.9:1	43–50
1982	310	OHC 4 (E15)	90.8 (1488)	Dual throat downdraft	N.A.	N.A.	2.92 x 3.228	9.0:1	43–50
	Stanza	OHC 4 (CA20)		Dual throat downdraft	N.A.	N.A.	N.A.	N.A.	50–60

NOTE: Specifications given are for United States except California.
N.A.: Not available at time of publication

Crankshaft and Connecting Rod Specifications
All measurements given in inches

Year	Engine Model	Crankshaft Main Brg Journal Dia	Main Brg Oil Clearance	Shaft End-Play	Thrust on No.	Connecting Rod Bearings Journal Dia	Oil Clearance	Side Clearance
1976–78	A14	1.966–1.967	0.0008–0.002	0.002–0.006	3	1.7701–1.7706	0.0008–0.002	0.008–0.012
1979–81	A14, A15	1.9666–1.9671	0.001–0.0035	0.002–0.0059	3	1.7701–1.7706	0.0012–0.0031	0.008–0.012
1982	E15	1.9663–1.9671	①	0.002–0.007	3	1.5730–1.5738	0.0012–0.0024	0.004–0.0146
	CA20	2.0847–2.0852	0.0016–0.0024	0.002–0.007	3	1.7701–1.7706	0.0008–0.0024	0.008–0.012

① #1 & 5: 0.0012–0.0030
#2, 3, 4: 0.0012–0.0036

ENGINE AND ENGINE REBUILDING

Piston and Ring Specifications
All measurements in inches

Year	Engine Model	Piston Clearance	Ring Gap Top Compression	Ring Gap Bottom Compression	Ring Gap Oil Control	Ring Side Clearance Top Compression	Ring Side Clearance Bottom Compression	Ring Side Clearance Oil Control
1976–78	A14	0.0009–0.002	0.008–0.014	0.006–0.012	0.012–0.035	0.002–0.003	0.001–0.002	Combined ring
1979–80	A14	0.001–0.002	0.008–0.014	0.006–0.012	0.012–0.035	0.002–0.003	0.001–0.002	Snug
1981	A15	0.0010–0.0018	0.0079–0.0138	0.0059–0.0118	0.0118–0.0354	0.0016–0.0028	0.0012–0.0024	0.0039
1982	E15	0.0010–0.0018	0.0098–0.0157	0.0059–0.0018	0.0118–0.0354	0.0016–0.0029	0.0012–0.0025	Snug
1982	CA20	0.0009–0.0017	0.0079–0.0138	0.0059–0.0118	0.0118–0.0354	0.0016–0.0029	0.0012–0.0025	0.0020–0.0057

ENGINE AND ENGINE REBUILDING 43

Valve Specifications

Year	Model	Seat Angle (deg)	Spring Test Pressure lbs. @ in.	Free Length (in.)	Stem-to-Guide Clearance (in.) Intake	Stem-to-Guide Clearance (in.) Exhaust	Stem Diameter (in.) Intake	Stem Diameter (in.) Exhaust
1976–78	A14	45°	52.7 @ 1.52	1.83	0.0006–0.0018	0.0016–0.0028	0.3138–0.3144	0.3128–0.3134
1979–82	A14, A15	45°30′	52.7 @ 1.19	1.83	0.0006–0.0018	0.0016–0.0028	0.3134–0.3140	0.3128–0.3134
	E15	45°30′	128 @ 1.189	1.839	0.0008–0.0020	0.0018–0.0030	0.2744–0.2750	0.2734–0.2740
	CA20	45°30′	①	②	0.0008–0.0021	0.0016–0.0029	0.2742–0.2748	0.2734–0.2740

① Inner: 24 @ 1.38
   Outer: 47 @ 1.58

② Inner: 1.7362
   Outer: 1.9677

Torque Specifications
All readings in ft. lbs.

Engine Model	Cylinder Head Bolts	Main Bearing Bolts	Rod Bearing Bolts	Crankshaft Pulley Bolt	Flywheel to Crankshaft Bolts	Manifolds Intake	Manifolds Exhaust
A14, A15, E15	51–54	36–43	23–27	108–145 ②	58–65 ①	11–14	11–14
CA20	51–58	33–40	22–27	90–98	72–80	13–16	13–17

① 1976–78 A14: 54–61 ft. lbs.
② E15: 83–108

1. Speedometer cable
2. Shift rod
3. Select rod

F10, 310 speedometer cable and shift rod removal

F10, 310 exhaust pipe removal

8. Unbolt the exhaust pipe from the exhaust manifold. There are three bolts which attach the pipe to the manifold and bolts which attach the pipe support to the engine.
9. Unbolt the axle shafts from the differential.
10. Remove the buffer rods from the engine. Do not alter the length of the rods.
11. Unbolt the engine from the engine mounts. Unbolt the transmission mount.
12. Attach a sling to the engine and remove it.
13. Installation is the reverse of removal.

F10, 310 axle shaft removal

A series head bolt loosening sequence

A series head bolt tightening sequence

1. Link support
2. Radius link

F10 radius link support

If the buffer rod length has not been altered, it should still be correct.

Cylinder Head

REMOVAL AND INSTALLATION

NOTE: *To prevent distortion or warping of the cylinder head, allow the engine to cool completely before removing the head bolts.*

A14 and A15 Overhead Valve Engines

To remove the cylinder head on OHV engines:
1. Drain the coolant.
2. Disconnect the battery ground cable.
3. Remove the upper radiator hose. Remove the water outlet elbow and the thermostat.
4. Remove the air cleaner, carburetor, rocker arm cover, and both manifolds.
5. Remove the spark plugs.
6. Disconnect the temperature gauge connection.
7. Remove the head bolts and remove the head and rocker arm assembly together. Rap the head with a mallet to loosen it from the block. Remove the head and discard the gasket.
8. Remove the pushrods, keeping them in order.

To replace the cylinder head on OHV engines,
1. Make sure that head and block surfaces are clean. Check the cylinder head surface with a straightedge and a feeler gauge for flatness. If the head is warped more than 0.004 in., it must be trued. If this is not done, there will probably be a leak. The block surface should also be checked in the same way. If the block is warped more than 0.004 in., it must be trued.
2. Install a new head gasket. Most gaskets have a TOP marking. Make sure that the proper head gasket is used on the A12 so that no water passages are blocked off.
3. Install the head. Install the pushrods in their original locations. Install the rocker arm assembly. Loosen the rocker arm adjusting screws to prevent bending the pushrods when tightening the head bolts. Tighten the head bolts finger tight. One of the head bolts is smaller in diameter than the others. This bolt should be inserted in hole number one, center in the illustration.

CAUTION: *The above mentioned bolt is thinner than the others because it acts as the oil passageway for the rocker components. It must be inserted in the correct hole or the valve train will seize up after a few hundred miles.*

4. Refer to the "Torque Specifications" chart for the correct head bolt torque. Tighten the bolts to one third of the specified torque in the order shown in the head bolt tightening sequence illustration. Torque the rocker arm mounting bolts to 15–18 ft. lbs.
5. Tighten the bolts to two thirds of the specified torque in sequence.

ENGINE AND ENGINE REBUILDING

6. Tighten the bolts to the full specified torque in sequence.
7. Adjust the valves to the cold setting.
8. Reassemble the engine. Intake and exhaust manifold bolt torque for 1200 A12 engine is 7–10 ft. lbs., for all others 11–14 ft-lbs. Fill the cooling system. Start the engine and run it until normal temperature is reached. Remove the rocker arm cover. Torque the bolts in sequence once more. Check the valve clearances.
9. Retorque the head bolts after 600 miles of driving. Check the valve clearances after torquing, as this may disturb the settings.

E15 and CA20 Overhead Camshaft Engines

1. Turn the crankshaft so that the #1 cylinder is at TDC.
2. Drain the cooling system.
3. Remove the drive belts.
4. Remove the front cover.
5. Remove the water pump pulley.
6. Remove the crankshaft pulley.
7. Remove the distributor-to-canister vacuum tube.
8. Remove the alternator adjusting bracket.
9. Remove the drive belt tensioner and camshaft sprocket.
10. Remove the water pump.
11. Remove the oil pump.
12. Loosen the cylinder head bolts in the sequence shown.
13. Lift off the head.
14. Installation is the reverse of removal. When installing the bolts, tighten the two center bolts temporarily to 15 ft. lb. Install all the head bolts loosely. After the timing

E series head bolt loosening sequence

E series head bolt tightening sequence

CA20 head bolt loosening sequence

CA20 head bolt tightening sequence

belt and front cover have been installed, torque all the head bolts in the sequence shown to the specification given in the torque chart.

OVERHAUL

Cylinder head overhaul should be referred to a competent automotive machine shop. Valve guides and seats are removable and oversizes are available from Datsun. For procedures, see overhaul section at the end of this chapter.

Rocker Shaft

REMOVAL AND INSTALLATION

1. Remove rocker cover.
2. On A series engines, loosen rocker adjusting bolts and push adjusting screws away from pushrods.
3. Unbolt and remove the rocker shaft assembly.
4. To install, reverse the above. Tighten the rocker shaft bolts to 14–18 ft. lbs. on A series engines; 13–16 ft. lbs. on CA20 engines; 12–15 ft. lbs. on E series engines, in a circular sequence. Adjust the valves.

NOTE: *Both the intake and the exhaust valve springs are the uneven pitch type. That is, the springs have narrow coils at the bottom and wide coils at the top. The narrow coils (painted white) must be the side making contact on the cylinder head surface.*

46 ENGINE AND ENGINE REBUILDING

CA20 engine outer components

For overhead camshaft engine rocker removal and installation, see Camshaft Removal and Installation section in this chapter.

Intake Manifold

REMOVAL AND INSTALLATION

1. Remove the air cleaner assembly together with all of the attending hoses.
2. Disconnect the throttle linkage and fuel and vacuum lines from the carburetor.
3. The carburetor can be removed from the manifold at this point or can be removed as an assembly with the intake manifold.
4. On the A series engines, disconnect the intake and exhaust manifold unless you are removing both. Loosen the intake manifold attaching nuts, working from the two ends toward the center, and then remove them.
5. Remove the intake manifold from the engine.
6. Install the intake manifold in the reverse order of removal.

Exhaust Manifold

REMOVAL AND INSTALLATION

1. Remove the air cleaner assembly, if necessary for access. Remove the heat shield, if present.
2. Disconnect the exhaust pipe from the exhaust manifold. Disconnect the intake manifold from the exhaust manifold (A-series engines only) unless you are removing both.

ENGINE AND ENGINE REBUILDING 47

CA20 engine internal components

3. Remove all temperature sensors, air induction pipes and other attachments from the manifold.
4. Loosen and remove the exhaust manifold attaching nuts and remove the manifold from the engine.
5. Install the exhaust manifold in the reverse order of removal.

Timing Chain Cover
REMOVAL AND INSTALLATION
A14, A15 Overhead Valve Engines

1. Remove the radiator. Loosen the alternator adjustment and remove the belt. Loosen the air pump adjustment and remove the belt on engines with the air pump system.

48   ENGINE AND ENGINE REBUILDING

E series engine outer components

2. Remove the fan and water pump.

3. Bend back the locktab from the crankshaft pulley nut. Remove the nut by affixing a heavy wrench and rapping the wrench with a hammer. The nut must be unscrewed in the opposite direction of normal engine rotation. Pull off the pulley.

4. It is recommended that the oil pan be removed or loosened before the front cover is removed.

5. Unbolt and remove the timing chain cover.

6. Replace the crankshaft oil seal in the cover. Most models use a felt seal.

7. Reverse the procedure to install, using new gaskets. Apply sealant to both sides of the timing cover gasket. Front cover bolt torque is 4 ft. lbs., water pump bolt torque is 7–10 ft. lbs., and oil pan bolt torque is 4 ft. lbs.

ENGINE AND ENGINE REBUILDING 49

Timing Chain and Camshaft

REMOVAL AND INSTALLATION
A14 A15 Overhead Valve Engines

It is recommended that this operation be done with the engine removed from the vehicle.
1. Remove the timing chain cover.
2. Unbolt and remove the chain tensioner.
3. Remove the camshaft sprocket retaining bolt.
4. Pull off the camshaft sprocket, easing off the crankshaft sprocket at the same time. Remove both sprockets and chain as an assembly. Be careful not to lose the shims and oil slinger from behind the crankshaft sprocket.
5. Remove the distributor, distributor drive spindle, pushrods, and valve lifters.

50 ENGINE AND ENGINE REBUILDING

E series engine internal components

NOTE: *The lifters cannot be removed until the camshaft has been removed.*

Remove the oil pump and pump driveshaft.

6. Unbolt and remove the camshaft locating plate.

7. Remove the camshaft carefully. This will be easier if the block is inverted to prevent the lifters from falling down.

8. The camshaft bearings can be pressed out and replaced. They are available in undersizes, should it be necessary to regrind the camshaft journals.

9. Reinstall the camshaft. If the locating

ENGINE AND ENGINE REBUILDING

plate has an oil hole, it should be to the right of the engine. The locating plate is marked with the word LOWER and an arrow. Locating plate bolt torque is 3–4 ft. lbs. Be careful to engage the drive pin in the rear end of the camshaft with the slot in the oil pump driveshaft.

10. Camshaft end-play can be measured after temporarily replacing the camshaft sprocket and securing bolt.

The engines have standard end-play specifications of 0.0004–0.002 in. with a service limit of 0.004 in. If the end-play is excessive, replace the locating plate. New plates are available in several sizes.

11. If the crankshaft or camshaft has been replaced, install the sprockets temporarily and make sure that they are parallel. Adjust by shimming under the crankshaft sprocket.

12. Assemble the sprockets and chain, aligning them.

13. Turn the crankshaft until the keyway and the No. 1 piston is at top dead center. Install the sprockets and chain. The oil slinger behind the crankshaft sprocket must be replaced with the concave surface to the front. If the chain and sprocket installation is correct, the sprocket marks must be aligned between the shaft centers when the No. 1 piston is at top dead center. Engine camshaft

52 ENGINE AND ENGINE REBUILDING

A series engine components

ENGINE AND ENGINE REBUILDING 53

Wood wedge used to hold the timing chain in place

Wedge the chain with a wood block (arrow)

A series engine timing mark alignment

E series engine valve timing mark alignment

CA20 valve timing mark alignment

sprocket retaining bolt torque is 33–36 ft. lbs.

14. The rest of the reassembly procedure is the reverse of disassembly. Engine chain tensioner bolt torque is 4–6 ft. lbs.

Timing Belt and Camshaft
REMOVAL AND INSTALLATION
E15 and CA20 Overhead Camshaft Engines

1. Disconnect the battery ground cable.
2. Remove the drive belts.
3. Remove the front cover.
4. Bring the engine around to TDC on the #1 piston. Note the alignment of the timing marks on the camshaft sprocket, belt and crankshaft sprocket. See the accompanying pictures for correct alignment.
5. Remove the timing belt by loosening the belt tensioner and removing the camshaft sprocket. Remove the rocker arm cover.
6. Remove rocker arm shaft(s) and remove camshaft.
7. Installation is the reverse of removal. Coat the camshaft with engine oil prior to installation.
8. When installing the camshaft, make sure that the protruding dowel is at the top on the front face of the shaft. See the accompanying picture for correct timing mark alignment. On the CA20, torque the camshaft sprocket bolts to 36–40 ft. lbs.; on the E15, torque the camshaft pulley bolt to 4–6 ft. lbs. (48–60 in. lb.)

Pistons and Connecting Rods
REMOVAL AND INSTALLATION
All Engines

1. Remove the cylinder head.
2. Remove the oil pan.

54 ENGINE AND ENGINE REBUILDING

3. Remove any carbon buildup from the cylinder wall at the top end of the piston travel with a ridge reamer tool.

4. Position the piston to be removed at the bottom of its stroke so that the connecting rod bearing cap can be reached easily from under the engine.

5. Unscrew the connecting rod bearing cap nuts and remove the cap and lower half of the bearing.

6. Push the piston and connecting rod up and out of the cylinder block with a length of wood. Use care not to scratch the cylinder wall with the connecting rod or the wooden tool.

7. Keep all of the components from each cylinder together and install them in the cylinder from which they were removed.

8. Coat the bearing face of the connecting rod and the outer face of the pistons with engine oil.

9. See the illustrations for the correct placement of the piston rings for your model and year Datsun.

10. Turn the crankshaft until the rod journal of the particular cylinder you are working on is brought to the TDC position.

11. With the piston and rings clamped in a ring compressor, the notched mark on the head of the piston toward the front of the engine, and the oil hole side of the connecting rod toward the fuel pump side of the engine, push the piston and connecting rod assembly into the cylinder bore until the big bearing end of the connecting rod contacts and is seated on the rod journal of the crankshaft. Use care not to scratch the cylinder wall with the connecting rod.

12. Push down farther on the piston and turn the crankshaft while the connecting rod rides around on the crankshaft rod journal. Turn the crankshaft until the crankshaft rod journal is at BDC (bottom dead center).

13. Align the mark on the connecting rod bearing cap with that on the connecting rod and tighten the bearing cap bolts to the specified torque.

14. Install all of the piston/connecting rod assemblies in the manner outlined above and assemble the oil pan and cylinder head to the engine in the reverse order of removal.

IDENTIFICATION AND POSITIONING

The pistons are marked with a number or "F" in the piston head. When installed in the engine the number or "F" markings are to be facing toward the front of the engine.

The connecting rods are installed in the engine with the oil hole facing toward the fuel pump side (right) of the engine.

NOTE: *It is advisable to number the pistons, connecting rods, and bearing caps in some manner so that they can be reinstalled in the same cylinder, facing in the same direction from which they are removed.*

CA20 piston and rod alignment

E series engine piston and rod alignment

A series engine piston and rod alignment

Piston ring arrangement

ENGINE AND ENGINE REBUILDING

ENGINE LUBRICATION

Oil Pan

REMOVAL AND INSTALLATION

All Engines

To remove the oil pan it will be necessary to unbolt the motor mounts and jack the engine to gain clearance. Drain the oil, remove the attaching screws, and remove the oil pan and gasket. Install the oil pan in the reverse order with a new gasket, tightening the screws to 4–7 ft. lbs.

Rear Main Oil Seal

REPLACEMENT

In order to replace the rear main oil seal, the rear main bearing cap must be removed. Removal of the rear main bearing cap requires the use of a special rear main bearing cap puller. Also, the oil seal is installed with a special crankshaft rear oil seal drift. Unless these or similar tools are available to you, it is recommended that the oil seal be replaced by a Datsun service center.

1. Remove the engine and transmission assembly from the vehicle.
2. Remove the transmission from the engine. Remove the oil pan.

Installing rear main seal

CA20 oil pump

CA20 oil pump installed

A series oil pump removal

3. Remove the clutch from the flywheel.
4. Remove the flywheel from the crankshaft.
5. Remove the rear main bearing cap together with the bearing cap side seals.
6. Remove the rear main oil seal from around the crankshaft.
7. Apply lithium grease around the sealing lip of the oil seal and install the seal around the crankshaft using a suitable tool.
8. Apply sealer to the rear main bearing cap as indicated, install the rear main bearing cap, and tighten the cap bolts to 33–40 ft. lbs.
9. Apply sealant to the rear main bearing cap side seals and install the side seals, driving the seals into place with a suitable drift.
10. Assemble the engine and install it in the vehicle in the reverse order of removal.

Oil Pump

REMOVAL AND INSTALLATION

A Series Engines

1. Drain the engine oil.
2. Remove the front stabilizer bar if it is in the way of removing the oil pump.
3. Remove the splash shield.
4. Remove the oil pump body with the drive spindle assembly.

5. Install the A-series oil pump in the reverse order of removal.

6. Fill the pump housing with engine oil, then align the punch mark on the spindle with the hole in the oil pump.

7. With a new gasket placed over the drive spindle, install the oil pump and drive spindle assembly so that the projection on the top of the drive spindle is located in the 11:25 o'clock position.

8. Install the distributor with the metal tip of the rotor pointing toward the No. 1 spark plug tower of the distributor cap.

9. Assemble the remaining components in the reverse order of removal.

E15 Engine

1. Loosen alternator lower bolts.
2. Remove alternator belt and adjusting bar bolt.
3. Move the alternator out of the way and support it safely.
4. Disconnect the oil pressure gauge harness.
5. Remove the pump assembly.
6. For installation, fill the pump with clean engine oil and rotate it several times.
7. Install the pump on the engine using a new gasket. Torque the pump mounting bolts to 7–9 ft. lbs.

CA20 Engine

1. Drain the oil and remove the oil pan.
2. Remove the water pump belt, crankshaft pulley and crankshaft damper.
3. Remove the timing belt, crankshaft sprocket and timing belt tensioner.
4. Remove the oil pump.
5. Installation is the reverse of removal. Fill the pump with clean engine oil and rotate it several times prior to installation. After aligning its locating notches with those of the crankshaft, install the pump along the locating notch. Apply RTV sealant to the front oil seal end of the pan prior to installation.

ENGINE COOLING

Radiator

REMOVAL AND INSTALLATION

A Series Engines

NOTE: *On some models it may be necessary to remove the front grille.*

1. Drain the engine coolant into a clean container.

2. Disconnect the upper and lower radiator hoses and the expansion tank hose.
3. If the fan has a shroud, unbolt the shroud and move it back, hanging it over the fan.
4. Remove the radiator mounting bolts and the radiator.
5. Installation is the reverse of removal. Fill the automatic transmission to the proper level. Fill the cooling system.

E15 Engine

1. Drain the cooling system.
2. Unbolt and set aside the power steering pump.
3. Disconnect the upper and lower radiator hoses.
4. Remove the lower hose adapter.
5. Disconnect and cap the automatic transmission cooling lines.
6. Disconnect the fan wires and remove the radiator.
7. Installation is the reverse of removal.

CA20 Engine

1. Drain the cooling system.
2. Disconnect the upper and lower radiator hoses and the coolant reserve tank hose.
3. Disconnect the water temperature switch connector and the fan wiring.
4. Remove the radiator.
5. Installation is the reverse of removal.

Water Pump

REMOVAL AND INSTALLATION

A Series Engines

1. Drain the engine coolant into a clean container.
2. Loosen the four bolts retaining the fan shroud to the radiator and remove the shroud.
3. Loosen the belt, then remove the fan and pulley from the water pump hub.
4. Remove the bolts retaining the pump and remove the pump together with the gasket from the front cover.

A series water pump removal

ENGINE AND ENGINE REBUILDING 57

5. Remove all traces of gasket material and install the water pump in the reverse order with a new gasket and sealer. Tighten the bolts uniformly.

E15 Engines

1. Drain the cooling system.
2. Remove the power steering drive belt.
3. Remove the power steering pump.
4. Remove the water pump drive belt.
5. Remove the water pump pulley.
6. Remove the water pump.
7. Installation is the reverse of removal. Always use a new gasket. Torque the bolts to 6–10 ft. lbs.

E series water pump removal

CA20 Engine

1. Drain the cooling system.
2. Remove the front cover.
3. Remove the water pump drive belt.
4. Remove the water pump pulley.
5. Remove the water pump.
6. Installation is the reverse of removal. Always use a new gasket. Torque the mounting bolts to 9–12 ft. lbs.

Thermostat

REMOVAL AND INSTALLATION
All Engines

1. Drain the engine coolant into a clean container so that the level is below the thermostat housing.
2. Disconnect the upper radiator hose at the water outlet.
3. Loosen the two securing nuts and remove the water outlet, gasket, and the thermostat from the thermostat housing.
4. Install the thermostat in the reverse order of removal, using a new gasket with sealer and with the thermostat spring toward the inside of the engine.

1980 and later thermostat: place the jiggle valve toward the top

ENGINE REBUILDING

Most procedures involved in rebuilding an engine are fairly standard, regardless of the type of engine involved. This section is a guide to accepted rebuilding procedures. Examples of standard rebuilding practices are illustrated and should be used along with specific details concerning your particular engine, found earlier in this chapter.

The procedures given here are those used by any competent rebuilder. Obviously some of the procedures cannot be performed by the do-it-yourself mechanic, but are provided so that you will be familiar with the services that should be offered by rebuilding or machine shops. As an example, in most instances, it is more profitable for the home mechanic to remove the cylinder heads, buy the necessary parts (new valves, seals, keepers, keys, etc.) and deliver these to a machine shop for the necessary work. In this way you will save the money to remove and install the cylinder head and the mark-up on parts.

On the other hand, most of the work involved in rebuilding the lower end is well within the scope of the do-it-yourself mechanic. Only work such as hot-tanking, actually boring the block or Magnafluxing (invisible crack detection) need be sent to a machine shop.

Tools

The tools required for basic engine rebuilding should, with a few exceptions, be those included in a mechanic's tool kit. An accurate torque wrench, and a dial indicator (reading in thousandths) mounted on a universal base should be available. Special tools, where required, are available from the major tool suppliers. The services of a competent automotive machine shop must also be readily available.

Precautions

Aluminum has become increasingly popular for use in engines, due to its low weight and excellent heat transfer characteristics. The following precautions must be observed when handling aluminum (or any other) engine parts:
—Never hot-tank aluminum parts.
—Remove all aluminum parts (identification tags, etc.) from engine parts before hot-tanking (otherwise they will be removed during the process).
—Always coat threads lightly with engine oil or anti-seize compounds before installation, to prevent seizure.
—Never over-torque bolts or spark plugs in aluminum threads. Should stripping occur, threads can be restored using any of a number of thread repair kits available (see next section).

Inspection Techniques

Magnaflux and Zyglo are inspection techniques used to locate material flaws, such as stress cracks. Magnaflux is a magnetic process, applicable only to ferrous materials. The Zyglo process coats the matrial with a fluorescent dye penetrant, and any material may be tested using Zyglo. Specific checks of suspected surface cracks may be made at lower cost and more readily using spot check dye. The dye is sprayed onto the suspected area, wiped off, and the area is then sprayed with a developer. Cracks then will show up brightly.

Overhaul

The section is divided into two parts. The first, Cylinder Head Reconditioning, assumes that the cylinder head is removed from the engine, all manifolds are removed, and the cylinder head is on a workbench. The camshaft should be removed from overhead cam cylinder heads. The second section, Cylinder Block Reconditioning, covers the block, pistons, connecting rods and crankshaft. It is assumed that the engine is mounted on a work stand, and the cylinder head and all accessories are removed.

Procedures are identified as follows:
Unmarked—Basic procedures that must be performed in order to successfully complete the rebuilding process.
Starred (*)—Procedures that should be performed to ensure maximum performance and engine life.
Double starred (**)—Procedures that may be performed to increase engine performance and reliability.

When assembling the engine, any parts that will be in frictional contact must be pre-lubricated, to provide protection on initial start-up. Any product specifically formulated for this purpose may be used. NOTE: *Do not use engine oil.* Where semi-permanent (locked but removable) installation of bolts or nuts is desired, threads should be cleaned and located with Loctite® or a similar product (non-hardening).

ENGINE AND ENGINE REBUILDING 59

Repairing Damaged Threads

Several methods of repairing damaged threads are available. Heli-Coil® (shown here), Keenserts® and Microdot® are among the most widely used. All involve basically the same principle—drilling out stripped threads, tapping the hole and installing a pre-wound insert—making welding, plugging and oversize fasteners unnecessary.

Two types of thread repair inserts are usually supplied—a standard type for most Inch Coarse, Inch Fine, Metric Coarse and Metric Fine thread sizes and a spark plug type to fit most spark plug port sizes. Consult the individual manufacturer's catalog to determine exact applications. Typical thread repair kits will contain a selection of pre-wound threaded inserts, a tap (corresponding to the outside diameter threads of the insert) and an installation tool. Spark plug inserts usually differ because they require a tap equipped with pilot threads and a combined reamer/tap section. Most manufacturers also supply blister-packed thread repair inserts separately in addition to a master kit containing a variety of taps and inserts plus installation tools.

Before effecting a repair to a threaded hole, remove any snapped, broken or damaged bolts or studs. Penetrating oil can be used to free frozen threads; the offending item can be removed with locking pliers or with a screw or stud extractor. After the hole is clear, the thread can be repaired, as follows:

Drill out the damaged threads with specified drill. Drill completely through the hole or to the bottom of a blind hole

With the tap supplied, tap the hole to receive the thread insert. Keep the tap well oiled and back it out frequently to avoid clogging the threads

Damaged bolt holes can be repaired with thread repair inserts

Standard thread repair insert (left) and spark plug thread insert (right)

Screw the threaded insert onto the installation tool until the tang engages the slot. Screw the insert into the tapped hole until it is ¼–½ turn below the top surface. After installation break off the tang with a hammer and punch

Standard Torque Specifications and Fastener Markings

The Newton-metre has been designated the world standard for measuring torque and will gradually replace the foot-pound and kilogram-meter. In the absence of specific torques, the following chart can be used as a guide to the maximum safe torque of a particular size/grade of fastener.

- There is no torque difference for fine or coarse threads.
- Torque values are based on clean, dry threads. Reduce the value by 10% if threads are oiled prior to assembly.
- The torque required for aluminum components or fasteners is considerably less.

U. S. BOLTS

SAE Grade Number		1 or 2			5			6 or 7		

Bolt Markings
Manufacturer's marks may vary—number of lines always 2 less than the grade number.

Usage		Frequent			Frequent			Infrequent		
Bolt Size (inches)—(Thread)		Maximum Torque			Maximum Torque			Maximum Torque		
	Ft-Lb	kgm	Nm	Ft-Lb	kgm	Nm	Ft-Lb	kgm	Nm
¼—20	5	0.7	6.8	8	1.1	10.8	10	1.4	13.5
—28	6	0.8	8.1	10	1.4	13.6			
5⁄16—18	11	1.5	14.9	17	2.3	23.0	19	2.6	25.8
—24	13	1.8	17.6	19	2.6	25.7			
⅜—16	18	2.5	24.4	31	4.3	42.0	34	4.7	46.0
—24	20	2.75	27.1	35	4.8	47.5			
7⁄16—14	28	3.8	37.0	49	6.8	66.4	55	7.6	74.5
—20	30	4.2	40.7	55	7.6	74.5			
½—13	39	5.4	52.8	75	10.4	101.7	85	11.75	115.2
—20	41	5.7	55.6	85	11.7	115.2			
9⁄16—12	51	7.0	69.2	110	15.2	149.1	120	16.6	162.7
—18	55	7.6	74.5	120	16.6	162.7			
⅝—11	83	11.5	112.5	150	20.7	203.3	167	23.0	226.5
—18	95	13.1	128.8	170	23.5	230.5			
¾—10	105	14.5	142.3	270	37.3	366.0	280	38.7	379.6
—16	115	15.9	155.9	295	40.8	400.0			
⅞—9	160	22.1	216.9	395	54.6	535.5	440	60.9	596.5
—14	175	24.2	237.2	435	60.1	589.7			
1—8	236	32.5	318.6	590	81.6	799.9	660	91.3	894.8
—14	250	34.6	338.9	660	91.3	849.8			

ENGINE AND ENGINE REBUILDING

METRIC BOLTS

NOTE: *Metric bolts are marked with a number indicating the relative strength of the bolt. These numbers have nothing to do with size.*

Description	Torque ft-lbs (Nm)			
Thread size x pitch (mm)	Head mark—4		Head mark—7	
6 x 1.0	2.2–2.9	(3.0–3.9)	3.6–5.8	(4.9–7.8)
8 x 1.25	5.8–8.7	(7.9–12)	9.4–14	(13–19)
10 x 1.25	12–17	(16–23)	20–29	(27–39)
12 x 1.25	21–32	(29–43)	35–53	(47–72)
14 x 1.5	35–52	(48–70)	57–85	(77–110)
16 x 1.5	51–77	(67–100)	90–120	(130–160)
18 x 1.5	74–110	(100–150)	130–170	(180–230)
20 x 1.5	110–140	(150–190)	190–240	(160–320)
22 x 1.5	150–190	(200–260)	250–320	(340–430)
24 x 1.5	190–240	(260–320)	310–410	(420–550)

NOTE: *This engine rebuilding section is a guide to accepted rebuilding procedures. Typical examples of standard rebuilding procedures are illustrated. Use these procedures along with the detailed instructions earlier in this chapter, concerning your particular engine.*

Cylinder Head Reconditioning

Procedure	Method
Remove the cylinder head:	See the engine service procedures earlier in this chapter for details concerning specific engines.
Identify the valves:	Invert the cylinder head, and number the valve faces front to rear, using a permanent felt-tip marker.
Remove the rocker arms (OHV engines only):	Remove the rocker arms with shaft(s) or balls and nuts. Wire the sets of rockers, balls and nuts together, and identify according to the corresponding valve.
Remove the camshaft (OHC engines only):	See the engine service procedures earlier in this chapter for details concerning specific engines.
Remove the valves and springs:	Using an appropriate valve spring compressor (depending on the configuration of the cylinder head), compress the valve springs. Lift out the keepers with needlenose pliers, release the compressor, and remove the valve, spring, and spring retainer. See the engine service procedures earlier in this chapter for details concerning specific engines.

62 ENGINE AND ENGINE REBUILDING

Cylinder Head Reconditioning

Procedure	Method
Check the valve stem-to-guide clearance: *Check the valve stem-to-guide clearance*	Clean the valve stem with lacquer thinner or a similar solvent to remove all gum and varnish. Clean the valve guides using solvent and an expanding wire-type valve guide cleaner. Mount a dial indicator so that the stem is at 90° to the valve stem, as close to the valve guide as possible. Move the valve off its seat, and measure the valve guide-to-stem clearance by rocking the stem back and forth to actuate the dial indicator. Measure the valve stems using a micrometer, and compare to specifications, to determine whether stem or guide wear is responsible for excessive clearance. NOTE: *Consult the Specifications tables earlier in this chapter.*
De-carbon the cylinder head and valves: *Remove the carbon from the cylinder head with a wire brush and electric drill*	Chip carbon away from the valve heads, combustion chambers, and ports, using a chisel made of hardwood. Remove the remaining deposits with a stiff wire brush. NOTE: *Be sure that the deposits are actually removed, rather than burnished.*
Hot-tank the cylinder head (cast iron heads only): CAUTION: *Do not hot-tank aluminum parts.*	Have the cylinder head hot-tanked to remove grease, corrosion, and scale from the water passages. NOTE: *In the case of overhead cam cylinder heads, consult the operator to determine whether the camshaft bearings will be damaged by the caustic solution.*
Degrease the remaining cylinder head parts:	Clean the remaining cylinder head parts in an engine cleaning solvent. Do not remove the protective coating from the springs.
Check the cylinder head for warpage: 1 & 3 CHECK DIAGONALLY 2 CHECK ACROSS CENTER *Check the cylinder head for warpage*	Place a straight-edge across the gasket surface of the cylinder head. Using feeler gauges, determine the clearance at the center of the straight-edge. If warpage exceeds .003″ in a 6″ span, or .006″ over the total length, the cylinder head must be resurfaced. NOTE: *If warpage exceeds the manufacturer's maximum tolerance for material removal, the cylinder head must be replaced.* When milling the cylinder heads of V-type engines, the intake manifold mounting position is altered, and must be corrected by milling the manifold flange a proportionate amount.

ENGINE AND ENGINE REBUILDING

Cylinder Head Reconditioning

Procedure	Method
*Knurl the valve guides: Cut-away view of a knurled valve guide	*Valve guides which are not excessively worn or distorted may, in some cases, be knurled rather than replaced. Knurling is a process in which metal is displaced and raised, thereby reducing clearance. Knurling also provides excellent oil control. The possibility of knurling rather than replacing valve guides should be discussed with a machinist.
Replace the valve guides: NOTE: *Valve guides should only be replaced if damaged or if an oversize valve stem is not available.* A—VALVE GUIDE I.D. B—LARGER THAN THE VALVE GUIDE O.D. WASHERS A—VALVE GUIDE I.D. B—LARGER THAN THE VALVE GUIDE O.D. Valve guide installation tool using washers for installation	See the engine service procedures earlier in this chapter for details concerning specific engines. Depending on the type of cylinder head, valve guides may be pressed, hammered, or shrunk in. In cases where the guides are shrunk into the head, replacement should be left to an equipped machine shop. In other cases, the guides are replaced using a stepped drift (see illustration). Determine the height above the boss that the guide must extend, and obtain a stack of washers, their I.D. similar to the guide's O.D., of that height. Place the stack of washers on the guide, and insert the guide into the boss. NOTE: *Valve guides are often tapered or beveled for installation.* Using the stepped installation tool (see illustration), press or tap the guides into position. Ream the guides according to the size of the valve stem.
Replace valve seat inserts:	Replacement of valve seat inserts which are worn beyond resurfacing or broken, if feasible, must be done by a machine shop.
Resurface (grind) the valve face: FOR DIMENSIONS, REFER TO SPECIFICATIONS CHECK FOR BENT STEM DIAMETER VALVE FACE ANGLE 1/32" MINIMUM THIS LINE PARALLEL WITH VALVE HEAD Critical valve dimensions	Using a valve grinder, resurface the valves according to specifications given earlier in this chapter. CAUTION: *Valve face angle is not always identical to valve seat angle.* A minimum margin of Valve grinding by machine

64 ENGINE AND ENGINE REBUILDING

Cylinder Head Reconditioning

Procedure	Method
	$1/32''$ should remain after grinding the valve. The valve stem top should also be squared and resurfaced, by placing the stem in the V-block of the grinder, and turning it while pressing lightly against the grinding wheel. **NOTE:** *Do not grind sodium filled exhaust valves on a machine. These should be hand lapped.*
Resurface the valve seats using reamers or grinder: Valve seat width and centering Reaming the valve seat with a hand reamer	Select a reamer of the correct seat angle, slightly larger than the diameter of the valve seat, and assemble it with a pilot of the correct size. Install the pilot into the valve guide, and using steady pressure, turn the reamer clockwise. **CAUTION:** *Do not turn the reamer counterclockwise.* Remove only as much material as necessary to clean the seat. Check the concentricity of the seat (following). If the dye method is not used, coat the valve face with Prussian blue dye, install and rotate it on the valve seat. Using the dye marked area as a centering guide, center and narrow the valve seat to specifications with correction cutters. **NOTE:** *When no specifications are available, minimum seat width for exhaust valves should be $5/64''$, intake valves $1/16''$.* After making correction cuts, check the position of the valve seat on the valve face using Prussian blue dye.
	To resurface the seat with a power grinder, select a pilot of the correct size and coarse stone of the proper angle. Lubricate the pilot and move the stone on and off the valve seat at 2 cycles per second, until all flaws are gone. Finish the seat with a fine stone. If necessary the seat can be corrected or narrowed using correction stones.
Check the valve seat concentricity: Check the valve seat concentricity with a dial gauge	Coat the valve face with Prussian blue dye, install the valve, and rotate it on the valve seat. If the entire seat becomes coated, and the valve is known to be concentric, the seat is concentric.
	*Install the dial gauge pilot into the guide, and rest of the arm on the valve seat. Zero the gauge, and rotate the arm around the seat. Run-out should not exceed .002''.

ENGINE AND ENGINE REBUILDING 65

Cylinder Head Reconditioning

Procedure	Method
*Lap the valves: NOTE: *Valve lapping is done to ensure efficient sealing of resurfaced valves and seats.* **Lapping the valves by hand** **Home-made valve lapping tool**	*Invert the cylinder head, lightly lubricate the valve stems, and install the valves in the head as numbered. Coat valve seats with fine grinding compound, and attach the lapping tool suction cup to a valve head. NOTE: *Moisten the suction cup.* Rotate the tool between the palms, changing position and lifting the tool often to prevent grooving. Lap the valve until a smooth, polished seat is evident. Remove the valve and tool, and rinse away all traces of grinding compound. **Fasten a suction cup to a piece of drill rod, and mount the rod in a hand drill. Proceed as above, using the hand drill as a lapping tool. CAUTION: *Due to the higher speeds involved when using the hand drill, care must be exercised to avoid grooving the seat.* Lift the tool and change direction of rotation often.
Check the valve springs: NOT MORE THAN 5/64" CLOSED COIL END DOWNWARD **Check the valve spring free length and squareness** **Check the valve spring test pressure**	Place the spring on a flat surface next to a square. Measure the height of the spring, and rotate it against the edge of the square to measure distortion. If spring height varies (by comparison) by more than $1/16''$ or if distortion exceeds $1/16''$, replace the spring. **In addition to evaluating the spring as above, test the spring pressure at the installed and compressed (installed height minus valve lift) height using a valve spring tester. Springs used on small displacement engines (up to 3 liters) should be $\mp$ 1 lb of all other springs in either position. A tolerance of $\mp$ 5 lbs is permissible on larger engines.

ENGINE AND ENGINE REBUILDING

Cylinder Head Reconditioning

Procedure	Method
*Install valve stem seals: Install valve stem seals	* Due to the pressure differential that exists at the ends of the intake valve guides (atmospheric pressure above, manifold vacuum below), oil is drawn through the valve guides into the intake port. This has been alleviated somewhat since the addition of positive crankcase ventilation, which lowers the pressure above the guides. Several types of valve stem seals are available to rocker arms and balls, and install them on the the stem and guide boss, while others require that the boss be machined. Recently, Teflon guide seals have become popular. Consult a parts supplier or machinist concerning availability and suggested usages. NOTE: *When installing seals, ensure that a small amount of oil is able to pass the seal to lubricate the valve guides; otherwise, excessive wear may result.*
Install the valves:	See the engine service procedures earlier in this chapter for details concerning specific engines. 　Lubricate the valve stems, and install the valves in the cylinder head as numbered. Lubricate and position the seals (if used) and the valve springs. Install the spring retainers, compress the springs, and insert the keys using needle-nose pliers or a tool designed for this purpose. NOTE: *Retain the keys with wheel bearing grease during installation.*
Check valve spring installed height: Measure the valve spring installed height (A) with a modified steel rule Valve spring installed height (A)	Measure the distance between the spring pad and the lower edge of the spring retainer, and compare to specifications. If the installed height is incorrect, add shim washers between the spring pad and the spring. CAUTION: *Use only washers designed for this purpose.*
Install the camshaft (OHC engines only) and check end-play:	See the engine service procedures earlier in this chapter for details concerning specific engines.

ENGINE AND ENGINE REBUILDING 67

Cylinder Head Reconditioning

Procedure	Method
Inspect the rocker arms, balls, studs, and nuts (OHV engines only): *Stress cracks in the rocker nuts* (SMALL FRACTURES)	Visually inspect the rocker arms, balls, studs, and nuts for cracks, galling, burning, scoring, or wear. If all parts are intact, liberally lubricate the rocker arms and balls, and install them on the cylinder head. If wear is noted on a rocker arm at the point of valve contact, grind it smooth and square, removing as little material as possible. Replace the rocker arm if excessively worn. If a rocker stud shows signs of wear, it must be replaced (see below). If a rocker nut shows stress cracks, replace it. If an exhaust ball is galled or burned, substitute the intake ball from the same cylinder (if it is intact), and install a new intake ball. **NOTE:** *Avoid using new rocker balls on exhaust valves.*
Replacing rocker studs (OHV engines only): *Extracting a pressed-in rocker stud* (AS STUB BEGINS TO PULL UP, IT WILL BE NECESSARY TO REMOVE THE NUT AND ADD MORE WASHERS — ⅜" NUT — FLAT WASHERS) *Ream the stud bore for oversize rocker studs*	In order to remove a threaded stud, lock two nuts on the stud, and unscrew the stud using the lower nut. Coat the lower threads of the new stud with Loctite, and install. Two alternative methods are available for replacing pressed in studs. Remove the damaged stud using a stack of washers and a nut (see illustration). In the first, the boss is reamed .005–.006" oversize, and an oversize stud pressed in. Control the stud extension over the boss using washers, in the same manner as valve guides. Before installing the stud, coat it with white lead and grease. To retain the stud more positively drill a hole through the stud and boss, and install a roll pin. In the second method, the boss is tapped, and a threaded stud installed.
Inspect the rocker shaft(s) and rocker arms (OHV engines only) *Check the rocker arm-to-rocker shaft contact area* (ROCKER ARM — SHAFT — CONTACT POINT)	Remove rocker arms, springs and washers from rocker shaft. **NOTE:** *Lay out parts in the order as they are removed.* Inspect rocker arms for pitting or wear on the valve contact point, or excessive bushing wear. Bushings need only be replaced if wear is excessive, because the rocker arm normally contacts the shaft at one point only. Grind the valve contact point of rocker arm smooth if necessary, removing as little material as possible. If excessive material must be removed to smooth and square the arm, it should be replaced. Clean out all oil holes and passages in rocker shaft. If shaft is grooved or worn, replace it. Lubricate and assemble the rocker shaft.

ENGINE AND ENGINE REBUILDING

Cylinder Head Reconditioning

Procedure	Method
Inspect the pushrods (OHV engines only):	Remove the pushrods, and, if hollow, clean out the oil passages using fine wire. Roll each pushrod over a piece of clean glass. If a distinct clicking sound is heard as the pushrod rolls, the rod is bent, and must be replaced. *The length of all pushrods must be equal. Measure the length of the pushrods, compare to specifications, and replace as necessary.
Inspect the valve lifters (OHV engines only): CHECK FOR CONCAVE WEAR ON FACE OF TAPPET USING TAPPET FOR STRAIGHT EDGE Check the lifter face for squareness	Remove lifters from their bores, and remove gum and varnish, using solvent. Clean walls of lifter bores. Check lifters for concave wear as illustrated. If face is worn concave, replace lifter, and carefully inspect the camshaft. Lightly lubricate lifter and insert it into its bore. If play is excessive, an oversize lifter must be installed (where possible). Consult a machinist concerning feasibility. If play is satisfactory, remove, lubricate, and reinstall the lifter.
*Testing hydraulic lifter leak down (OHV engines only):	Submerge lifter in a container of kerosene. Chuck a used pushrod or its equivalent into a drill press. Position container of kerosene so pushrod acts on the lifter plunger. Pump lifter with the drill press, until resistance increases. Pump several more times to bleed any air out of lifter. Apply very firm, constant pressure to the lifter, and observe rate at which fluid bleeds out of lifter. If the fluid bleeds very quickly (less than 15 seconds), lifter is defective. If the time exceeds 60 seconds, lifter is sticking. In either case, recondition or replace lifter. If lifter is operating properly (leak down time 15–60 seconds), lubricate and install it.

Cylinder Block Reconditioning

Procedure	Method
Checking the main bearing clearance: PLASTIGAGE® Plastigage® installed on the lower bearing shell	Invert engine, and remove cap from the bearing to be checked. Using a clean, dry rag, thoroughly clean all oil from crankshaft journal and bearing insert. NOTE: *Plastigage® is soluble in oil; therefore, oil on the journal or bearing could result in erroneous readings.* Place a piece of Plastigage along the full length of journal, reinstall cap, and torque to specifications. NOTE: *Specifications are given in the engine specifications earlier in this chapter.* Remove bearing cap, and determine bearing clearance by comparing width of Plastigage to the scale on Plastigage envelope. Journal taper is determined by comparing width of the Plastigage strip near its ends. Rotate crankshaft 90° and retest, to determine journal eccentricity. NOTE: *Do not rotate crankshaft with Plastigage*

ENGINE AND ENGINE REBUILDING   69

Cylinder Block Reconditioning

Procedure	Method
Measure Plastigage® to determine main bearing clearance	*installed*. If bearing insert and journal appear intact, and are within tolerances, no further main bearing service is required. If bearing or journal appear defective, cause of failure should be determined before replacement.
	* Remove crankshaft from block (see below). Measure the main bearing journals at each end tiwce (90° apart) using a micrometer, to determine diameter, journal taper and eccentricity. If journals are within tolerances, reinstall bearing caps at their specified torque. Using a telescope gauge and micrometer, measure bearing I.D. parallel to piston axis and at 30° on each side of piston axis. Subtract journal O.D. from bearing I.D. to determine oil clearance. If crankshaft journals appear defective, or do not meet tolerances, there is no need to measure bearings; for the crankshaft will require grinding and/or undersize bearings will be required. If bearing appears defective, cause for failure should be determined prior to replacement.
Check the connecting rod bearing clearance:	Connecting rod bearing clearance is checked in the same manner as main bearing clearance, using Plastigage. Before removing the crankshaft, connecting rod side clearance also should be measured and recorded.
	* Checking connecting rod bearing clearance, using a micrometer, is identical to checking main bearing clearance. If no other service is required, the piston and rod assemblies need not be removed.
Remove the crankshaft: Match the connecting rod to the cylinder with a number stamp	Using a punch, mark the corresponding main bearing caps and saddles according to position (i.e., one punch on the front main cap and saddle, two on the second, three on the third, etc.). Using number stamps, identify the corresponding connecting rods and caps, according to cylinder (if no numbers are present). Remove the main and connecting rod caps, and place sleeves of plastic tubing or vacuum hose over the connecting rod bolts, to protect the journals as the crankshaft is removed. Lift the crankshaft out of the block. Match the connecting rod and cap with scribe marks

ENGINE AND ENGINE REBUILDING

Cylinder Block Reconditioning

Procedure	Method
Remove the ridge from the top of the cylinder: *Cylinder bore ridge*	In order to facilitate removal of the piston and connecting rod, the ridge at the top of the cylinder (unworn area; see illustration) must be removed. Place the piston at the bottom of the bore, and cover it with a rag. Cut the ridge away using a ridge reamer, exercising extreme care to avoid cutting too deeply. Remove the rag, and remove cuttings that remain on the piston. CAUTION: *If the ridge is not removed, and new rings are installed, damage to rings will result.*
Remove the piston and connecting rod: *Push the piston out with a hammer handle*	Invert the engine, and push the pistons and connecting rods out of the cylinders. If necessary, tap the connecting rod boss with a wooden hammer handle, to force the piston out. CAUTION: *Do not attempt to force the piston past the cylinder ridge* (see above).
Service the crankshaft:	Ensure that all oil holes and passages in the crankshaft are open and free of sludge. If necessary, have the crankshaft ground to the largest possible undersize.
	**Have the crankshaft Magnafluxed, to locate stress cracks. Consult a machinist concerning additional service procedures, such as surface hardening (e.g., nitriding, Tuftriding) to improve wear characteristics, cross drilling and chamfering the oil holes to improve lubrication, and balancing.
Removing freeze plugs:	Drill a small hole in the middle of the freeze plugs. Thread a large sheet metal screw into the hole and remove the plug with a slide hammer.
Remove the oil gallery plugs:	Threaded plugs should be removed using an appropriate (usually square) wrench. To remove soft, pressed in plugs, drill a hole in the plug, and thread in a sheet metal screw. Pull the plug out by the screw using pliers.
Hot-tank the block: NOTE: *Do not hot-tank aluminum parts.*	Have the block hot-tanked to remove grease, corrosion, and scale from the water jackets. NOTE: *Consult the operator to determine whether the camshaft bearings will be damaged during the hot-tank process.*

ENGINE AND ENGINE REBUILDING

Cylinder Block Reconditioning

Procedure	Method

Check the block for cracks:	Visually inspect the block for cracks or chips. The most common locations are as follows:
	    Adjacent to freeze plugs.
	    Between the cylinders and water jackets.
	    Adjacent to the main bearing saddles.
	    At the extreme bottom of the cylinders.
	Check only suspected cracks using spot check dye (see introduction). If a crack is located, consult a machinist concerning possible repairs.

	** Magnaflux the block to locate hidden cracks. If cracks are located, consult a machinist about feasibility of repair.
Install the oil gallery plugs and freeze plugs:	Coat freeze plugs with sealer and tap into position using a piece of pipe, slightly smaller than the plug, as a driver. To ensure retention, stake the edges of the plugs. Coat threaded oil gallery plugs with sealer and install. Drive replacement soft plugs into block using a large drift as driver.
	* Rather than reinstalling lead plugs, drill and tap the holes, and install threaded plugs.
Check the bore diameter and surface:	Visually inspect the cylinder bores for roughness, scoring, or scuffing. If evident, the cylinder bore must be bored or honed oversize to eliminate imperfections, and the smallest possible oversize piston used. The new pistons should be given to the machinist with the block, so that the cylinders can be bored or honed exactly to the piston size (plus clearance). If no flaws are evident, measure the bore diameter using a telescope gauge and micrometer, or dial gauge, parallel and perpendicular to the engine centerline, at the top (below the ridge) and bottom of the bore. Subtract the bottom measurements from the top to determine taper, and the parallel to the centerline measurements from the perpendicular measurements to determine eccentricity. If the measurements are not within specifications, the cylinder must be bored or honed, and an oversize piston installed. If the measurements are within specifications the cylinder may be used as is, with only finish honing (see below).

Measure the cylinder bore with a dial gauge

Cylinder bore measuring points (A—AT RIGHT ANGLE TO CENTERLINE OF ENGINE; B—PARALLEL TO CENTERLINE OF ENGINE)

Measure the cylinder bore with a telescope gauge

Measure the telescope gauge with a micrometer to determine the cylinder bore

72 ENGINE AND ENGINE REBUILDING

Cylinder Block Reconditioning

Procedure	Method
	NOTE: *Prior to submitting the block for boring, perform the following operation(s).*
Check the cylinder block bearing alignment: **Check the main bearing saddle alignment**	Remove the upper bearing inserts. Place a straightedge in the bearing saddles along the centerline of the crankshaft. If clearance exists between the straightedge and the center saddle, the block must be alignbored.
*Check the deck height:	The deck height is the distance from the crankshaft centerline to the block deck. To measure, invert the engine, and install the crankshaft, retaining it with the center main cap. Measure the distance from the crankshaft journal to the block deck, parallel to the cylinder centerline. Measure the diameter of the end (front and rear) main journals, parallel to the centerline of the cylinders, divide the diameter in half, and subtract it from the previous measurement. The results of the front and rear measurements should be identical. If the difference exceeds .005″, the deck height should be corrected. NOTE: *Block deck height and warpage should be corrected at the same time.*
Check the block deck for warpage:	Using a straightedge and feeler gauges, check the block deck for warpage in the same manner that the cylinder head is checked (see Cylinder Head Reconditioning). If warpage exceeds specifications, have the deck resurfaced. NOTE: *In certain cases a specification for total material removal (Cylinder head and block deck) is provided. This specification must not be exceeded.*
Clean and inspect the pistons and connecting rods: RING EXPANDER **Remove the piston rings**	Using a ring expander, remove the rings from the piston. Remove the retaining rings (if so equipped) and remove piston pin. NOTE: *If the piston pin must be pressed out, determine the proper method and use the proper tools; otherwise the piston will distort.* Clean the ring grooves using an appropriate tool, exercising care to avoid cutting too deeply. Thoroughly clean all carbon and varnish from the piston with solvent. CAUTION: *Do not use a wire brush or caustic solvent on pistons.* Inspect the pistons for scuffing, scoring, cracks, pitting, or excessive ring groove wear. If wear is evident, the piston must be replaced. Check the connecting rod length by measuring the rod from the inside of the large end to the

ENGINE AND ENGINE REBUILDING

Cylinder Block Reconditioning

Procedure	Method
Clean the piston ring grooves (RING GROOVE CLEANER)	inside of the small end using calipers (see illustration). All connecting rods should be equal length. Replace any rod that differs from the others in the engine.
	*Have the connecting rod alignment checked in an alignment fixture by a machinist. Replace any twisted or bent rods.
Check the connecting rod length (arrow)	*Magnaflux the connecting rods to locate stress cracks. If cracks are found, replace the connecting rod.
Fit the pistons to the cylinders: **Measure the piston prior to fitting** (90°)	Using a telescope gauge and micrometer, or a dial gauge, measure the cylinder bore diameter perpendicular to the piston pin, 2½" below the deck. Measure the piston perpendicular to its pin on the skirt. The difference between the two measurements is the piston clearance. If the clearance is within specifications or slightly below (after boring or honing), finish honing is all that is required. If the clearance is excessive, try to obtain a slightly larger piston to bring clearance within specifications. Where this is not possible, obtain the first oversize piston, and hone (or if necessary, bore) the cylinder to size.
Assemble the pistons and connecting rods: **Install the piston pin lock-rings (if used)**	Inspect piston pin, connecting rod small end bushing, and piston bore for galling, scoring, or excessive wear. If evident, replace defective part(s). Measure the I.D. of the piston boss and connecting rod small end, and the O.D. of the piston pin. If within specifications, assemble piston pin and rod. *CAUTION: If piston pin must be pressed in, determine the proper method and use the proper tools; otherwise the piston will distort.* Install the lock rings; ensure that they seat properly. If the parts are not within specifications, determine the service method for the type of engine. In some cases, piston and pin are serviced as an assembly when either is defective. Others specify reaming the piston and connecting rods for an oversize pin. If the connecting rod bushing is worn, it may in many cases be replaced. Reaming the piston and replacing the rod bushing are machine shop operations.

ENGINE AND ENGINE REBUILDING

Cylinder Block Reconditioning

Procedure	Method
Clean and inspect the camshaft: *Check the camshaft for straightness*	Degrease the camshaft, using solvent, and clean out all oil holes. Visually inspect cam lobes and bearing journals for excessive wear. If a lobe is questionable, check all lobes as indicated below. If a journal or lobe is worn, the camshaft must be reground or replaced. NOTE: *If a journal is worn, there is a good chance that the bushings are worn.* If lobes and journals appear intact, place the front and rear journals in V-blocks, and rest a dial indicator on the center journal. Rotate the camshaft to check straightness. If deviation exceeds .001″, replace the camshaft. *Check the camshaft lobes with a micrometer, by measuring the lobes from the nose to base and again at 90° (see illustration). The lift is determined by subtracting the second measurement from the first. If all exhaust lobes and all intake lobes are not identical, the camshaft must be reground or replaced. *Camshaft lobe measurement*
Replace the camshaft bearings (OHV engines only): *Camshaft bearing removal and installation tool (OHV engines only)*	If excessive wear is indicated, or if the engine is being completely rebuilt, camshaft bearings should be replaced as follows: Drive the camshaft rear plug from the block. Assemble the removal puller with its shoulder on the bearing to be removed. Gradually tighten the puller nut until bearing is removed. Remove remaining bearings, leaving the front and rear for last. To remove front and rear bearings, reverse position of the tool, so as to pull the bearings in toward the center of the block. Leave the tool in this position, pilot the new front and rear bearings on the installer, and pull them into position: Return the tool to its original position and pull remaining bearings into position. NOTE: *Ensure that oil holes align when installing bearings.* Replace camshaft rear plug, and stake it into position to aid retention.
Finish hone the cylinders:	Chuck a flexible drive hone into a power drill, and insert it into the cylinder. Start the hone, and move it up and down in the cylinder at a rate which will produce approximately a 60° cross-hatch pattern. NOTE: *Do not extend the hone below the cylin-*

ENGINE AND ENGINE REBUILDING

Cylinder Block Reconditioning

Procedure	Method
Cylinder bore after honing (CROSS HATCH PATTERN, 50°-60°)	*der bore*. After developing the pattern, remove the hone and recheck piston fit. Wash the cylinders with a detergent and water solution to remove abrasive dust, dry, and wipe several times with a rag soaked in engine oil.
Check piston ring end-gap: *Check the piston ring end gap*	Compress the piston rings to be used in a cylinder, one at a time, into that cylinder, and press them approximately 1″ below the deck with an inverted piston. Using feeler gauges, measure the ring end-gap, and compare to specifications. Pull the ring out of the cylinder and file the ends with a fine file to obtain proper clearance. **CAUTION:** *If inadequate ring end-gap is utilized, ring breakage will result.*
Install the piston rings: *Check the piston ring side clearance* (PISTON RING, FEELER GAUGE, RING GROOVE)	Inspect the ring grooves in the piston for excessive wear or taper. If necessary, recut the grooves(s) for use with an overwidth ring or a standard ring and spacer. If the groove is worn uniformly, overwidth rings, or standard rings and spacers may be installed without recutting. Roll the outside of the ring around the groove to check for burrs or deposits. If any are found, remove with a fine file. Hold the ring in the groove, and measure side clearance. If necessary, correct as indicated above. **NOTE:** *Always install any additional spacers above the piston ring.* The ring groove must be deep enough to allow the ring to seat below the lands (see illustration). In many cases, a "go-no-go" depth gauge will be provided with the piston rings. Shallow grooves may be corrected by recutting, while deep grooves require some type of filler or expander behind the piston. Consult the piston ring sup-

Cylinder Block Reconditioning

Procedure	Method
	plier concerning the suggested method. Install the rings on the piston, lowest ring first, using a ring expander. **NOTE:** *Position the ring as specified by the manufacturer.* Consult the engine service procedures earlier in this chapter for details concerning specific engines.
Install the camshaft (OHV engines only):	Liberally lubricate the camshaft lobes and journals, and install the camshaft. **CAUTION:** *Exercise extreme care to avoid damaging the bearings when inserting the camshaft.* Install and tighten the camshaft thrust plate retaining bolts. See the engine service procedures earlier in this chapter for details concerning specific engines.
Check camshaft end-play (OHV engines only): Check the camshaft end-play with a feeler gauge DIAL INDICATOR CAMSHAFT Check the camshaft end-play with a dial indicator	Using feeler gauges, determine whether the clearance between the camshaft boss (or gear) and backing plate is within specifications. Install shims behind the thrust plate, or reposition the camshaft gear and retest endplay. In some cases, adjustment is by replacing the thrust plate. See the engine service procedures earlier in this chapter for details concerning specific engines. *Mount a dial indicator stand so that the stem of the dial indicator rests on the nose of the camshaft, parallel to the camshaft axis. Push the camshaft as far in as possible and zero the gauge. Move the camshaft outward to determine the amount of camshaft endplay. If the endplay is not within tolerance, install shims behind the thrust plate, or reposition the camshaft gear and retest. See the engine service procedures earlier in this chapter for details concerning specific engines.
Install the rear main seal:	See the engine service procedures earlier in this chapter for details concerning specific engines.
Install the crankshaft: INSTALLING BEARING SHELL REMOVING BEARING SHELL **Remove or install the upper bearing insert using a roll-out pin**	Thoroughly clean the main bearing saddles and caps. Place the upper halves of the bearing inserts on the saddles and press into position. **NOTE:** *Ensure that the oil holes align.* Press the corresponding bearing inserts into the main bearing caps. Lubricate the upper main bearings, and lay the crankshaft in position. Place a strip of Plastigage on each of the crankshaft journals, install the main caps, and torque to specifications. Remove the main caps, and compare the Plastigage to the scale on the Plastigage envelope. If clearances are within tolerances, remove the Plastigage, turn the crankshaft 90°, wipe off all oil and retest. If all clearances are correct, re-

ENGINE AND ENGINE REBUILDING

Cylinder Block Reconditioning

Procedure	Method
Home-made bearing roll-out pin (60°, 5/8")	move all Plastigage, thoroughly lubricate the main caps and bearing journals, and install the main caps. If clearances are not within tolerance, the upper bearing inserts may be removed, without removing the crankshaft, using a bearing roll out pin (see illustration). Roll in a bearing that will provide proper clearance, and retest. Torque all main caps, excluding the thrust bearing cap, to specifications. Tighten the thrust bearing cap finger tight. To properly align the thrust bearing, pry the crankshaft the extent of its axial travel several times, the last movement held toward the front of the engine, and torque the thrust bearing cap to specifications. Determine the crankshaft end-play (see below), and bring within tolerance with thrust washers.

Aligning the thrust bearing
(PRY CRANKSHAFT FORWARD — PRY CAP BACKWARD — TIGHTEN CAP)

Procedure	Method
Measure crankshaft end-play:	Mount a dial indicator stand on the front of the block, with the dial indicator stem resting on the nose of the crankshaft, parallel to the crankshaft axis. Pry the crankshaft the extent of its travel rearward, and zero the indicator. Pry the crankshaft forward and record crankshaft end-play. **NOTE:** *Crankshaft end-play also may be measured at the thrust bearing, using feeler gauges (see illustration).*

Check the crankshaft end-play with a dial indicator

Check the crankshaft end-play with a feeler gauge

78 ENGINE AND ENGINE REBUILDING

Cylinder Block Reconditioning

Procedure	Method
Install the pistons: USE A SHORT PIECE OF 3/8" HOSE AS A GUIDE **Use lengths of vacuum hose or rubber tubing to protect the crankshaft journals and cylinder walls during piston installation** RING COMPRESSOR **Install the piston using a ring compressor**	Press the upper connecting rod bearing halves into the connecting rods, and the lower halves into the connecting rod caps. Position the piston ring gaps according to specifications (see car section), and lubricate the pistons. Install a ring compressor on a piston, and press two long (8") pieces of plastic tubing over the rod bolts. Using the tubes as a guide, press the pistons into the bores and onto the crankshaft with a wooden hammer handle. After seating the rod on the crankshaft journal, remove the tubes and install the cap finger tight. Install the remaining pistons in the same manner. Invert the engine and check the bearing clearance at two points (90° apart) on each journal with Plastigage. NOTE: *Do not turn the crankshaft with Plastigage installed.* If clearance is within tolerances, remove *all* Plastigage, thoroughly lubricate the journals, and torque the rod caps to specifications. If clearance is not within specifications, install different thickness bearing inserts and recheck. CAUTION: *Never shim or file the connecting rods or caps.* Always install plastic tube sleeves over the rod bolts when the caps are not installed, to protect the crankshaft journals.
Check connecting rod side clearance: **Check the connecting rod side clearance with a feeler gauge**	Determine the clearance between the sides of the connecting rods and the crankshaft, using feeler gauges. If clearance is below the minimum tolerance, the rod may be machined to provide adequate clearance. If clearance is excessive, substitute an unworn rod, and recheck. If clearance is still outside specifications, the crankshaft must be welded and reground, or replaced.
Inspect the timing chain (or belt):	Visually inspect the timing chain for broken or loose links, and replace the chain if any are found. If the chain will flex sideways, it must be replaced. Install the timing chain as specified. Be sure the timing belt is not stretched, frayed or broken. NOTE: *If the original timing chain is to be reused, install it in its original position.*

ENGINE AND ENGINE REBUILDING

Cylinder Block Reconditioning

Procedure	Method
Check timing gear backlash and runout (OHV engines):	Mount a dial indicator with its stem resting on a tooth of the camshaft gear (as illustrated). Rotate the gear until all slack is removed, and zero the indicator. Rotate the gear in the opposite direction until slack is removed, and record gear backlash. Mount the indicator with its stem resting on the edge of the camshaft gear, parallel to the axis of the camshaft. Zero the indicator, and turn the camshaft gear one full turn, recording the runout. If either backlash or runout exceed specifications, replace the worn gear(s).

Check the camshaft gear backlash

Check the camshaft gear run-out

Completing the Rebuilding Process

Following the above procedures, complete the rebuilding process as follows:

Fill the oil pump with oil, to prevent cavitating (sucking air) on initial engine start up. Install the oil pump and the pickup tube on the engine. Coat the oil pan gasket as necessary, and install the gasket and the oil pan. Mount the flywheel and the crankshaft vibration damper or pulley on the crankshaft. NOTE: *Always use new bolts when installing the flywheel.* Inspect the clutch shaft pilot bushing in the crankshaft. If the bushing is excessively worn, remove it with an expanding puller and a slide hammer, and tap a new bushing into place.

Position the engine, cylinder head side up. Lubricate the lifters, and install them into their bores. Install the cylinder head, and torque it as specified. Insert the pushrods (where applicable), and install the rocker shaft(s) (if so equipped) or position the rocker arms on the pushrods. Adjust the valves.

Install the intake and exhaust manifolds, the carburetor(s), the distributor and spark plugs. Adjust the point gap and the static ignition timing. Mount all accessories and install the engine in the car. Fill the radiator with coolant, and the crankcase with high quality engine oil.

Break-in Procedure

Start the engine, and allow it to run at low speed for a few minutes, while checking for leaks. Stop the engine, check the oil level, and fill as necessary. Restart the engine, and fill the cooling system to capacity. Check the point dwell angle and adjust the ignition timing and the valves. Run the engine at low to medium speed (800–2500 rpm) for approximately ½ hour, and retorque the cylinder head bolts. Road test the car, and check again for leaks.

Follow the manufacturer's recommended engine break-in procedure and maintenance schedule for new engines.

Emission Controls and Fuel System

EMISSION CONTROLS

There are three types of automotive pollutants; crankcase fumes, exhaust gases and gasoline evaporation. The equipment that is used to limit these pollutants is commonly called emission control equipment.

Crankcase Emission Controls

The crankcase emission control equipment consists of a positive crankcase ventilation valve (PCV), a closed or open oil filler cap and hoses to connect this equipment.

When the engine is running, a small portion of the gases which are formed in the combustion chamber during combustion leak by the piston rings and enter the crankcase. Since these gases are under pressure they tend to escape from the crankcase and enter into the atmosphere. If these gases were allowed to remain in the crankcase for any length of time, they would contaminate the engine oil and cause sludge to build up. If the gases are allowed to escape into the atmosphere, they would pollute the air, as they contain unburned hydrocarbons. The crankcase emission control equipment recycles these gases back into the engine combustion chamber where they are burned.

Crankcase gases are recycled in the following manner: while the engine is running, clean filtered air is drawn into the crankcase through the carburetor air filter and then through a hose leading to the rocket cover. As the air passes through the crankcase it picks up the combustion gases and carries them out of the crankcase, up through the PCV valve and into the intake manifold. After they enter the intake manifold they are drawn into the combustion chamber and burned.

The most critical component in the system is the PCV valve. This vacuum controlled valve regulates the amount of gases which are recycled into the combustion chamber. At low engine speeds the valve is partially closed, limiting the flow of gases into the intake manifold. As engine speed increases, the valve opens to admit greater quantities of the gases into the intake manifold. If the valve should become blocked or plugged, the gases will be prevented from escaping from the crankcase by the normal route. Since these gases are under pressure, they will find their own way out of the crankcase. This alternate route is usually a weak oil seal or gasket in the engine. As the gas escapes by the gasket, it also creates an oil leak. Besides causing oil leaks, a clogged PCV valve also allows these gases to remain in the crankcase for an extended

EMISSION CONTROLS AND FUEL SYSTEM

49 states A series engine emission control systems

EMISSION CONTROLS AND FUEL SYSTEM

EMISSION CONTROLS AND FUEL SYSTEM 83

84 EMISSION CONTROLS AND FUEL SYSTEM

California E series engine emission control systems

period of time, promoting the formation of sludge in the engine.

The above explanation and the troubleshooting procedure which follows applies to all engines with PCV systems.

TESTING

Check the PCV system hoses and connections, to see that there are no leaks; then replace or tighten, as necessary.

To check the valve, remove it and blow through both of its ends. When blowing from the side which goes toward the intake manifold, very little air should pass through it. When blowing from the crankcase (valve cover) side, air should pass through freely.

Replace the valve with a new one, if the valve fails to function as outlined.

NOTE: *Do not attempt to clean or adjust the valve; replace it with a new one.*

REMOVAL AND INSTALLATION

To remove the PCV valve, simply loosen the hose clamp and remove the valve from the manifold-to-crankcase hose and intake mani-

EMISSION CONTROLS AND FUEL SYSTEM 85

49 states E series engine emission control systems

fold. Install the PCV valve in the reverse order of removal.

Evaporative Emission Control System

The system used on 1976 and later models consists of sealed fuel tank, vapor-liquid separator (certain models only), vapor vent line, carbon canister, vacuum signal line and a canister purge line.

In operation, fuel vapors and/or liquid are routed to the liquid/vapor separator or check valve where liquid fuel is directed back into the fuel tank as fuel vapors flow into the charcoal filled canister. The charcoal absorbs and stores the fuel vapors when the engine is not running or is at idle. When the throttle valves in the carburetor (or air intakes for fuel injection) are opened, vacuum from above the throttle valves is routed through a vacuum signal line to the purge control valve on the canister. The control valve opens and allows the fuel vapors to be drawn from the canister through a purge line and into the intake manifold and the combustion chambers.

INSPECTION AND SERVICE

Check the hoses for proper connections and damage. Replace as necessary. Check the va-

EMISSION CONTROLS AND FUEL SYSTEM

Canadian E series engine emission control systems

por separator tank for fuel leaks, distortion and dents, and replace as necessary.

Carbon Canister and Purge Control Valve

To check the operation of the carbon canister purge control valve, disconnect the rubber hose between the canister control valve and the T-fitting, at the T-fitting. Apply vacuum to the hose leading to the control valve. The vacuum condition should be maintained indefinitely. If the control valve leaks, remove the top cover of the valve and check for a dislocated or cracked diaphragm. If the diaphragm is damaged, a repair kit containing a new diaphragm, retainer, and spring is available and should be installed.

The carbon canister has an air filter in the bottom of the canister. The filter element should be checked once a year or every 12,000 miles; more frequently if the car is operated in dusty areas. Replace the filter by pulling it out of the bottom of the canister and installing a new one.

EMISSION CONTROLS AND FUEL SYSTEM

California CA20 engine emission control systems

REMOVAL AND INSTALLATION

Removal and installation of the various evaporative emission control system components consists of disconnecting the hoses, loosening retaining screws, and removing the part which is to be replaced or checked. Install in the reverse order. When replacing hose, make sure that it is fuel and vapor resistant.

Spark Timing Control System

The spark timing control system has been used in different forms on Datsuns since 1972. The first system, Transmission Controlled Spark System (TCS) was used on most Datsuns through 1979. This system consists of a thermal vacuum valve, a vacuum switching valve, a high gear detecting switch, and a

88 EMISSION CONTROLS AND FUEL SYSTEM

49 states CA20 engine emission control systems

number of vacuum hoses. Basically the system is designed to retard full spark advance except when the car is in high gear and the engine is at normal operating temperature. At all other times, the spark advance is retarded to one degree or another.

The 1980–82 Spark Timing Control System replaces the TCS system. The major difference is that it works solely from engine water temperature changes rather than a transmission-mounted switch. The system includes a thermal vacuum valve, a vacuum delay valve, and attendant hoses. It performs the same function as the earlier TCS system; to retard full spark advance at times when high levels of pollutants would otherwise be given off.

INSPECTION AND ADJUSTMENTS

Normally the TCS and Spark Timing Control systems should be trouble-free. However, if you suspect a problem in the system, first check to make sure all wiring (if so equipped) and hoses are connected and free from dirt. Also check to make sure the distributor vacuum advance is working properly. If everything appears all right, connect a timing light to the engine and make sure the initial timing

EMISSION CONTROLS AND FUEL SYSTEM

49 states high altitude CA20 engine emission control systems

is correct. On vehicles with the TCS system, run the engine until it reaches normal operating temperature, and then have an assistant sit in the car and shift the transmission through all the gears slowly. If the system is functioning properly, the timing will be 10 to 15 degrees advanced in high gear (compared to the other gear positions). If the system is still not operating correctly, you will have to check for continuity at all the connections with a test light.

To test the Spark Timing Control System, connect a timing light and check the ignition timing while the temperature gauge is in the "cold" position. Write down the reading. Allow the engine to run with the timing light attached until the temperature needle reaches the center of the gauge. As the engine is warming up, check with the timing light to make sure the ignition timing retards. When the temperature needle is in the middle of the gauge, the ignition timing should adv-

EMISSION CONTROLS AND FUEL SYSTEM

Adjusting the TOCS pressure

ance from its previous position. If the ignition timing does not change, replace the thermal vacuum valve.

Early Fuel Evaporation System

The Early Fuel Evaporation System is used on the A-series engines. The system's purpose is to heat the air/fuel mixture when the engine is below normal operating temperature. 1976–79 engines use a system much akin to the old style exhaust manifold heat riser. The only adjustment necessary is to occasionally lubricate the counterweight. Other than that, the system should be trouble-free.

The 1980–82 engines use coolant water heat instead of exhaust gas heat to pre-warm the fuel mixture. This system should be trouble-free.

Throttle Opener Control System (TOCS)

The Throttle Opener Control System (TOCS) used on A-series engines (except 1980 California) reduces hydrocarbon emissions during coasting conditions.

High manifold vacuum during coasting prevents the complete combustion of the air/fuel mixture because of the reduced amount of air. This condition will result in a large amount of HC emission. Enriching the air/fuel mixture for a short time (during the high vacuum condition) will reduce the emission of the HC.

However, enriching the air/fuel mixture with only the mixture adjusting screw will cause poor engine idle or invite an increase in the carbon monoxide (CO) content of the exhaust gases.

The TOCS system consists of a servo diaphragm, vacuum control valve, throttle opener solenoid valve, speed detecting switch and amplifier on manual transmission models. Automatic transmission models use an inhibitor and inhibitor relay in the place of the speed detecting switch and amplifier. At the moment when the manifold vacuum increases, as during deceleration, the vacuum control valve opens to transfer the manifold vacuum to the servo diaphragm chamber, and the carburetor throttle valve opens slightly. Under this condition, the proper amount of fresh air is sucked into the combustion chamber. As a result, a more thorough ignition takes place, burning much of the HC in the exhaust gases.

Automatic Temperature Controlled Air Cleaner

The rate of fuel atomization varies with the temperature of the air that the fuel is being mixed with. The air/fuel ratio cannot be held constant for efficient fuel combustion with a wide range of air temperatures. Cold air being drawn into the engine causes a denser and richer air/fuel mixture, inefficient fuel atomization, and thus, more hydrocarbons in the exhaust gas. Hot air being drawn into the engine causes a leaner air/fuel mixture and more efficient atomization and combustion for less hydrocarbons in the exhaust gases.

The automatic temperature controlled air cleaner is designed so that the temperature of the ambient air being drawn into the engine is automatically controlled, to hold the temperature of the air and, consequently, the fuel/air ratio at a constant rate for efficient fuel combustion.

A temperature sensing vacuum switch controls vacuum applied to a vacuum motor operating a valve in the intake snorkle of the air cleaner. When the engine is cold or the air being drawn into the engine is cold, the vacuum motor opens the valve, allowing air heated by the exhaust manifold to be drawn into the engine. As the engine warms up, the temperature sensing unit shuts off the vacuum applied to the vacuum motor which allows the valve to close, shutting off the heated air and allowing cooler, outside (under hood) air to be drawn into the engine.

TESTING

When the air around the temperature sensor of the unit mounted inside the air cleaner

CHILTON'S
FUEL ECONOMY & TUNE-UP TIPS

Tune-Up • Spark Plug Diagnosis • Emission Controls
Fuel System • Cooling System • Tires and Wheels
General Maintenance

55 WAYS TO IMPROVE FUEL ECONOMY

CHILTON'S FUEL ECONOMY & TUNE-UP TIPS

Fuel economy is important to everyone, no matter what kind of vehicle you drive. The maintenance-minded motorist can save both money and fuel using these tips and the periodic maintenance and tune-up procedures in this Repair and Tune-Up Guide.

There are more than 130,000,000 cars and trucks registered for private use in the United States. Each travels an average of 10-12,000 miles per year, and, in total they consume close to 70 billion gallons of fuel each year. This represents nearly 2/3 of the oil imported by the United States each year. The Federal government's goal is to reduce consumption 10% by 1985. A variety of methods are either already in use or under serious consideration, and they all affect your driving and the cars you will drive. In addition to "down-sizing", the auto industry is using or investigating the use of electronic fuel delivery, electronic engine controls and alternative engines for use in smaller and lighter vehicles, among other alternatives to meet the federally mandated Corporate Average Fuel Economy (CAFE) of 27.5 mpg by 1985. The government, for its part, is considering rationing, mandatory driving curtailments and tax increases on motor vehicle fuel in an effort to reduce consumption. The government's goal of a 10% reduction could be realized — and further government regulation avoided — if every private vehicle could use just 1 less gallon of fuel per week.

How Much Can You Save?

Tests have proven that almost anyone can make at least a 10% reduction in fuel consumption through regular maintenance and tune-ups. When a major manufacturer of spark plugs sur-

TUNE-UP

1. Check the cylinder compression to be sure the engine will really benefit from a tune-up and that it is capable of producing good fuel economy. A tune-up will be wasted on an engine in poor mechanical condition.
2. Replace spark plugs regularly. New spark plugs alone can increase fuel economy 3%.
3. Be sure the spark plugs are the correct type (heat range) for your vehicle. See the Tune-Up Specifications.

Heat range refers to the spark plug's ability to conduct heat away from the firing end. It must conduct the heat away in an even pattern to avoid becoming a source of pre-ignition, yet it must also operate hot enough to burn off conductive deposits that could cause misfiring.

The heat range is usually indicated by a number on the spark plug, part of the manufacturer's designation for each individual spark plug. The numbers in bold-face indicate the heat range in each manufacturer's identification system.

Manufacturer	Typical Designation
AC	R **45** TS
Bosch (old)	WA **145** T30
Bosch (new)	HR **8** Y
Champion	RBL **15** Y
Fram/Autolite	**415**
Mopar	P-**62** PR
Motorcraft	BRF-**42**
NGK	BP **5** ES-15
Nippondenso	W **16** EP
Prestolite	14GR **5** 2A

Periodically, check the spark plugs to be sure they are firing efficiently. They are excellent indicators of the internal condition of your engine.

On AC, Bosch (new), Champion, Fram/Autolite, Mopar, Motorcraft and Prestolite, a higher number indicates a hotter plug. On Bosch (old), NGK and Nippondenso, a higher number indicates a colder plug.

4. Make sure the spark plugs are properly gapped. See the Tune-Up Specifications in this book.
5. Be sure the spark plugs are firing efficiently. The illustrations on the next 2 pages show you how to "read" the firing end of the spark plug.
6. Check the ignition timing and set it to specifications. Tests show that almost all cars

veyed over 6,000 cars nationwide, they found that a tune-up, on cars that needed one, increased fuel economy over 11%. Replacing worn plugs alone, accounted for a 3% increase. The same test also revealed that 8 out of every 10 vehicles will have some maintenance deficiency that will directly affect fuel economy, emissions or performance. Most of this mileage-robbing neglect could be prevented with regular maintenance.

Modern engines require that all of the functioning systems operate properly for maximum efficiency. A malfunction anywhere wastes fuel. You can keep your vehicle running as efficiently and economically as possible, by being aware of your vehicles operating and performance characteristics. If your vehicle suddenly develops performance or fuel economy problems it could be due to one or more of the following:

PROBLEM	POSSIBLE CAUSE
Engine Idles Rough	Ignition timing, idle mixture, vacuum leak or something amiss in the emission control system.
Hesitates on Acceleration	Dirty carburetor or fuel filter, improper accelerator pump setting, ignition timing or fouled spark plugs.
Starts Hard or Fails to Start	Worn spark plugs, improperly set automatic choke, ice (or water) in fuel system.
Stalls Frequently	Automatic choke improperly adjusted and possible dirty air filter or fuel filter.
Performs Sluggishly	Worn spark plugs, dirty fuel or air filter, ignition timing or automatic choke out of adjustment.

Check spark plug wires on conventional point type ignition for cracks by bending them in a loop around your finger.

Be sure that spark plug wires leading to adjacent cylinders do not run too close together. (Photo courtesy Champion Spark Plug Co.)

have incorrect ignition timing by more than 2°.

7. If your vehicle does not have electronic ignition, check the points, rotor and cap as specified.

8. Check the spark plug wires (used with conventional point-type ignitions) for cracks and burned or broken insulation by bending them in a loop around your finger. Cracked wires decrease fuel efficiency by failing to deliver full voltage to the spark plugs. One misfiring spark plug can cost you as much as 2 mpg.

9. Check the routing of the plug wires. Misfiring can be the result of spark plug leads to adjacent cylinders running parallel to each other and too close together. One wire tends to pick up voltage from the other causing it to fire "out of time".

10. Check all electrical and ignition circuits for voltage drop and resistance.

11. Check the distributor mechanical and/or vacuum advance mechanisms for proper functioning. The vacuum advance can be checked by twisting the distributor plate in the opposite direction of rotation. It should spring back when released.

12. Check and adjust the valve clearance on engines with mechanical lifters. The clearance should be slightly loose rather than too tight.

SPARK PLUG DIAGNOSIS

Normal

APPEARANCE: This plug is typical of one operating normally. The insulator nose varies from a light tan to grayish color with slight electrode wear. The presence of slight deposits is normal on used plugs and will have no adverse effect on engine performance. The spark plug heat range is correct for the engine and the engine is running normally.

CAUSE: Properly running engine.

RECOMMENDATION: Before reinstalling this plug, the electrodes should be cleaned and filed square. Set the gap to specifications. If the plug has been in service for more than 10-12,000 miles, the entire set should probably be replaced with a fresh set of the same heat range.

Oil Deposits

APPEARANCE: The firing end of the plug is covered with a wet, oily coating.

CAUSE: The problem is poor oil control. On high mileage engines, oil is leaking past the rings or valve guides into the combustion chamber. A common cause is also a plugged PCV valve, and a ruptured fuel pump diaphragm can also cause this condition. Oil fouled plugs such as these are often found in new or recently overhauled engines, before normal oil control is achieved, and can be cleaned and reinstalled.

RECOMMENDATION: A hotter spark plug may temporarily relieve the problem, but the engine is probably in need of work.

Incorrect Heat Range

APPEARANCE: The effects of high temperature on a spark plug are indicated by clean white, often blistered insulator. This can also be accompanied by excessive wear of the electrode, and the absence of deposits.

CAUSE: Check for the correct spark plug heat range. A plug which is too hot for the engine can result in overheating. A car operated mostly at high speeds can require a colder plug. Also check ignition timing, cooling system level, fuel mixture and leaking intake manifold.

RECOMMENDATION: If all ignition and engine adjustments are known to be correct, and no other malfunction exists, install spark plugs one heat range colder.

Carbon Deposits

APPEARANCE: Carbon fouling is easily identified by the presence of dry, soft, black, sooty deposits.

CAUSE: Changing the heat range can often lead to carbon fouling, as can prolonged slow, stop-and-start driving. If the heat range is correct, carbon fouling can be attributed to a rich fuel mixture, sticking choke, clogged air cleaner, worn breaker points, retarded timing or low compression. If only one or two plugs are carbon fouled, check for corroded or cracked wires on the affected plugs. Also look for cracks in the distributor cap between the towers of affected cylinders.

RECOMMENDATION: After the problem is corrected, these plugs can be cleaned and reinstalled if not worn severely.

Photos Courtesy Champion Spark Plug Co.

MMT Fouled

APPEARANCE: Spark plugs fouled by MMT (Methycyclopentadienyl Maganese Tricarbonyl) have reddish, rusty appearance on the insulator and side electrode.

CAUSE: MMT is an anti-knock additive in gasoline used to replace lead. During the combustion process, the MMT leaves a reddish deposit on the insulator and side electrode.

RECOMMENDATION: No engine malfunction is indicated and the deposits will not affect plug performance any more than lead deposits (see Ash Deposits). MMT fouled plugs can be cleaned, regapped and reinstalled.

High Speed Glazing

APPEARANCE: Glazing appears as shiny coating on the plug, either yellow or tan in color.

CAUSE: During hard, fast acceleration, plug temperatures rise suddenly. Deposits from normal combustion have no chance to fluff-off; instead, they melt on the insulator forming an electrically conductive coating which causes misfiring.

RECOMMENDATION: Glazed plugs are not easily cleaned. They should be replaced with a fresh set of plugs of the correct heat range. If the condition recurs, using plugs with a heat range one step colder may cure the problem.

Ash (Lead) Deposits

APPEARANCE: Ash deposits are characterized by light brown or white colored deposits crusted on the side or center electrodes. In some cases it may give the plug a rusty appearance.

CAUSE: Ash deposits are normally derived from oil or fuel additives burned during normal combustion. Normally they are harmless, though excessive amounts can cause misfiring. If deposits are excessive in short mileage, the valve guides may be worn.

RECOMMENDATION: Ash-fouled plugs can be cleaned, gapped and reinstalled.

Detonation

APPEARANCE: Detonation is usually characterized by a broken plug insulator.

CAUSE: A portion of the fuel charge will begin to burn spontaneously, from the increased heat following ignition. The explosion that results applies extreme pressure to engine components, frequently damaging spark plugs and pistons.

Detonation can result by over-advanced ignition timing, inferior gasoline (low octane) lean air/fuel mixture, poor carburetion, engine lugging or an increase in compression ratio due to combustion chamber deposits or engine modification.

RECOMMENDATION: Replace the plugs after correcting the problem.

Photos Courtesy Fram Corporation

EMISSION CONTROLS

13. Be aware of the general condition of the emission control system. It contributes to reduced pollution and should be serviced regularly to maintain efficient engine operation.

14. Check all vacuum lines for dried, cracked or brittle conditions. Something as simple as a leaking vacuum hose can cause poor performance and loss of economy.

15. Avoid tampering with the emission control system. Attempting to improve fuel econ-

FUEL SYSTEM

Check the air filter with a light behind it. If you can see light through the filter it can be reused.

Extremely clogged filters should be discarded and replaced with a new one.

18. Replace the air filter regularly. A dirty air filter richens the air/fuel mixture and can increase fuel consumption as much as 10%. Tests show that 1/3 of all vehicles have air filters in need of replacement.

19. Replace the fuel filter at least as often as recommended.

20. Set the idle speed and carburetor mixture to specifications.

21. Check the automatic choke. A sticking or malfunctioning choke wastes gas.

22. During the summer months, adjust the automatic choke for a leaner mixture which will produce faster engine warm-ups.

COOLING SYSTEM

29. Be sure all accessory drive belts are in good condition. Check for cracks or wear.

30. Adjust all accessory drive belts to proper tension.

31. Check all hoses for swollen areas, worn spots, or loose clamps.

32. Check coolant level in the radiator or expansion tank.

33. Be sure the thermostat is operating properly. A stuck thermostat delays engine warm-up and a cold engine uses nearly twice as much fuel as a warm engine.

34. Drain and replace the engine coolant at least as often as recommended. Rust and scale

TIRES & WHEELS

38. Check the tire pressure often with a pencil type gauge. Tests by a major tire manufacturer show that 90% of all vehicles have at least 1 tire improperly inflated. Better mileage can be achieved by over-inflating tires, but never exceed the maximum inflation pressure on the side of the tire.

39. If possible, install radial tires. Radial tires deliver as much as 1/2 mpg more than bias belted tires.

40. Avoid installing super-wide tires. They only create extra rolling resistance and decrease fuel mileage. Stick to the manufacturer's recommendations.

41. Have the wheels properly balanced.

omy by tampering with emission controls is more likely to worsen fuel economy than improve it. Emission control changes on modern engines are not readily reversible.

16. Clean (or replace) the EGR valve and lines as recommended.

17. Be sure that all vacuum lines and hoses are reconnected properly after working under the hood. An unconnected or misrouted vacuum line can wreak havoc with engine performance.

---

23. Check for fuel leaks at the carburetor, fuel pump, fuel lines and fuel tank. Be sure all lines and connections are tight.

24. Periodically check the tightness of the carburetor and intake manifold attaching nuts and bolts. These are a common place for vacuum leaks to occur.

25. Clean the carburetor periodically and lubricate the linkage.

26. The condition of the tailpipe can be an excellent indicator of proper engine combustion. After a long drive at highway speeds, the inside of the tailpipe should be a light grey in color. Black or soot on the insides indicates an overly rich mixture.

27. Check the fuel pump pressure. The fuel pump may be supplying more fuel than the engine needs.

28. Use the proper grade of gasoline for your engine. Don't try to compensate for knocking or "pinging" by advancing the ignition timing. This practice will only increase plug temperature and the chances of detonation or pre-ignition with relatively little performance gain.

Increasing ignition timing past the specified setting results in a drastic increase in spark plug temperature with increased chance of detonation or preignition. Performance increase is considerably less. (Photo courtesy Champion Spark Plug Co.)

---

that form in the engine should be flushed out to allow the engine to operate at peak efficiency.

35. Clean the radiator of debris that can decrease cooling efficiency.

36. Install a flex-type or electric cooling fan, if you don't have a clutch type fan. Flex fans use curved plastic blades to push more air at low speeds when more cooling is needed; at high speeds the blades flatten out for less resistance. Electric fans only run when the engine temperature reaches a predetermined level.

37. Check the radiator cap for a worn or cracked gasket. If the cap does not seal properly, the cooling system will not function properly.

---

42. Be sure the front end is correctly aligned. A misaligned front end actually has wheels going in different directions. The increased drag can reduce fuel economy by .3 mpg.

43. Correctly adjust the wheel bearings. Wheel bearings that are adjusted too tight increase rolling resistance.

Check tire pressures regularly with a reliable pocket type gauge. Be sure to check the pressure on a cold tire.

GENERAL MAINTENANCE

Check the fluid levels (particularly engine oil) on a regular basis. Be sure to check the oil for grit, water or other contamination.

A vacuum gauge is another excellent indicator of internal engine condition and can also be installed in the dash as a mileage indicator.

44. Periodically check the fluid levels in the engine, power steering pump, master cylinder, automatic transmission and drive axle.

45. Change the oil at the recommended interval and change the filter at every oil change. Dirty oil is thick and causes extra friction between moving parts, cutting efficiency and increasing wear. A worn engine requires more frequent tune-ups and gets progressively worse fuel economy. In general, use the lightest viscosity oil for the driving conditions you will encounter.

46. Use the recommended viscosity fluids in the transmission and axle.

47. Be sure the battery is fully charged for fast starts. A slow starting engine wastes fuel.

48. Be sure battery terminals are clean and tight.

49. Check the battery electrolyte level and add distilled water if necessary.

50. Check the exhaust system for crushed pipes, blockages and leaks.

51. Adjust the brakes. Dragging brakes or brakes that are not releasing create increased drag on the engine.

52. Install a vacuum gauge or miles-per-gallon gauge. These gauges visually indicate engine vacuum in the intake manifold. High vacuum = good mileage and low vacuum = poorer mileage. The gauge can also be an excellent indicator of internal engine conditions.

53. Be sure the clutch is properly adjusted. A slipping clutch wastes fuel.

54. Check and periodically lubricate the heat control valve in the exhaust manifold. A sticking or inoperative valve prevents engine warm-up and wastes gas.

55. Keep accurate records to check fuel economy over a period of time. A sudden drop in fuel economy may signal a need for tune-up or other maintenance.

© 1980 Chilton Book Company, Radnor, PA 19089

EMISSION CONTROLS AND FUEL SYSTEM

1. Air inlet pipe
2. Vacuum motor ass'y
3. Temperature sensor ass'y
4. Hot air pipe
5. Air control valve
6. Idle compresator

Automatic temperature controlled air cleaner

housing reaches 100°F, the sensor should block the flow of vacuum to the air control valve vacuum motor. When the temperature around the temperature sensor is below 100°F, the sensor should allow vacuum to pass onto the air valve vacuum motor thus blocking off the air cleaner snorkle to under hood (unheated) air.

When the temperature around the sensor is above 118°F, the air control valve should be completely open to under hood air.

If the air cleaner fails to operate correctly, check for loose or broken vacuum hoses. If the hoses are not the cause, replace the vacuum motor in the air cleaner.

Exhaust Gas Recirculation (EGR)

This system is used on all models. Exhaust gas recirculation is used to reduce combustion temperatures in the engine, thereby reducing the oxides of nitrogen emissions.

An EGR valve is mounted on the center of the intake manifold. The recycled exhaust gas is drawn into the bottom of the intake manifold riser portion through the exhaust manifold heat stove and EGR valve. A vacuum diaphragm is connected to a timed signal port at the carburetor flange.

As the throttle valve is opened, vacuum is applied to the EGR valve vacuum diaphragm. When the vacuum reaches about 2 in. Hg, the diaphragm moves against spring pressure and is in a fully up position at 8 in. Hg of vacuum. As the diaphragm moves up,

it opens the exhaust gas metering valve which allows exhaust gas to be pulled into the engine intake manifold. The system does not operate when the engine is idling because the exhaust gas recirculation would cause a rough idle.

A thermal vacuum valve inserted in the engine thermostat housing controls the application of the vacuum to the EGR valve. When the engine coolant reaches a predetermined temperature, the thermal vacuum valve opens and allows vacuum to be routed to the EGR

Typical EGR system

valve. Below the predetermined temperature, the thermal vacuum valve closes and blocks vacuum to the EGR valve.

All 1978–79 models have a B.P.T. valve installed between the EGR valve and the thermal vacuum valve. The B.P.T. valve has a diaphragm which is raised or lowered by exhaust back pressure. The diaphragm opens or closes an air bleed, which is connected into the EGR vacuum line. High pressure results in higher levels of EGR, because the diaphragm is raised, closing off the air bleed, which allows more vacuum to reach and open the EGR valve. Thus, the amount of recirculated exhaust gas varies with exhaust pressure.

1980–82 models use a V.V.T. valve (venturi vacuum transducer valve) instead of the B.P.T. valve. The V.V.T. valve monitors exhaust pressure and carburetor vacuum in order to activate the diaphragm which controls the throttle vacuum applied to the EGR control valve. This system expands the operating range of the EGR unit, as well as increasing the EGR flow rate as compared to the B.P.T. unit.

Many Datsuns are equipped with an EGR warning system which signals via a light in the dashboard that the EGR system may need service. The EGR warning light should come on every time the starter is engaged as a test to make sure the bulb is not blown. The system uses a counter which works in conjunction with the odometer, and lights the warning signal after the vehicle has traveled a predetermined number of miles.

To reset the counter, which is mounted in the engine compartment, remove the grommet installed in the side of the counter and insert the tip of a small screwdriver into the hole. Press down on the knob inside the hole. Reinstall the grommet.

TESTING

1. Remove the EGR valve and apply enough vacuum to the diaphragm to open the valve.
2. The valve should remain open for over 30 seconds after the vacuum is removed.
3. Check the valve for damage, such as warpage, cracks, and excessive wear around the valve and seat.
4. Clean the seat with a brush and compressed air and remove any deposits from around the valve and port (seat).
5. To check the operation of the thermal vacuum valve, remove the valve from the engine and apply vacuum to the ports of the valve. The valve should not allow vacuum to pass.
6. Place the valve in a container of water with a thermometer and heat the water. When the temperature of the water reaches 134°–145°F, remove the valve and apply vacuum to the ports; the valve should allow vacuum to pass through it.
7. To test the B.P.T. valve installed on 1978 and later models, disconnect the two vacuum hoses from the valve. Plug one of the ports. While applying pressure to the bottom of the valve, apply vacuum to the unplugged port and check for leakage. If any exists, replace the valve.
8. To test the check valve installed in some 1978 and later models, remove the valve and blow into the side which connects to the EGR valve. Air should flow. When air is applied to the other side, air flow resistance should be greater. If not, replace the valve.
9. To check the V.V.T. valve which replaces the B.T.P. valve on some 1980–82 models, disconnect the top and bottom center hoses and apply a vacuum to the top hose. Check for leaks. If a leak is present, replace the valve.

Mixture Ratio Rich-Lean and EGR Large-Small Exchange System (1980–82 California Engines)

This system controls the air-fuel mixture ratio and the amount of recirculated exhaust gas (manual transmission models only) in accordance with the engine coolant temperature and car speed. The system consists of a vacuum switching valve, a power valve, a speed detecting switch located in the speedometer, a speed detecting switch amplifier and a water temperature switch.

When the coolant temperature is above 122°F and the car is traveling at least 40 miles per hour, the vacuum switching valve is on and acts to lean down the fuel mixture. It also allows a small amount of EGR to be burned on manual transmission cars. When the coolant temperature is above 122°F but the vehicle is traveling less than 40 miles per hour, the vacuum switching valve is off and allows the mixture to richen. It also allows a large amount of EGR to be burned in manual transmission models. When coolant temperature is below 122°F the vacuum switching valve is always on and acts to lean down the fuel mixture.

EMISSION CONTROLS AND FUEL SYSTEM

Checking the vacuum switch on 1980 and later models

TESTING

Warm up the engine and jack up the drive wheels of the vehicle. Support the raised end of the car on jack stands and chock the wheels still on the ground. Start the engine and shift the transmission into TOP speed and maintain a speedometer speed higher than 50 MPH. Pinch the hose running from the vacuum switching valve to the air cleaner and see if the engine speed decreases and operates erratically. Shift the transmission into 3RD speed and run the car at a speed lower than 30 MPH. Disconnect the vacuum hose running between the vacuum switching valve and the power valve, by detaching it at the power valve and blocking its open end with your finger. The engine should operate erratically. If the expected engine reaction in both of these tests does not happen, check all wiring connections and hoses for breaks and blockage.

Air Injection Reactor System

In gasoline engines, it is difficult to completely burn the air/fuel mixture through normal combustion in the combustion chambers. Under certain operating conditions, unburned fuel is exhausted into the atmosphere.

The air injection reactor system is designed so that ambient air, pressurized by the air pump, is injected through the injection nozzles into the exhaust ports near each exhaust valve. The exhaust gases are at high temperatures and ignite when brought into contact with the oxygen. Unburned fuel is then burned in the exhaust ports and manifold.

In 1976 California models utilized a secondary system consisting of an air control valve which limits injection of secondary air and an emergency relief valve which controls the supply of secondary air. This system protects the catalytic converter from overheating. In 1977 the function of these two valves was taken by a single combined air control (C.A.C.) valve.

All engines with the air pump system have a series of minor alterations to accommodate the system. These are:

1. Special close-tolerance carburetor. Most engines require a slightly rich idle mixture adjustment.
2. Distributor with special advance curve. Ignition timing is retarded about 10° at idle in most cases.
3. Cooling system changes such as larger fan, higher fan speed, and thermostatic fan clutch. This is required to offset the increase in temperature caused by retarded timing at idle.
4. Faster idle speed.
5. Heated air intake on some engines.

The only periodic maintenance required on the air pump system is replacement of the air filter element and adjustment of the drive belt.

TESTING

Air Pump

If the air pump makes an abnormal noise and cannot be corrected without removing the pump from the vehicle, check the following in sequence:

1. Turn the pulley ¾ of a turn in the clockwise direction and ¼ of a turn in the counterclockwise direction. If the pulley is binding and if rotation is not smooth, a defective bearing is indicated.
2. Check the inner wall of the pump body, vanes and rotor for wear. If the rotor has abnormal wear, replace the air pump.
3. Check the needle roller bearing for wear and damage. If the bearings are defective, the air pump should be replaced.
4. Check and replace the rear side seal if abnormal wear or damage is noticed.
5. Check and replace the carbon shoes holding the vanes if they are found to be worn or damaged.
6. A deposit of carbon particles on the inner wall of the pump body and vanes is normal, but should be removed with compressed air before reassembling the air pump.

EMISSION CONTROLS AND FUEL SYSTEM

Check Valve

Remove the check valve from the air pump discharge line. Test it for leakage by blowing air into the valve from the air pump side and from the air manifold side. Air should only pass through the valve from the air pump side if the valve is functioning normally. A small amount of air leakage from the manifold side can be overlooked. Replace the check valve if it is found to be defective.

Anti-Backfire Valve

Disconnect the rubber hose connecting the mixture control valve with the intake manifold and plug the hose. If the mixture control valve is operating correctly, air will continue to blow out the mixture control valve for a few seconds after the accelerator pedal is fully depressed (engine running) and released quickly. If air continues to blow out for more than five seconds, replace the mixture control valve.

Air Pump Relief Valve

Disconnect the air pump discharge hose leading to the exhaust manifold. With the engine running, restrict the air-flow coming from the pump. The air pump relief valve should vent the pressurized air to the atmosphere if it is working properly.

NOTE: *When performing this test do not completely block the discharge line of the air pump as damage may result if the relief valve fails to function properly.*

Air Injection Nozzles

Check around the air manifold for air leakage with the engine running at 2,000 rpm. If air is leaking from the eye joint bolt, retighten or replace the gasket. Check the air nozzles for restrictions by blowing air into the nozzles.

Hoses

Check and replace hoses if they are found to be weakened or cracked. Check all hose connections and clips. Be sure that the hoses are not in contact with other parts of the engine.

Emergency Air Relief Valve

1. Warm up the engine.
2. Check all hoses for leaks, kinks, improper connections, etc.
3. Run the engine up to 2000 rpm under no load. No air should be discharged from the valve.
4. Disconnect the vacuum hose from the valve. This is the hose which runs to the intake manifold. Run the engine up to 2000 rpm. Air should be discharged from the valve. If not, replace it.

Combined Air Control Valve

1. Check all hoses for leaks, kinks, and improper connections.
2. Thoroughly warm up the engine.
3. With the engine idling, check for air discharge from the relief opening in the air cleaner case.
4. Disconnect and plug the vacuum hose from the valve. Air should be discharged from the valve with the engine idling. If the disconnected vacuum hose is not plugged, the engine will stumble.
5. Connect a hand-operated vacuum pump to the vacuum fitting on the valve and apply 7.8–9.8 in. Hg. of vacuum. Run the engine speed up to 3000 rpm. No air should be discharged from the valve.
6. Disconnect and plug the air hose at the check valve, with the conditions as in the preceding step. This should cause the valve to discharge air. If not, or if any of the conditions in this procedure are not met, replace the valve.

Electric Choke

The purpose of the electric choke, is to shorten the time the choke is in operation after the engine is started, thus shortening the time of high HC output.

An electric heater warms the bimetal spring which controls the opening and closing of the choke valve. The heater starts to heat as soon as the engine starts.

Catalytic Converter

This system is used on all 1975–78 models delivered in California in addition to all 1978–82 models. Through catalytic action, it changes residual hydrocarbons and carbon monoxide in the exhaust gas into carbon dioxide and water before the exhaust gas is discharged into the atmosphere.

NOTE: *Only unleaded fuel must be used with catalytic converters; lead in fuel will quickly pollute the catalyst and render it useless.*

The emergency air relief valve is used as a catalyst protection device. When the temperature of the catalyst goes above maximum

EMISSION CONTROLS AND FUEL SYSTEM

operating temperature, the temperature sensor signals the switching module to activate the emergency air relief valve. This stops air injection into the exhaust manifold and lowers he temperature of the catalyst.

Certain late 1970's catalyst-equipped models have a floor temperature warning system which emits a warning if the catalytic converter or engine becomes overly hot or malfunctions, causing floor temperature to rise.

FUEL SYSTEM

Fuel Pump

The fuel pump is a mechanically-operated, diaphragm-type driven by the fuel pump eccntric on the camshaft.

Design of the fuel pump permits disassembly, cleaning, and repair or replacement of defective parts.

TESTING

1. Disconnect the line between the carburetor and the pump at the carburetor.
2. Connect a fuel pump pressure gauge into the line.
3. Start the engine. The pressure should be between 3.0 and 3.9 psi. There is usually enough gas in the float bowl to perform this test.
4. If the pressure is ok, perform a capacity test. Remove the gauge from the line. Use a graduated container to catch the gas from the fuel line. Fill the carburetor float bowl with gas. Run the engine for one minute at about 1,000 rpm. The pump should deliver 600cc in one minute or less.

REMOVAL AND INSTALLATION

1. Disconnect the two fuel lines from the fuel pump. Be sure to keep the line leading from the fuel tank up high to prevent the excess loss of fuel.
2. Remove the two fuel pump mounting nuts and remove the fuel pump assembly from the side of the engine.
3. Install the fuel pump in the reverse order of removal, using a new gasket and sealer on the mating surface.

Carburetor

The carburetor used is a two-barrel downdraft type with a low-speed (primary) side and a high-speed (secondary) side.

1. Packing
2. Valve assembly
3. Retainer
4. Screw
5. Diaphragm assembly
6. Diaphragm spring
7. Retainer
8. Diaphragm assembly
9. Complete-body lower
10. Screw
11. Washer-spring
12. Fuel pump cap
13. Cap gasket
14. Connector-inlet
15. Connector-outlet
16. Rocker arm spring
17. Nut
18. Washer-spring
19. Washer-plain
20. Gasket
21. Spacer
22. Rocker pin
23. Spacer
24. Rocker arm

A series engine fuel pump

All models have an electrically-operated anti-dieseling solenoid. As the ignition switch is turned off, the valve is energized and shuts off the supply of fuel to the idle circuit of the carburetor.

REMOVAL AND INSTALLATION

1. Remove the air cleaner.
2. Disconnect the fuel and vacuum lines from the carburetor.
3. Remove the throttle lever.
4. Remove the four nuts and washers retaining the carburetor to the manifold.

EMISSION CONTROLS AND FUEL SYSTEM

CA20 engine fuel pump

E series engine fuel pump

5. Lift the carburetor from the manifold.
6. Remove and discard the gasket used between the carburetor and the manifold.
7. Install the carburetor in the reverse order of removal, using a new carburetor base gasket.

THROTTLE LINKAGE ADJUSTMENT

On all models, make sure the throttle is wide open when the accelerator pedal is floored. Some models have an adjustable accelerator pedal stop to prevent strain on the linkage.

DASHPOT ADJUSTMENT

A dashpot is used on carburetors of all cars with automatic transmissions and many late model manual transmission models. The dashpot slowly closes the throttle on automatic transmissions to prevent stalling and serves as an emission control device on all late model vehicles.

The dashpot should be adjusted to contact the throttle lever on deceleration at approximately 2,000–2,300 rpm for A series and 2,300–2,500 rpm for E15 engines.

Dashpot adjustment

NOTE: *Before attempting to adjust the dashpot, make sure the idle speed, timing and mixture adjustments are correct.*

SECONDARY THROTTLE LINKAGE ADJUSTMENT

All Datsun carburetors discussed in this book are two stage type carburetors. On this type of carburetor, the engine runs on the primary barrel most of the time, with the secondary barrel being used for acceleration purposes. When the throttle valve on the primary side opens to an angle of approximately 50 degrees (from its fully closed position), the secondary throttle valve is pulled open by the connecting linkage. The fifty degree angle of throttle valve opening works out to a clearance measurement of somewhere between 0.26–0.32 in. between the throttle valve and the carburetor body. The easiest way to measure this is to use a drill bit. Drill bits from size H to size P (standard letter size drill bits) should fit. Check the appendix in the back of the book for the exact size of the various drill bits. If an adjustment is necessary, bend the connecting link between the two linkage assemblies.

1. Roller
2. Connecting lever
3. Return plate
4. Adjust plate
5. Throttle chamber
6. Throttle valve

Secondary throttle linkage adjustment

FLOAT LEVEL ADJUSTMENT

The fuel level is normal if it is within the lines on the window glass of the float chamber (or the sight glass) when the vehicle is resting on level ground and the engine is off.

If the fuel level is outside the lines, remove the float housing cover. Have an absorbent cloth under the cover to catch the fuel

Float level adjustment

from the fuel bowl. Adjust the float level by bending the needle seat on the float.

The needle valve should have an effective stroke of about 0.0591 in. When necessary, the needle valve stroke can be adjusted by bending the float stopper.

NOTE: *Be careful not to bend the needle valve rod when installing the float and baffle plate, if removed.*

FAST IDLE ADJUSTMENT

1. With the carburetor removed from the vehicle, place the upper side of the fast idle screw on the second step of the fast idle cam and measure the clearance between the throttle valve and the wall of the throttle valve chamber at the center of the throttle valve. Check it against the following specifications:
- 1976–78 F10: 0.0287–0.0343 in.
- 1979–80 310: 0.0283–0.0350 in.
- 1981 310: 0.0287–0.0343 in.
- 1982 310: 0.0287–0.0343 in. MT
            0.0393–0.0449 in. AT
- 1982 Stanza: 0.0260–0.0315 in.

"M/T" means manual transmission. "A/T" means automatic transmission.

NOTE: *The first step of the fast idle adjustment procedure is not absolutely necessary.*

2. Install the carburetor on the engine.
3. Start the engine and measure the fast idle rpm with the engine at operating temperature. The cam should be at the 2nd step.
- 1976–78 F10: 1900–2700 rpm
- 1979–81 310: 49 states 2400–3200 rpm
            Calif. 2300–3100 rpm
            Canada 1900–2700 rpm
- 1982 310: 49 states 2400–3200 rpm
            Calif. 2300–3100 rpm
            Canada 1900–2700 MT
            2400–3200 AT

4. To adjust the fast idle speed, turn the fast idle adjusting screw counterclockwise to increase the fast idle speed and clockwise to decrease the fast idle speed.

98 EMISSION CONTROLS AND FUEL SYSTEM

E series fast idle adjustment

AUTOMATIC CHOKE ADJUSTMENT

1. With the engine cold, make sure the choke is fully closed (press the gas pedal all the way to the floor and release).
2. Check the choke linkage for binding. The choke plate should be easily opened and closed with your finger. If the choke sticks or binds, it can usually be freed with a liberal application of a carburetor cleaner made for the purpose. A couple of quick squirts of the right stuff normally does the trick.

If not, the carburetor will have to be disassembled for repairs.

3. The choke is correctly adjusted when the index mark on the choke housing (notch) aligns with the center mark on the carburetor body. If the setting is incorrect, loosen the three screws clamping the choke body in place and rotate the choke cover left or right until the marks align. Tighten the screws carefully to avoid cracking the housing.

CHOKE UNLOADER ADJUSTMENT

NOTE: *The choke must be cold for this adjustment.*

1. Close the choke valve completely.
2. Hold the choke valve closed by stretching a rubber band between the choke piston lever and a stationary part of the carburetor.
3. Open the throttle lever fully.
4. Adjustment is made by bending the unloader tongue. Adjust the gap between the choke plate and the carburetor body to:
- F10: 0.079 in.
- 310: 0.0929 in.
- Stanza: 0.0965 in.

VACUUM BREAK ADJUSTMENT

1. With the engine cold, close the choke completely.
2. Pull the vacuum break stem straight up as far as it will go.
3. Check the clearance between the choke plate and the carburetor wall. Clearance should be:
- A and E series: .0669 in. USA
  .0587 in. Canada
- CA20 series: .1347 in.

4. Adjustment is made on Canadian models by bending the connecting rod; on USA models by removing the plastic plug from the adjusting screw hole and turning the adjusting screw.

ACCELERATOR PUMP ADJUSTMENT

If a smooth constant stream of fuel is not injected into the carburetor bore when the throttle is opened the accelerator pump needs adjustment.

1. Remove the carburetor from the engine.
2. Check the gap between the primary throttle valve and the inner wall of the carburetor when the pump lever comes in contact with the piston pin. This is the stroke limiter gap. It should be .05 in. If not, bend the stroke limiter.
3. Fill the carburetor bowl with fuel.

EMISSION CONTROLS AND FUEL SYSTEM

Vacuum break adjustment

Accelerator pump adjustment

4. Fully open the choke.

5. Place a calibrated container under the throttle bore. Slowly open and close the throttle (full open to full closed) ten times keeping the throttle open 3 seconds each time. Measure the amount of fuel in the container. The amount should be .3–.5 ml or .010–.018 oz. If not, and the stroke limiter gap is correct, replace the accelerator pump unit.

ANTI-DIESELING SOLENOID

Check this valve if the engine continues to run after the key has been turned off.

1. Run the engine at idle speed and disconnect the lead wire at the anti-dieseling solenoid. The engine should stop.

2. If the engine does not stop, check the harness for current at the solenoid. If current is present, replace the solenoid. Installation

100 EMISSION CONTROLS AND FUEL SYSTEM

A series engine carburetor

torque for the solenoid is 13–16 ft.lbs. for A and E series engines and 13–25 ft. lb. for CA20 engines.

OVERHAUL

Efficient carburetion depends greatly on careful cleaning and inspection during overhaul, since dirt, gum, water, or varnish in or on the carburetor parts are often responsible for poor performance.

Overhaul your carburetor in a clean, dust-free area. Carefully disassemble the carburetor, referring often to the exploded views. Keep all similar and look-alike parts segregated during disassembly and cleaning to avoid accidental interchange during assembly. Make a note of all jet sizes.

When the carburetor is disassembled, wash all parts (except diaphragms, electric choke units, pump plunger, and any other plastic, leather, fiber, or rubber parts) in clean carburetor solvent. Do not leave parts in the sol-

EMISSION CONTROLS AND FUEL SYSTEM 101

E series engine carburetor

vent any longer than is necessary to sufficiently loosen the deposits. Excessive cleaning may remove the special finish from the float bowl and choke valve bodies, leaving these parts unfit for service. Rinse all parts in clean solvent and blow them dry with compressed air to allow them to air dry. Wipe clean all cork, plastic, leather, and fiber parts with a clean, lint-free cloth.

Blow out all passages and jets with compressed air and be sure that there are no restrictions or blockages. Never use wire or similar tools to clean jets and valves separately to avoid accidental interchange.

Check all parts for wear or damage. If wear or damage is found, replace the defective parts. Especially check the following:

1. Check the float needle and seat for wear. If wear is found, replace the complete assembly.

2. Check the float hinge pin for wear and the float(s) for dents or distortion. Replace the float if fuel has leaked into it.

3. Check the throttle and choke shaft bores

102 EMISSION CONTROLS AND FUEL SYSTEM

Carburetor Specifications

Year	Engine	Vehicle Model	Carb Model	Main Jet # Primary	Main Jet # Secondary	Main Air Bleed # Primary	Main Air Bleed # Secondary	Slow Jet # Primary	Slow Jet # Secondary	Float Level (in.)	Power Jet #
1976	A14 California	F10	DCH306-17	105	145	95	80	45	50	0.75	40
	A14 (Federal)	F10	DCH306-16	103	145	95	80	45	50	0.75	40
1977	A14 California	F10	DCH306-17A	106	145	95	80	45	50	0.75	40
	A14 (Federal)	F10	DCH306-16A	105	145	95	80	45	50	0.75	40
1978	A14 (California)	F10	DCH306-65	106	145	95	80	45	50	0.75	40
	A14 (Federal)	F10	DCH306-64	105	145	95	80	45	50	0.75	40
1979	A14 (California)	310	DCH306-75	107	145	95	80	45	50	0.75	43
	A14 (Federal)	310	DCH306-76	105	145	110	80	45	50	0.75	40
1980	A14 (California)	310	DCH306-112	107	145	80	80	45	50	0.75	38

EMISSION CONTROLS AND FUEL SYSTEM

1981	A14 (Federal)	310	DCH306-102	107	143	65	60	45	50	0.75	43
	A15 (Federal)	310	DCR306-103	114	125	80	80	45	50	0.75	35
	A15 (California)	310	DCR306-113	113	125	60	80	45	50	0.75	35
	A15 (Canada)	310	DCR306-123	100	145	70	80	43	70	0.75	40
1982	E15 (Federal)	310	DCR306-130	116	125	80	80	45	50	0.47	38
	E15 (California)	310	DCR306-140	114	125	60	80	45	50	0.47	38
	E15 (Canada)	310	DCR306-150MT	100	120	70	60	43	80	0.47	40
	E15 (Canada)	310	DCR306-151AT	100	120	70	60	43	80	0.47	40
	CA20 (Fed. & Canada)	Stanza	DCR342-33	111	160	90	60	47	100	0.91	45
	CA20 (California)	Stanza	DCR342-31	113	160	90	60	47	100	0.91	45

104 EMISSION CONTROLS AND FUEL SYSTEM

A. Choke chamber
B. Carburetor body
C. Throttle chamber
1. Lock lever
2. Filter set screw
3. Fuel nipple
4. Fuel filter
5. Needle valve body
6. Needle valve
7. Power valve
8. Secondary main air bleed
9. Primary main air bleed
10. B.C.D.D.
11. Secondary slow air bleed
12. Secondary main jet
13. Plug
14. Secondary slow jet
15. Primary throttle valve
16. Idle compensator
17. Accelerating pump parts
18. Plug for accelerating mechanism
19. Plug
20. Spring
21. Primary slow jet
22. Primary and secondary small venturi
23. Throttle adjusting screw
24. Throttle adjusting screw spring
25. Secondary throttle valve
26. Accelerating pump lever
27. Anti-dieseling solenoid valve
28. Blind plug
29. Idle adjusting screw
30. Idle adjusting screw spring
31. Choke connecting rod
32. Diaphragm chamber parts
33. Throttle valve switch
34. Float

CA20 engine carburetor

for wear or an out-of-round condition. Damage or wear to the throttle arm, shaft, or shaft bore will often require replacement of the throttle body. These parts require a close tolerance of fit; wear may allow air leakage, which could affect starting and idling.

NOTE: *Throttle shafts and bushings are not included in overhaul kits. They can be purchased separately.*

4. Inspect the idle mixture adjusting needles for burrs or grooves. Any such condition requires replacement of the needle, since you will not be able to obtain a satisfactory idle.

5. Test the accelerator pump check valves. They should pass air one way but not the other. Test for proper seating by blowing and sucking on the valve. Replace the valve if necessary. If the valve is satisfactory, wash the valve again to remove breath moisture.

6. Check the bowl cover for warped surfaces with a straightedge.

7. Closely inspect the valves and seats for wear and damage, replacing as necessary.

8. After the carburetor is assembled, check the choke valve for freedom of operation.

Carburetor overhaul kits are recommended for each overhaul. These kits contain all gaskets and new parts to replace those that deteriorate most rapidly. Failure to replace all parts supplied with the kit (especially gaskets) can result in poor performance later.

Some carburetor manufactures supply overhaul kits of three basic types: minor repair; major repair; and gasket kits. Basically, they contain the following:

Minor Repair Kits:
- All gaskets
- Float needle valve
- Volume control screw
- All diaphragms
- Spring for the pump diaphragm

Major Repair Kits:
- All jets and gaskets
- All diaphragms
- Float needle valve
- Volume control screw
- Pump ball valve
- Main jet carrier
- Float

Gasket Kits:
- All gaskets

After cleaning and checking all components, reassemble the carburetor, using new parts and referring to the exploded view. When reassembling, make sure that all screws and jets are tight in their seats, but do not overtighten as the tips will be distorted. Tighten all screws gradually in rotation. Do not tighten needle valves into their seats; uneven jetting will result. Always use new gaskets. Be sure to adjust the float level when reassembling.

Cooling Fan 1982 U.S.A. Models

This device was installed to lower the temperature of the fuel in the fuel lines and carburetor. After a brief shut-down, the fuel would bubble and cause a surging or hesitation on re-start until cooler fuel entered the carburetor. The cooling fan will turn on automatically after shut down of the engine if the coolant temperature of the engine is above 172°F and will run for up to 17 minutes. The fan cools the fuel in the carburetor and lines.

REMOVAL AND INSTALLATION

1. Disconnect the lead wires at the fan.
2. Remove the fan and bracket.
3. Installation is the reverse of removal.

Fuel Tank

REMOVAL AND INSTALLATION

F10 Sedan and Hatchback

1. Disconnect the battery ground cable.
2. Drain the fuel into a suitable container.
3. Disconnect the filler hose, the air vent hose, fuel return hose, and fuel outlet hose.
4. Disconnect the wires from the sending unit.
5. Remove the bolts securing the fuel tank and remove the tank.
6. Installation is in the reverse order of removal.

F10 Wagon

The removal procedure is the same as that for the sedan and hatchback. However, when removing the fuel tank bolts, it is easier if you start at the three bolts at the front of the tank.

310

1. Disconnect the battery ground cable.
2. Remove the drain plug and drain the fuel.
3. Disconnect the filler tube and filler hose from the fuel tank.
4. Disconnect the hoses attached to the fuel tank near the filler hose and at the bottom front of the tank.
5. Loosen the tension on the parking brake

106 EMISSION CONTROLS AND FUEL SYSTEM

→ VAPOR
--- AIR

FOR SEDAN AND HATCHBACK

FOR SPORT WAGON

1. Fuel tank
2. Fuel outlet hose
3. Fuel return hose
4. Evaporation hose to fuel tank
5. Air vent line
6. Evaporation hose to engine
7. Filler hose
8. Filler cap
9. Separator
10. Limit valve
11. Vent cleaner

F10 fuel tank

1. Fuel tank
2. Fuel suction hose
3. Fuel return hose
4. Evaporation hose
5. Vent tube
6. Filler hose
7. Filler tube
8. Filler cap
9. Fuel check valve
10. Breather tube

FUEL RETURN TUBE
EVAPORATION TUBE
FUEL SUCTION TUBE
BRAKE TUBE
SECTION A-A

VACUUM SIGNAL LINE
CANISTER PURGE LINE

11. Drain hose
12. Fuel tank gauge unit
13. Grommet
14. Fuel filter
15. Carbon canister

310 fuel tank

EMISSION CONTROLS AND FUEL SYSTEM 107

and disconnect the wire on the fuel tank gauge unit.

6. Remove the retaining bolts and remove the tank by sliding it forward and down.

Installation is the reverse of removal.

Stanza

1. Drain the tank.
2. Remove the rear seat cushion.
3. Remove the inspection cover.
4. Disconnect the gauge wiring.
5. Disconnect the hoses.
6. Remove the tank protector.
7. Remove the tank.
8. Installation is the reverse of removal.

Chassis Electrical

HEATER

Heater Assembly
REMOVAL AND INSTALLATION

F10

1. Disconnect the battery ground cable.
2. Drain the engine coolant and remove the heater hoses.
3. Remove the defroster hoses from each side of the heater assembly.
4. Remove the cable retaining clamps and remove the cables for the intake and floor doors.
5. Disconnect the three pole connector.
6. Remove the four heater retaining screws. Remove the heater.
7. Installation is in the reverse order of removal.

310 without A/C

1. Disconnect the battery ground cable.
2. Set the temperature lever to the HOT position and drain the engine coolant.
3. Remove the instrument panel assembly. See the following section for instructions.
4. Disconnect the control cables and rod from the heater unit. Disconnect the heater motor harness.
5. Disconnect the inlet and the outlet heater hoses from the engine compartment.
6. Remove the two lower and three upper bolts attaching the heater and blower units to the vehicle. The air conditioning unit is on the passenger's side of the vehicle. It does not have to be removed to remove the heater and blower units.
7. Remove the heater and blower units.
8. Installation is the reverse of removal.

Stanza without A/C

1. Remove the instrument panel.
2. Disconnect the heater hoses and vacuum tube in the engine compartment.
3. Remove the heater control assembly.
4. Unbolt and remove the heater unit.
5. Installation is the reverse of removal.

310 with A/C

1. Disconnect the battery ground.
2. Set the temperature control lever to HOT and drain the cooling system.
3. Remove the instrument panel.
4. Disconnect the hoses at the core.
5. Disconnect all wiring from the unit.
6. Loosen the band seal at the joint between the cooling and heater units.
7. Unbolt and remove the heater.

110 CHASSIS ELECTRICAL

1. Connector
2. Clip
3. Heater hose (inlet)
4. Defroster nozzle (R.H.)
5. Defroster duct (R.H.)
6. Heater switch
7. Heater control
8. Heater case (R.H.)
9. Heater core
10. Heater case (L.H.)
11. Heater hose (outlet)
12. Defroster nozzle (L.H.)
13. Defroster duct (L.H.)

F10 heater assembly

1. Heater case
2. Heater core
3. Water cock
4. Heater control
5. Blower case
6. Blower fan
7. Blower motor
8. Resistor
9. Air distributor
10. Defroster nozzle
11. Side defroster ducts L.H.
12. Side defroster ducts R.H.
13. Side ventilation ducts L.H.
14. Side ventilation duct R.H.

310 heater assembly

CHASSIS ELECTRICAL 111

Stanza heater assembly

Heater Blower
REMOVAL AND INSTALLATION
F10

1. Remove the heater unit as described above.

NOTE: *You may be able to remove the blower on some models without removing the heater unit from the vehicle.*

2. Remove the three or four screws holding the blower motor in the case and remove the motor with the fan attached.
3. Installation is the reverse of removal.

310

1. Disconnect the battery ground cable.
2. Remove the instrument panel lower cover on the driver's side.
3. Disconnect the wiring harness at the blower and wherever else it constricts removal of the blower motor.
4. Remove the control wire and rod from in front of the motor.
5. Remove the three screws holding the control assembly in front of the blower motor and move the assembly out of the way.
6. Remove the three blower motor attaching screws and then remove the blower motor with the fan attached.
7. Installation is the reverse of removal.

Stanza

1. Working in the engine compartment, disconnect the blower motor insulator upper fasteners.
2. Remove the blower motor retaining bolts.
3. Push the blower motor insulator down by hand and remove the motor.
4. Installation is the reverse of removal.

Heater Core
REMOVAL AND INSTALLATION
F10

1. Remove the heater assembly as described earlier.
2. Remove the sealing sponges. Unfasten the seven clips that hold the heater case together.
3. Remove the heater core from the cases.
4. Installation is the reverse of removal.

310

1. Remove the heater unit from the vehicle.

112 CHASSIS ELECTRICAL

2. Disconnect the inlet and outlet hoses from the core if you have not done so already.
3. Remove the clips securing the case halves and separate the halves.
4. Remove the heater core.
5. Installation is the reverse of removal.

Stanza

1. Remove pedal bracket mounting bolts, steering column mounting bolts, brake and clutch pedal cotter pins.
2. Move the pedal bracket and steering column to the left.
3. Disconnect the air mix door control cable and heater valve control lever, then remove the control lever.
4. Remove the core cover.
5. Disconnect the hoses at the core.
6. Installation is the reverse of removal. Be sure to bleed the system.

RADIO

REMOVAL AND INSTALLATION
F10

1. Remove the instrument cluster.
2. Detach all electrical connections.
3. Remove the radio knobs and retaining nuts.
4. Remove the rear support bracket.
5. Remove the radio.
6. Reverse the procedure for installation.

310 and Stanza

1. Disconnect the battery ground cable.
2. Remove the center bezel.
3. Loosen and remove the screws retaining the radio in place.
4. Remove the radio and disconnect the antenna feeder cable, power lines and speaker connections.
5. Installation is the reverse of removal.

WINDSHIELD WIPER MOTOR AND LINKAGE

REMOVAL AND INSTALLATION
F10

1. Disconnect the battery ground cable.
2. Lift the wiper arms, remove their attaching nuts and remove them.
3. Remove the meter cover.
4. Remove the glove box.
5. Remove the wiper motor attaching bolts.
6. Remove the ball joint connecting the motor shaft to the wiper link.
7. Remove the wiper motor from the cowl dash panel after disconnecting its wiring.
8. Remove the wiper pivot bolts from under the dashboard and remove the linkage.
9. Installation is the reverse of removal.
NOTE: *Make sure you install the wiper arms in the correct positions by running the system without the arms on, stopping it, then attaching the arms.*

1. Windshield wiper blade
2. Windshield wiper arm
3. Arm nut
4. Pivot
5. Connector rod
6. Wiper motor
7. Wiper motor bracket
8. Motor arm

F10 wiper system

CHASSIS ELECTRICAL 113

1. Windshield wiper arm
2. Windshield wiper blade
3. Pivot (R.H.)
4. Pivot (L.H.)
5. Windshield wiper motor assembly

310 and D Stanza wiper system

310 and Stanza

1. Disconnect the battery ground cable.
2. Open the hood and disconnect the motor wiring connection.
3. Unbolt the motor from the body.
4. Disconnect the wiper linkage from the motor and remove the motor.
5. Installation is the reverse of removal.

INSTRUMENT CLUSTER

REMOVAL AND INSTALLATION

F10

1. Disconnect the battery ground cable.
2. Disconnect the speedometer cable from the back of the speedometer.
3. Remove the package tray and disconnect the heater control cables from the heater.
4. Disconnect all wire harness connectors from the back of the instrument panel after noting their locations and tagging them.
5. Remove the choke knob and nut.
6. Remove the steering column bracket installation bolts.
7. Loosen the instrument panel upper attaching screws.
8. Remove the bolts securing the sides of the instrument panel.
9. Remove the bolts attaching the instrument panel to the pedal bracket.
10. Remove the instrument panel.
11. Installation is in the reverse order of removal.

310 and Stanza

1. Disconnect the battery terminals.
2. Remove the steering wheel and the steering column covers.
3. Remove the instrument cluster lid by removing its screws.
4. Remove the instrument cluster screws, pull the unit out and disconnect all wiring and cables from its rear. Mark the wires to avoid confusion during assembly. Be careful not to damage the printed circuit.
5. Remove the cluster.
6. Installation is the reverse of removal.

Speedometer Cable

REPLACEMENT

1. Remove any lower dash covers that may be in the way and disconnect the speedometer cable from the back of the speedometer.

114 CHASSIS ELECTRICAL

1. Meter
2. Radio
3. Glove box
4. Speaker
5. Instrument panel
6. Stay

F10 instrument panel

1. Instrument panel
2. Instrument pad
3. Cluster lid
4. Center bezel
5. Ash tray
6. Center ventilator
7. Striker
8. Glove lid
9. Side ventilator case
10. Key lock
11. Coin pocket

310 instrument panel

CHASSIS ELECTRICAL 115

SGL models

G models

Stanza instrument panels

NOTE: *On some models it may be easier to remove the instrument cluster to gain access to the cable.*

2. Pull the cable from the cable housing. If the cable is broken, the other half of the cable will have to be removed from the transmission end. Unscrew the retaining knob at the transmission and remove the cable from the transmission extension housing.

3. Lubricate the cable with graphite power

116　CHASSIS ELECTRICAL

(sold as speedometer cable lubricant) and feed the cable into the housing. It is best to start at the speedometer end and feed the cable down towards the transmission. It is also usually necessary to unscrew the transmission connection and install the cable end to the gear, then reconnect the housing to the transmission. Slip the cable end into the speedometer and reconnect the cable housing.

Ignition Switch

Ignition switch removal and installation procedures are covered in Chapter 7; Suspension and Steering.

LIGHTING

Headlights

REMOVAL AND INSTALLATION

NOTE: *Many Datsuns have radiator grilles which are unit-constructed to also serve as headlight frames. In this case, it will be necessary to remove the grille to gain access to the headlights.*

1. Remove the grille, if necessary.
2. Remove the headlight retaining ring screws. These are the three or four short screws in the assembly. There are also two longer screws at the top and side of the headlight which are used to aim the headlight. Do not tamper with these or the headlight will have to be re-aimed.
3. Remove the ring on round headlights by turning it clockwise.
4. Pull the headlight bulb from its socket and disconnect the electrical plug.
5. Connect the plug to the new bulb.

6. Position the headlight in the shell. Make sure that the word "TOP" is, indeed, at the top and that the knobs in the headlight lens engage the slots in the mounting shell.
7. Place the retaining ring over the bulb and install the screws.
8. Install the grille, if removed.

CIRCUIT PROTECTION

Fusible Links

A fusible link is a protective device used in an electrical circuit. When current increases beyond a certain amperage, the fusible metal wire of the link melts, thus breaking the electrical circuit and preventing further damage to the other components and wiring. Whenever a fusible link is melted because of a short circuit, correct the cause before installing a new link.

Use the following chart to locate the fusible link(s) on your Datsun.

All Datsun fusible links are the plug in kind. To replace them, simply unplug the bad link and insert the new one.

Most fusible links are found near the battery

Fusible Links

Year	Model	Number	Color/Protects	Location
1976–78	F10	2	Red/N.A. Green/N.A.	At positive battery terminal
1979–81	310	4	1 Red/Fuse block 3 Green/Ignition, lights, fan	Mounted on fender well beside battery
1982	310 Stanza	4	1 Red/Fuse block, alternator, air conditioner relay 3 Green/Ignition switch, fan and defogger, lights, carburetor cooling fan (U.S. models)	Mounted on fender well beside battery

CHASSIS ELECTRICAL

Fuse Box and Flasher Location

Year	Model	Fuse Box Location	Flasher Location
1976–78	F10	Below hood release knob	Under driver's side of dashboard①
1979–82	310 Stanza	Below hood release knob	Turn signal: Passenger side kick board Hazard: Driver's side at hood release

① Both the turn signal and the hazard flashers are side by side
NOTE: The original turn signal flasher unit is pink, and larger than the original hazard flasher unit, which is gold.

WIRING DIAGRAMS

Wiring diagrams have been left out of this book. As cars have become more complex, and available with longer and longer option lists, wiring diagrams have grown in size and complexity also. It has become virtually impossible to provide a readable reproduction in a reasonable number of pages.

Clutch and Transmission

6

MANUAL TRANSMISSION
F10
LINKAGE ADJUSTMENT

Four-Speed Models

1. The adjustment is made at the shift rods on the transmission. Loosen the adjusting nuts marked 1 and 2 in the illustration.
2. Measure the clearance between the shift lever marked 3 in the illustration and the transmission case. Make sure the shift lever is pushed completely into the transmission case. The clearance is marked "A" in the illustration.
3. Place the transmission in fourth gear. Shift lever 3 should now be fully downward.
4. Increase the initial clearance "A" by 8 mm (0.31).
5. Push lever 4 fully upward. Now tighten nut 1 until it makes contact with trunnion 7. Then back the nut off one full turn and tighten it with nut 2.

F10 4-speed linkage is adjusted in sequence at the numbered points

CLUTCH AND TRANSMISSION 119

F10 5-speed linkage is adjusted in sequence at the numbered points

Five Speed Models

1. Loosen locknuts 1, 2, 3, and 4.
2. Make sure shift lever 5 is pushed completely into the transmission case, then move it back 8 mm (0.31 in.).
3. Place the car in third gear.
4. Push select lever 6 fully down. Turn nut 3 until it comes into contact with trunnion 9. Back the nut off one or two turns, and then tighten nut 3 with nut 4. Tighten nuts 1 and 2.

310
LINKAGE ADJUSTMENT
Four and Five-Speed Models

Adjustment can be made by adjusting the select lever.

1. Loosen the adjusting nuts at each end of the control rod lever near the bottom of the linkage.
2. Set the shift control lever in the Neutral position.
3. Fully push the shift lever (transmission side) in the direction P1, as shown in the illustration. On the four speed transmission, pull the lever back about 8 mm (0.31 in.). On the five speed, pull the shift lever back 11.5 mm (0.453 in.). With the select lever held in the above position, move the shift lever in direction P2, which engages third gear on four speed transmissions and second gear on five speed transmissions.
4. Push the control rod select lever as far as it will go in direction P3, then turn the upper adjusting nut until it touches the trunnion. Turn the nut a quarter turn more, and lock the select lever with the other adjusting nut.
5. Operate the shift control lever in the car to see if it shifts smoothly through the gears.

310 4-speed linkage

120 CLUTCH AND TRANSMISSION

310 5-speed linkage

REMOVAL AND INSTALLATION

F10, and 1979–80 310

You must remove the engine/transmission unit as a whole. Refer to chapter 3 for procedures.

After removal, remove the bolts holding the transmission to the engine and separate by pulling the transmission towards the clutch housing.

Removing the transmission mounting bracket on F10 and early 310 models

Separating the clutch housing from the engine on F10 and early 310 models

NOTE: *The clutch assembly will remain attached to the engine.*
Installation is the reverse of removal.
CAUTION: *If the clutch has been removed, it will have to be re-aligned, and when connecting drive shafts, insert O-rings between the differential side flanges and the drive shafts.*

1981–82 310 and Stanza

1. Remove the battery. On Stanza, remove the radiator reservoir.
2. Drain the transmission.
3. Remove the driveshafts from the transaxle.

NOTE: *Take care not to damage the seal lips. After the driveshafts are removed, insert a dummy shaft into each opening so that the side gears don't fall into the case.*

4. Remove the distributor, air induction tube, EGR tube and exhaust manifold cover.
5. Remove the heater hose clamp.
6. Remove the clutch control cable from the lever.
7. Disconnect the speedometer cable at the case.
8. Disconnect all wiring from the case. On Stanza, remove the wheel well liner.

Separating the control rod and the support rod on 1982 310

Engine gusset removal on 1982 310

CLUTCH AND TRANSMISSION

310 and Stanza right engine mount

310 and Stanza rear mounting bracket

9. Separate the control rod and support rod from the case. On Stanza, disconnect the exhaust pipe at the manifold.
10. Place a jackstand under the engine oil pan to take up the engine weight.
11. Take up the transaxle weight with a floor jack.
12. Remove the engine gusset bolts.
13. On 5-speed models, remove the engine right side and rear mounting brackets.
14. Attach a shop crane to the transaxle at the clutch control cable bracket.
15. Unbolt the transaxle from the engine. On 5-speed models, pull the engine to the right and slide the transaxle away from the engine.
16. Lift the engine from the car.
17. Installation is the reverse of removal. Note the following points:
   a. Clean all mating surfaces.
   b. Apply EP chassis lube to the splines on the clutch disc and input shaft.
   c. Fill transaxle with 80W–90 gear oil. Apply sealant to the threads of the filler and drain plugs.
   d. Engine-to-transaxle bolt torque is 12–15 ft. lbs.

CLUTCH

ADJUSTMENT

Refer to the Clutch Specifications Chart for clutch pedal height above floor and pedal free play.

1. Adjust pedal height here
2. Adjust pedal free-play here
MG. Lubricate with multipurpose grease here
H. is pedal height
h. is free-play

Hydraulic clutch adjusting points

LOCK NUT
16–22 N-M
(1.6–2.2 KG-M,
12–16 FT-LB)

Stanza clutch pedal adjustment: H is the pedal height, A is the pedal free-play

122 CLUTCH AND TRANSMISSION

1982 310 clutch pedal adjustment: H is the pedal height, A is the pedal free-play

All models through 1981 have a hydraulically operated clutch. Pedal height is usually adjusted with a stopper limiting the upward travel of the pedal. Pedal free-play is adjusted at the master cylinder pushrod. If the pushrod is nonadjustable, free-play is adjusted by placing shims between the master cylinder and the firewall. On a few models, pedal free play can also be adjusted at the operating (slave) cylinder pushrod. Pushrods are available in three lengths for the F10 and the 310. 1982 models have a cable-actuated mechanical clutch.

Clutch Specifications

Year	Model	Pedal Height Above Floor (in.)	Pedal Free-Play (in.)
All	F10	6.9	0.23–0.55
1979–81	310	7.15	0.04–0.20
1982	310	7.27	0.43–0.83
1982	Stanza	6.00	0.43–0.63

REMOVAL AND INSTALLATION

F10 and 1979–80 310

Because of the configuration of the transmission/drive shaft system (transaxle), the transmission is impossible to remove from the car without removing the engine.

Due to this problem, Datsun has made provisions for clutch service through an access plate (cover) on the top of the housing. The engine and transmission need not be removed to permit repair or replacement.

NOTE: *The clutch cover and pressure plate are balanced as a unit. If replacement is necessary, replace both parts.*

1. Disconnect the following cables, wires and hoses:
   Battery ground cable
   Fresh air duct
   Engine harness connectors on the clutch housing
   Ignition wire between the coil and the distributor
   Carbon canister hoses

2. Remove the inspection plate from the top of the clutch housing and remove the six bolts holding the clutch cover.

NOTE: *In order to reach all six bolts, you are going to have to jack up the car and, as you loosen the bolts, rotate the right front wheel with the car in top gear. This will rotate the clutch cover.*

CAUTION: *Be sure to loosen the bolts evenly in order.*

3. Rotate the steering wheel all the way to the right and remove the inspection plate inside the right wheel well.

4. Disconnect the withdrawal lever and remove the six bolts on the bearing house. Reaching through the wheel well inspection hole, pull out the primary drive gear assembly.

NOTE: *To remove the withdrawal lever pin you must first remove the E-ring that holds it to the bearing housing.*

5. After removing the drive gear, go back to the engine compartment and lift the clutch cover and disc assembly out through the open section of the clutch housing. You may also remove the diaphragm at the same time.

6. Remove the strap holding the pressure plate to the clutch cover and remove the clutch from the center.

NOTE: *The strap must be replaced in the same position it had before removal. Mark the relative position before removal. In-*

CLUTCH AND TRANSMISSION 123

1. Flywheel
2. Diaphragm spring
3. Pressure plate
4. Clutch disc
5. Clutch cover
6. Pushrod
7. Release bearing
8. Withdrawal lever
9. Rubber cover

F10 and 1979–80 310 clutch

stalling it out of position will cause an imbalance.

Installation is the reverse of removal. But, you must observe the following:

1. Paying particular attention to the alignment marks, reassemble the disc and cover to the pressure plate. Tighten the strap bolts to 5–6 ft. lbs. (F10), 7–9 ft. lbs. (310).

2. Put the diaphragm spring and cover assembly onto the flywheel and screw the bolts in with your fingers.

NOTE: *These bolts should remain loose enough to shift the assembly when installing the drive gear. There are a pair of aligning pins on the flywheel.*

3. Install the drive gear assembly by aligning the disc hub with the gear spline. After alignment, tighten the cover bolts to 5–7.2 ft. lbs.

NOTE: *There are two aligning pins on the flywheel.*

Removing the primary drive gear

124 CLUTCH AND TRANSMISSION

Stanza and 1981-82 310

1. Remove the transaxle.
2. Insert a clutch disc centering tool into the clutch disc hub for support.
3. Loosen the pressure plate bolts evenly, a little at a time to prevent distortion.
4. Remove the clutch assembly.
5. Installation is the reverse of removal. Apply a light coating of chassis lube to the clutch disc splines and the input shaft. Use a centering tool to aid installation. Torque the pressure plate bolts in a criss-cross pattern, a little at a time each to 12-15 ft. lbs.

Clutch Master Cylinder

REMOVAL AND INSTALLATION

1. Disconnect the clutch pedal arm from the pushrod.
2. Disconnect the clutch hydraulic line from the master cylinder.
   NOTE: *Take precautions to keep brake fluid from coming in contact with any painted surfaces.*
3. Remove the nuts attaching the master cylinder and remove the master cylinder and pushrod toward the engine compartment side.
4. Install the master cylinder in the reverse order of removal and bleed the clutch hydraulic system.

OVERHAUL

1. Remove the master cylinder from the vehicle.
2. Drain the clutch fluid from the master cylinder reservoir.
3. Remove the boot and circlip and remove the pushrod.
4. Remove the stopper, piston, cup and return spring.
5. Clean all of the parts in clean brake fluid.
6. Check the master cylinder and piston for wear, corrosion and scores and replace the parts as necessary. Light scoring and glaze can be removed with crocus cloth soaked in brake fluid.

1. Bleeder screw
2. Cylinder body
3. Piston cup
4. Piston
5. Dust cover
6. Push rod
7. Lock nut
8. Push nut

Typical slave cylinder

1. Reservoir cap
2. Reservoir
3. Reservoir band
4. Cylinder body
5. Valve assembly
6. Valve spring
7. Spring seat
8. Return spring
9. Piston cup
10. Piston
11. Push rod
12. Stopper
13. Stopper ring
14. Dust cover
15. Nut

Typical master cylinder

CLUTCH AND TRANSMISSION

7. Generally, the cup seal should be replaced each time the master cylinder is disassembled. Check the cup and replace it if it is worn, fatigued, or damaged.

8. Check the clutch fluid reservoir, filler cap, dust cover and the pipe for distortion and damage and replace the parts as necessary.

9. Lubricate all new parts with clean brake fluid.

10. Reassemble the master cylinder parts in the reverse order of disassembly, taking note of the following:
   a. Reinstall the cup seal carefully to prevent damaging the lipped portions;
   b. Adjust the height of the clutch pedal after installing the master cylinder in position on the vehicle;
   c. Fill the master cylinder and clutch fluid reservoir and then bleed the clutch hydraulic system.

Clutch Slave Cylinder

REMOVAL AND INSTALLATION

1. Remove the slave cylinder attaching bolts and the pushrod from the shaft fork.
2. Disconnect the flexible fluid hose from the slave cylinder and remove the unit from the vehicle.
3. Install the slave cylinder in the reverse order of removal and bleed the clutch hydraulic system.

OVERHAUL

1. Remove the slave cylinder from the vehicle.
2. Remove the pushrod and boot.
3. Force out the piston by blowing compressed air into the slave cylinder at the hose connection.

NOTE: *Be careful not to apply excess air pressure to avoid possible injury.*

4. Clean all of the parts in clean brake fluid.
5. Check and replace the slave cylinder bore and piston if wear or severe scoring exists. Light scoring and glaze can be removed with crocus cloth soaked in brake fluid.
6. Normally the piston cup should be replaced when the slave cylinder is disassembled. Check the piston cup and replace it if it is found to be worn, fatigued or scored.
7. Replace the rubber boot if it is cracked or broken.
8. Lubricate all parts with clean brake fluid and assemble in reverse of disassembly. Bleed the system.

Driveshaft

REMOVAL AND INSTALLATION

The drive axles are variously called driveshafts or axles, or drive axles. Strictly speaking, they are not driveshafts, but drive axles. A special puller is necessary to remove the axles. The tool is illustrated here.

1. Jack up the car and support it with safety stands.
2. Remove the wheel and tire.
3. Pull out the cotter pin and then remove

Hub nut removal

1. Outside joint assembly (Birfield joint)
2. Band
3. Dust cover
4. Band
5. Inner ring
6. Cage
7. Ball
8. Outer ring
9. Plug
10. Inside joint assembly (Double offset joint)

Drive axle

126 CLUTCH AND TRANSMISSION

the wheel bearing nut. You'll have to hold the wheel hub still somehow while you do this.

4. Remove the bolts which secure the drive axle to the transaxle assembly. The drive axle is splined into the hub assembly and is removed from underneath the car.

5. Install the puller on the hub and remove the drive axle by screwing the tool inward. This will force the drive axle out the back of the hub assembly.

6. The drive axle is installed by lightly hammering it back into place in the hub assembly. Quite often, this is a difficult job since the splines are a tight fit. Unfortunately, there is no other way to do it unless you want to remove the steering knuckle and then press the shaft on. Light persistent tapping should get the job done.

7. The rest of the procedure is the reverse of removal. Be careful not to damage the grease seal. Torque the wheel bearing nut to 90–145 ft. lbs.

NOTE: *If you are going to remove the steering knuckle assembly along with the drive axle, see chapter 7, Suspension and Steering, for procedures.*

AUTOMATIC TRANSMISSION

Of all the vehicle covered in this book, only the 1982 310 and Stanza are available with an automatic transmission. This is the RN3F01A 3-speed unit.

THROTTLE WIRE ADJUSTMENT

The throttle wire is adjusted by means of double nuts on the carburetor side.

1. Loosen the adjusting nuts.
2. With the throttle fully opened, turn the threaded shaft inward as far as it will go and tighten the first nut against the bracket.

Throttle wire adjustment

3. Back off the first nut ½ turn and tighten the second nut against the bracket.
4. The throttle wire stroke between the threaded shaft and the cam should be 1.079–1.236 in.

CONTROL CABLE ADJUSTMENT

1. Place the control lever in Park.
2. Connect the control cable end to the lever in the transaxle unit, and tighten the cable securing bolt.
3. Move the lever to the 1 position. Make sure that the lever works smoothly and quietly.

Control cable adjustment

4. Place the lever in Park.
5. Make sure that the lever locks in Park. Remove the cable adjusting outer nut and loosen the inner nut. Connect the control cable to the trunnion and install the outer nut.
6. Pull on the cable a couple of times, then tighten the outer nut until it just contacts the bracket. Tighten the inner nut securely. The length of the cable between the inner end of the rubber boot and the outer end of the rod should be 4.75 in.
7. Check all parts to ensure smooth working order. Check the cable spring cotter pin to make sure that it is assembled as shown.

Correct positioning of the control lever cotter pin

CLUTCH AND TRANSMISSION

BAND ADJUSTMENT

1. Loosen the band adjuster locknut.
2. Tighten the anchor end pin locknut to 3–4 ft. lbs.
3. Back off the anchor end pin lock nut exactly 2½ turns.
4. Tighten the locknut to 12–16 ft. lbs. making absolutely certain that the anchor end pin locknut does not move.

REMOVAL AND INSTALLATION

The engine and transaxle have to be removed as a unit.

1. Remove the converter housing dust cover.
2. Unbolt the flex plate from the converter.
3. Make two chalk marks on the converter and flex plate for reassembly.
4. Remove the starter.
5. See the engine removal and installation section and remove the unit from the car.
6. Installation is the reverse of removal. Note the following:

   a. Align the previously made chalk marks when installing the converter. Measure the distance between the transmission housing end face and the converter face. The distance should be ⅞ inch.

   b. After installation, rotate the converter several times to ensure freedom of movement.

   c. Connect all wires and adjust all linkage points as previously described.

Suspension and Steering

FRONT SUSPENSION

All models covered in this book use Mac-Pherson strut front suspension. In this type of suspension, each strut combines the function of coil spring and shock absorber. The spindle is mounted to the lower part of the strut through a single ball joint. No upper suspension arm is required in this design. The spindle and lower control arm are located fore and aft by tension rods which attach to the chassis.

Springs and Shock Absorbers

TESTING SHOCK ABSORBER ACTION

Shock absorbers require replacement if the vehicle fails to recover quickly after a large bump is encountered. If there is a tendency for the vehicle to sway or nose dive excessively, or, sometimes, if the suspension is overly susceptible to vibration.

A good way to test the shocks is to intermittently apply downward pressure to one corner of the vehicle until it is moving up and down for almost the full suspension travel, then release it and watch the recovery. If the vechile bounces slightly about one more time and then comes to rest, the shock absorbers are serviceable. If the vehicle goes on bouncing, the shocks require replacement.

Strut

REMOVAL AND INSTALLATION

F10

1. Jack up the car and support it safely. Remove the wheel.
2. Disconnect and plug the brake hose. Remove the brake caliper as outlined in Chapter 8. Remove the disc and hub as described in this chapter.
3. Disconnect the tension rod and stabilizer bar from the transverse link.
4. Unbolt the steering arm. Pry the control arm down to detach it from the strut.
5. Place a jack under the bottom of the strut.
6. Open the hood and remove the nuts holding the top of of the strut.
7. Lower the jack slowly and cautiously until the strut assembly can be removed.
8. Reverse the procedure to install. The self-locking nuts holding the top of the strut must be replaced. Bleed the brakes.

310

1. Raise and support the car on jackstands.
2. Remove the wheel.
3. Remove the steering side rod from the knuckle arm using a ball joint remover.
4. Detach the brake tube from the strut.

SUSPENSION AND STEERING

1. Transverse link bushing
2. Transverse link
3. Connecting bolt
4. Stabilizer bracket
5. Stabilizer
6. Stabilizer bushing
7. Strut
8. Knuckle
9. Ball joint
10. O-ring
11. Gland packing assembly
12. Bound bumper
13. Coil spring
14. Dust cover
15. Spring seat
16. Grease seal
17. Thrust seat
18. Thrust plate
19. Mount insulator
20. Insulator cap

F10, 310 front suspension

5. Support the transverse link with a jackstand.
6. Detach the strut from the knuckle.
7. Working under the hood, remove the dust cap at the top of the strut. Loosen the strut piston rod locknut.
8. Support the strut, remove the three strut attaching nuts and remove the strut.
9. Installation is the reverse of removal. Torque the:
- Strut-to-body nuts: 11–17 ft. lbs.
- Strut-to-knuckle bolts: 24–33 ft. lbs.
- Side rod ball stud end: 40–47 ft. lbs.

Stanza

1. Raise and support the car on jackstands.
2. Remove the wheel.
3. Detach the brake tube from the strut.
4. Support the transverse link with a jackstand.
5. Detach the knuckle from the strut.
6. Loosen, but do not remove, the strut piston rod locknut.
7. Support the strut and remove the three upper attaching nuts. Remove the strut.
8. Installation is the reverse of removal. Torque the:
- Strut-to-body nuts: 23–31 ft. lbs.
- Piston rod locknut: 43–54 ft. lbs.
- Strut-to-knuckle bolts: 56–80 ft. lbs.

Coil Spring and Shock Absorber
REMOVAL AND INSTALLATION

CAUTION: *The coil springs are under considerable tension, and can exert enough*

130 SUSPENSION AND STEERING

Stanza front suspension

force to cause serious injury. Disassemble the struts only if the proper tools are available, and use extreme caution.

Coil springs on all models must be removed with the aid of a coil spring compressor. If you don't have one, don't try to improvise by using something else: you could risk injury. The Datsun coil spring compressor is Special Tool ST3565S001 or variations of that number. Basically, they are all the same tool. These are the recommended compressors, although they are probably not the only spring compressors which will work. Always follow manufacturer's instructions when operating a spring compressor. You can now buy cartridge type shock absorbers for many Datsuns: installation procedures are not the same as those given here. In this case, follow the instructions that come with the shock absorbers.

To remove the coil spring, you must first remove the strut assembly from the vehicle. See above for procedures.

1. Secure the strut assembly in a vise.
2. Attach the spring compressor to the spring, leaving the top few coils free.
3. Remove the dust cap from the top of the strut to expose the center nut, if a dust cap is provided.
4. Compress the spring just far enough to permit the strut insulator to be turned by hand. Remove the self-locking center nut.
5. Take out the strut insulator, strut bearing, oil seal, upper spring seat and bound bumper rubber from the top of the strut. Note their sequence of removal and be sure to assemble them in the same order.
6. Remove the spring with the spring compressor still attached.

Assembly is the reverse of disassembly. Observe the following. Make sure you assemble the unit with the shock absorber piston rod fully extended. When assembling, take care that the rubber spring seats, both top and bottom, and the spring are positioned in their grooves before releasing the spring.

7. To remove the shock absorber: Remove the dust cap, if so equipped, and push the piston rod down until it bottoms. With the piston in this position, loosen and remove the gland packing shock absorber retainer. This calls for Datsun Special Tool ST35500001, but you should be able to loosen it either with a pipe wrench or by tapping it around with a drift.

NOTE: *If the gland tube is dirty, clean it before removing it to prevent dirt from contaminating the fluid inside the strut tube.*

8. Remove the O-ring from the top of the piston guide and lift out the piston rod together with the cylinder. Drain all of the fluid from the strut and shock components into a suitable container. Clean all parts.

NOTE: *The piston rod, piston rod guide*

SUSPENSION AND STEERING

and cylinder are a matched set: single parts of this shock assembly should not be exchanged with parts of other assemblies.

Assembly is the reverse of disassembly with the following notes.

After installing the cylinder and piston rod assembly (the shock absorber kit) in the outer casing, remove the piston rod guide, if so equipped, from the cylinder and pour the correct amount of new fluid into the cylinder-and strut outer casing. To find this amount consult the instructions with your shock absorber kit. The amount of oil should be listed. Use only Nissan Genuine Strut Oil or its equivalent.

NOTE: *It is important that the correct amount of fluid be poured into the strut to assure correct shock absorber damping force.*

Install the O-ring, fluid and any other cylinder components. Fit the gland packing and tighten it after greasing the gland packing-to-piston rod mating surfaces.

NOTE: *When tightening the gland packing, extend the piston rod about 3 to 5 inches from the end of the outer casing to expel most of the air from the strut.*

After the kit is installed, bleed the air from the system in the following manner: hold the strut with its bottom end facing down. Pull the piston rod out as far as it will go. Turn the strut upside down and push the piston in as far as it will go. Repeat this procedure several times until an equal pressure is felt on both the pull out and the push in strokes of the piston rods. The remaining assembly is the reverse of disassembly.

Ball Joint

INSPECTION

The lower ball joint should be replaced when play becomes excessive. Datsun does not publish specifications on just what constitutes excessive play, relying instead on a method of determining the force (in inch pounds) required to keep the ball joing turning. This method is not very helpful to the backyard mechanic since it involves removing the ball joint, which is what we are trying to avoid in the first place. An effective way to determine ball joint play is to jack up the car until the wheel is just a couple of inches off the ground and the ball joint is unloaded (meaning you can't jack directly underneath the ball joint). Place a long bar under the tire and move the wheel and tire assembly up and down. Keep one hand on top of the tire while you are doing this. If there is over ¼ inch of play at the top of the tire, the ball joint is

1. Driveshaft
2. Strut assembly
3. Grease seal
4. Inner sheel bearing
5. Knuckle
6. Spacer
7. Outer wheel bearing
8. Grease seal
9. Rotor
10. Wheel hub
11. Hub nut
12. Ball joint
13. Transverse link assembly

F10, 310 front hub and knuckle

132 SUSPENSION AND STEERING

1. Driveshaft
2. Strut assembly
3. Grease seal (Inner)
4. Inner wheel bearing
5. Knuckle
6. Spacer
7. Outer wheel bearing
8. Grease seal (Outer)
9. Disc rotor
10. Wheel hub
11. Hub nut

Tightening torque: N·m (kg-m, ft-lb)
- Ⓐ 32 - 44 (3.3 - 4.5, 24 - 33)
- Ⓑ 29 - 39 (3 - 4, 22 - 29)
- Ⓒ 25 - 33 (2.5 - 3.4, 18 - 25)
- Ⓓ 118 - 196 (12 - 20, 87 - 145)
- Ⓔ 78 - 98 (8 - 10, 58 - 72)

Stanza front hub and knuckle

probably bad. This is assuming that the wheel bearings are in good shape and properly adjusted. As a double check on this, have someone watch the ball joint while you move the tire up and down with the bar. If you can see considerable play, besides feeling play at the top of the wheel, the ball joint needs replacing.

REMOVAL AND INSTALLATION
F10

1. Raise the car and support it on jack stands. Remove the wheel.
2. Remove the nut holding the ball stud to the knuckle and force out the stud with a ball joint fork, being careful not to damage the ball joint dust cover.
3. Remove the ball joint bolts and the ball joint.

Install the ball joint in the reverse order of removal. Tighten the ball stud attaching nut to 22–29 ft. lbs., and the ball joint to transverse link attaching bolts to 40–47 ft. lbs.

Ball joint removal

310 and Stanza

1. Jack up the car and support it on stands.
2. Remove the wheel.
3. Remove the driveshaft. Refer to chapter 6 for procedures.
4. Separate the ball joint from the steering knuckle with a ball joint remover, being careful not to damage the ball joint dust cover if the ball joint is to be used again.
5. Remove the other ball joint bolts from

SUSPENSION AND STEERING

the transverse link and remove the ball joint.
Installation is the reverse of removal. Tighten the ball stud attaching nut (from ball joint to steering knuckle) to 22–29 ft. lbs., and the Ball joint to transverse link bolts to 40–47 ft. lbs.

Lower Control Arm (Transverse Link) and Ball Joint

REMOVAL AND INSTALLATION

F10 and 310

CAUTION: *Always use new nuts.*
1. Raise and support the car on jackstands.
2. Remove the wheel.
3. Unbolt the transverse link from the ball joint.
4. Remove the nut attaching the stabilizer link to the transverse link.
5. Unbolt the transverse link from the subframe and remove it from the car.
6. Installation is the reverse of removal. Note the following torques:
 • Transverse link-to-sub frame: 42–51 ft. lbs.
 • Ball joint-to-transverse link: 40–47 ft. lbs.

Transverse link attaching points, F10 and 310

Unbolting transverse link from sub frame on F10 and 310

Stanza

CAUTION: *Always use new nuts.*
1. Raise and support the car on jackstands.
2. Remove the wheel.
3. Remove the lower ball joint.

Removing Stanza transverse link

Removing Stanza gusset

4. Remove the transverse link.
5. Remove the gusset.
6. Installation is the reverse of removal. When installing the link, tighten the nut securing the link spindle to the gusset. Final tightening should be made with the weight of the car on the wheels. Tightening torques are:
 • Gusset-to-body: 65–87 ft. lbs.
 • Transverse link securing nut: 65–80 ft. lbs.
 • Transverse link securing bolts: 65–87 ft. lbs.
 • Lower ball joint nuts: 40–51 ft. lbs.

Front End Alignment

CASTER AND CAMBER

Caster is the forward or rearward tilt of the upper end of the kingpin, or the upper ball joint, which results in a slight tilt of the steering axis forward or backward. Rearward tilt is referred to as a positive caster, while forward tilt is referred to as negative caster.

Camber is the inward or outward tilt from the vertical, measured in degrees, of the front wheels at the top. An outward tilt gives the wheel positive chamber. Proper camber is critical to assure even tire wear.

SUSPENSION AND STEERING

Wheel Alignment Specifications

Year	Model	Caster Range (deg)	Caster Preferred Setting (deg)	Camber Range (deg)	Camber Preferred Setting (deg)	Toe-In (in.)	Steering Axis Inclination (deg)	Wheel Pivot Ratio (deg) Inner Wheel	Wheel Pivot Ratio (deg) Outer Wheel
1976–78	F10	20'P–1°50'P	1°05'P	50'P–2°20'P	1°35'P	①	9°15'–10°45'	36°30'–39°30'	31°–34°
1979–82	310	25'P–1°55'P	1°05'P	15'P–1°45'P	1°P	0–0.08	11°10'–12°30'	36°30'–39°30'	29°30'–32°30'
1982	Stanza	40'P–2°10'P	1°15'P	45'N–45'P	0	0–0.08	N.A.	36–40	30–34

① 0–0.79 Radial tires
0.20–0.28 Bias tires
N.A.: Information not available

SUSPENSION AND STEERING

Since caster and camber are adjusted traditionally by adding or subtracting shims behind the upper control arms, and the Datsuns covered in this guide have replaced the upper control arm with the MacPherson strut, the only way to adjust caster and camber is to replace bent or worn parts of the front suspension.

TOE

Toe is the amount, measured in a fraction of an inch, that the wheels are closer together at one end than the other. Toe-in means that the front wheels are closer together at the front than the rear; toe-out means the rears are closer than the front. Datsuns are adjusted to have a slight amount of toe-in. Toe-in is adjusted by turning the tie-rod, which has a right-hand thread on one end and a left-hand thread on the other.

You can check your vehicle's toe-in yourself without special equipment if you make careful measurements. The wheels must be straight ahead.

1. Toe-in can be determined by measuring the distance between the center of the tire treads, at the front of the tire and at the rear. If the tread pattern of your car's tires makes this impossible, you can measure between the edges of the wheel rims, but make sure to move the car forward and measure in a couple of places to void errors caused by bent rims or wheel runout.
2. If the measurement is not within specifications, loosen the locknuts at both ends of the tie-rod (the driver's side locknut is left-hand threaded.
3. Turn the top of the tie-rod toward the front of the car to reduce toe-in, or toward the rear to increase it. When the correct dimension is reached, tighten the locknuts and check the adjustment.

NOTE: *The length of the tie-rods must always be equal to each other.*

STEERING ANGLE ADJUSTMENT

The maximum steering angle is adjusted by stopper bolts on the steering arms. Loosen the locknut on the stopper bolt, turn the stopped bolt in or out as required to obtain the proper maximum steering angle and retighten the locknut.

SUSPENSION HEIGHT

Suspension height is adjusted by replacing the springs. Various springs are available for adjustment.

REAR SUSPENSION

Springs

REMOVAL AND INSTALLATION
F10 Station Wagon

1. Jack up the car and support it with safety stands.
2. Remove the wheel and tire.
3. Remove the nuts from the lower portion of the shock absorber.
4. Remove the nuts from the U-bolts, and detach the bumper rubbers and the spring seat.
5. Jack up the axle until it clears the leaf spring.
6. Remove the hand brake clamp from the leaf spring.
7. Remove the front pin and shackle, and detach the spring from the body.
8. Installation is in the reverse order of removal.

F10 Sedan and Hatchback

1. Jack up the rear of the car and support it with safety stands.
2. Remove the wheels and tires.
3. Support the trailing arm with a jack.
4. Remove the upper and lower shock absorber nuts.
5. Lower the jack slowly and carefully. Remove the coil spring.
6. Installation is in the reverse order of removal.

Stanza

1. Raise and support the rear of the car on jackstands.
2. Remove the wheel.
3. Disconnect the brake tube and parking brake cable.
4. Remove the brake assembly and wheel bearing.
5. Detach the parallel links and radius rod from the strut.
6. Support the strut.
7. Remove the strut upper end nuts.
8. Remove the strut from the car.
9. Installation is the reverse of removal. Note the following torque values:
- Strut-to-parallel link: 65–87 ft. lb.
- Strut-to-radius rod: 54–69 ft. lb.
- Strut-to-body: 23–31 ft. lb.

136 SUSPENSION AND STEERING

1. Rear arm
2. Coil spring
3. Rubber seat
4. Shock absorber
5. Drum
6. Bumper
7. Bushing
8. Rear arm bolt

F10 sedan and hatchback rear suspension

1. Axle tube
2. U-bolt
3. Shock absorber
4. Bumper rubber
5. Shackle
6. Spring seat
7. Leaf spring
8. Front pin

F10 station wagon rear suspension

SUSPENSION AND STEERING 137

Stanza rear suspension

SUSPENSION AND STEERING

1. Rubber seat
2. Coil spring
3. Rear arm
4. Shock absorber

Tightening torque N·m (kg-m, ft-lb)

Ⓐ :   8 - 12 (0.8 - 1.2, 5.8 - 8.7)
Ⓑ : 15 - 24 (1.5 - 2.4, 11 - 17)

310 rear suspension

Shock Absorber

INSPECTION AND TESTING

Inspect and test the rear shock absorbers in the same manner as outlined for the front shock absorbers.

REMOVAL AND INSTALLATION

F10 and 310

1. Open the trunk and remove the cover panel to expose the shock mounts. Pry off the mount covers, if so equipped. On leaf spring models, jack up the rear of the vehicle and support the rear axle on stands.
2. Remove the two nuts holding the top of the shock absorber. Unbolt the bottom of the shock absorber.
3. Remove the shock absorber.
4. Installation is the reverse of removal.

STEERING

Steering Wheel

REMOVAL AND INSTALLATION

1. Position the wheels in the straight-ahead direction. The steering wheel should be right-side up and level.
2. Disconnect the battery ground cable.
3. Look at the back of your steering wheel. If there are countersunk screws in the back of the spokes, remove the screws and pull off the horn pad. Some models have a horn wire running from the pad to the steering wheel. Disconnect it.
   There are three other types of horn buttons or rings on Datsuns. The first simply pulls off. The Second, which is usually a large, semi-Triangular pad, must be pushed up, then pulled off. The third must be pushed in and turned clockwise.
4. Remove the rest of the horn switching mechanism, noting the relative location of the parts. Remove the mechanism only if it hinders subsequent wheel removal proceedures.
5. Match-mark the top of the steering column shaft and the steering wheel flange.
6. Remove the attaching nut and remove the steering wheel with a puller.
   CAUTION: *Do not strike the shaft with a hammer, which may cause the column to collapse.*
7. Install the steering wheel in the reverse order of removal, aligning the punch marks. Do not drive or hammer the wheel into place, or you may cause the collapsible steering column to collapse; in which case you'll have to buy a whole new steering column unit.
8. Tighten the steering wheel nut to 14–

SUSPENSION AND STEERING 139

1. Steering wheel
2. Steering lock
3. Column clamp
4. Steering column assembly
5. Lower bracket
6. Lower joint
7. Pinion gear housing

F10 and 310 steering column

18 ft. lbs. on the F10, 22–25 ft. lbs. on the 310 and 27–38 ft. lb. on the Stanza.

9. Reinstall the horn button, pad, or ring.

Turn Signal Switch

REMOVAL AND INSTALLATION

On some later model Datsuns, the turn signal switch is part of a combination switch. The whole unit is removed together.

1. Disconnect the battery ground cable.
2. Remove the steering wheel as previously outlined. Observe the "caution" on the collapsible steering column.
3. Remove the steering column covers.
4. Disconnect the electrical plugs from the switch.
5. Remove the retaining screws and remove the switch.
6. Installation is the reverse of removal. Many models have turn signal switches that have a tab which must fit into a hole in the steering shaft in order for the system to return the switch to the neutral position after the turn has been made. Be sure to align the tab and the hole when installing.

Steering Lock

REMOVAL AND INSTALLATION

The steering lock/ignition switch/warning buzzer assembly is attached to the steering column by special screws whose heads shear off on installation. The screws must be drilled out to remove the assembly. The ignition switch or warning switch can be replaced without removing the assembly. The ignition switch is on the back of the assembly, and the warning switch on the side. The warning buzzer, which sounds when the driver's door is opened with the steering unlocked, is located behind the instrument panel.

Tie-Rod Ends (Steering Side Rods)

REMOVAL AND INSTALLATION

You will need a ball joint remover for this operation.

1. Jack up the front of the vehicle and support it on jack stands.
2. Locate the faulty tie-rod end. It will have a lot of play in it and the dust cover will probably be ripped.

SUSPENSION AND STEERING

3. Remove the cotter key and nut from the tie-rod stud. Note the position of the steering linkage.
4. Loosen the locknut holding the tie-rod to the rest of the steering linkage.
5. Free the tie-rod ball joint from either the relay rod or steering knuckle by using a ball joint remover.
6. Unscrew and remove the tie rod end, counting the number of turns it takes to completely free it.
7. Install the new tie-rod end, turning it in exactly as far as you screwed out the old one. Make sure it is correctly positioned in relation to the rest of the steering linkage.
8. Fit the ball joint and nut, tighten them and install a new cotter pin.

Before finally tightening the tie-rod lock nut or clamp, adjust the toe-in of the vehicle. See section under "Front Suspension."

Power Steering Pump

REMOVAL AND INSTALLATION

1. Remove the hoses at the pump and plug the openings shut to prevent contamination. Position the disconnected lines in a raised attitude to prevent leakage.
2. Remove the pump belt.
3. Loosen the retaining bolts and any braces, and remove the pump.

Installation is the reverse of removal. Adjust the belt tension by referring to the "Belts" section in chapter one, "General Information and Maintenance." Bleed the system.

BLEEDING THE POWER STEERING SYSTEM

1. Fill the pump reservoir and allow to remain undisturbed for a few minutes.
2. Raise the car until the front wheels are clear of the ground.
3. With the engine off, quickly turn the wheels right and left several times, lightly contacting the stops.
4. Add fluid if necessary.
5. Start the engine and let it idle.
6. Repeat Steps 3 and 4 with the engine idling.
7. With the steering wheel all the way to the left, open the bleeder screw on the steering gear to allow the air to bleed. Close the screw when fluid is expelled.
8. Stop the engine, lower the car until the wheels just touch the ground. Start the engine, allow it to idle, and turn the wheels back and forth several times. Check the fluid level and refill if necessary.

Manual Steering Gear

REMOVAL AND INSTALLATION

F10 and 310

1. Raise and support the car on jackstands.
2. Remove the steering joint cover and remove the steering column-to-lower joint bolts.
3. Remove the bolt securing the lower joint to the steering pinion gear and disconnect the joint from the gear.
4. Remove the side rod ball stud nuts.
5. Remove the side rod ball studs with a ball joint remover.
6. Unclamp and remove the steering gear.
7. Installation is the reverse of removal. Note the following torques:
   • Side rod-to-kunckle arm: 40–47 ft. lb.
   • Gear housing clamp bolt: 16–25 ft. lb.
   • Lower joint-to-pinion gear: 17–22 ft. lb.
   • Lower joint-to-steering column: 17–22 ft. lb.
8. Check the wheel alignment.

Stanza

1. Raise and support the car on jackstands.
2. Remove the tie rod from the knuckle with a ball joint remover.
3. Loosen, but do not remove, the steering gear mounting bolts.
4. Remove the steering column lower joint.
5. Unbolt and remove the gear.
6. Installation is the reverse of removal. Note the following torques:
   • Tie rod-to-steering knuckle: 22–29 ft. lb.
   • Gear housing clamp bolt: 43–58 ft. lb.
   • Lower joint-to-pinion gear: 23–31 ft. lb.
   • Lower joint-to-steering column: 23–31 ft. lb.

Power Steering Gear

REMOVAL AND INSTALLATION

310

1. Raise and support the front of the car on jackstands.
2. Remove the lower joint cover and loosen, but do not, remove the bolts attaching the lower joint at the column.
3. Unbolt the lower joint from the steering pinion gear.
4. Unbolt and remove the side rod ball studs from the knuckle arms using a ball joint remover.

SUSPENSION AND STEERING 141

1. Nut
2. Cotter pin
3. Side rod outer socket assembly
4. Lock nut
5. Boot clamp
6. Boot
7. Snap ring
8. Steering rack bushing
9. Plate
10. Steering gear mount
11. Side rod inner socket assembly
12. Lock nut
13. Steering gear housing assembly
14. Steering clamp
15. Oil seal
16. Pinion bearing outer snap ring
17. Pinion bearing inner snap ring
18. Steering pinion bearing
19. Steering gear pinion
20. Steering rack gear
21. Retainer
22. Retainer spring
23. Adjust screw
24. Adjust screw lock nut
Tightening torque: N-m (kg-m, ft-lb)
Ⓐ 54-64 (5.5-6.5, 40-47)
Ⓑ 37-46 (3.8-4.7, 27-34)
Ⓒ 78-98 (8-10, 58-72)
Ⓓ 22-33 (2.2-3.4, 16-25)
Ⓔ 78-98 (8-10, 58-72)
Ⓕ 39-59 (4-6, 29-43)

F10 and 310 manual steering gear

5. Disconnect the hoses at the gear.
6. Unbolt and remove the gear linkage.
7. Installation is the reverse of removal. Note the following torque values:
- Side rod-to-knuckle arm: 40–47 ft. lb.
- Gear housing clamp bolt: 16–25 ft. lb.
- Gear housing-to-sub frame: 16–25 ft. lb.
- Lower joint-to-pinion gear: 17–22 ft. lb.
- Lower joint-to-steering column: 17–22 ft. lb.
- Hoses-to-gear: 36–51 ft. lb.

Stanza

1. Raise and support the car on jackstands.
2. Disconnect the hoses at the gear.
3. Unbolt and remove the side rod ball studs from the knuckle using a ball joint remover.
4. Remove the lower steering joint.
5. Remove the steering gear mounting bolts.
6. Remove the cylinder tubes.
7. Remove the steering gear and linkage.
8. Installation is the reverse of removal. Note the following torques:
- Tie rod-to-knuckle: 22–29 ft. lb.
- Gear housing clamp bolt: 43–58 ft. lb.
- Low pressure hose clip bolt: 9–617 in. lb.
- High pressure hose-to-gear: 29–36 ft. lb.

142 SUSPENSION AND STEERING

STEERING WHEEL
- Ⓣ 37-51 (3.8-5.2, 27-38)
- DO NOT STRIKE END OF STEERING COLUMN SHAFT WITH A HAMMER. STRIKING SHAFT WILL DAMAGE NEEDLE BEARING OR COLUMN SHAFT.
- BE CAREFUL NOT TO DAMAGE CANEL POLE.

MG SLIDING PORTION

Ⓣ 9-14 (0.9-1.4, 6.5-10.1)

Ⓣ 9-14 (0.9-1.4, 6.5-10.1)

STEERING COLUMN ASSEMBLY
- NEVER IN ANY CASE SHOULD UNDUE STRESS BE APPLIED TO STEERING COLUMN IN AXIAL DIRECTION.
- WHEN INSTALLING, DO NOT APPLY BENDING FORCE TO STEERING COLUMN.

STEERING LOCK

Ⓣ 3.4-4.4 (0.35-0.45, 2.5-3.3)

Ⓣ 31-42 (3.2-4.3, 23-31)

Ⓣ 39-49 (4.0-5.0, 29-36)

Ⓣ 29-39 (3.0-4.0, 22-29)

MANUAL STEERING GEAR ASSEMBLY (RP15L)

Ⓣ 29-49 (3.0-5.0, 22-36)

Ⓣ 3.7-5.0 (0.38-0.51, 2.7-3.7)

POWER STEERING OIL TANK

Ⓣ 3.7-5.0 (0.38-0.51, 2.7-3.7)

Ⓣ 3.1-4.3 (0.32-0.44, 2.3-3.2)

TIGHTEN BOLTS SECURELY

Ⓣ 59-78 (6.0-8.0, 43-58)

PRESSURE SWITCH

HOSE

ADJUSTING NUT

Ⓣ 5-8 (0.5-0.8, 3.6-5.8)

Ⓣ 31-42 (3.2-4.3, 23-31)

Ⓣ 31-42 (3.2-4.3, 23-31)

POWER STEERING GEAR ASSEMBLY (IPRP15L)

POWER STEERING OIL PUMP*

Ⓣ 49-69 (5.0-7.0, 36-51)

Ⓣ 1-2 (0.1-0.2, 0.7-1.4)

MG : MULTI-PURPOSE GREASE POINT
Ⓣ : N·M (KG-M, FT-LB)

Stanza steering system components

SUSPENSION AND STEERING   143

310 power steering gear

- POWER STEERING OIL PUMP
- LOW PRESSURE HOSE
- HIGH PRESSURE HOSE
- POWER STEERING GEAR AND LINKAGE

T: N-M (KG-M, FT-LB)

- T 3.7-4.9 (0.38-0.5, 2.7-3.6)
- T 3.7-4.9 (0.38-0.5, 2.7-3.6)
- T 29-49 (3-5, 22-36)
- T 31-42 (3.2-4.3, 23-31)
- T 31-42 (3.2-4.3, 23-31)
- T 22-33 (2.2-3.4, 16-25)
- T 22-33 (2.2-3.4, 16-25)
- T 3-5 (0.3-0.5, 2.2-3.6)
- T 49-69 (5-7, 36-51)
- T 54-64 (5.5-6.5, 40-47)

Brakes 08

BRAKE SYSTEM

Adjustment

To adjust the brakes, raise the wheels, disconnect the parking brake linkage from the rear wheels, apply the brakes hard a few times to center the drums, and proceed as follows:

NOTE: *Only certain types of drum brakes require adjustment; some drum brakes are automatically adjusted when the parking brake is applied. No disc brakes need adjustment—they are self adjusting.*

BOLT-TYPE ADJUSTER

Turn the adjuster bolt on the backing plate until the wheel can no longer be turned, then back off until the wheel is free of drag. Repeat the procedure on the other adjusted bolt on the same wheel. Some models may have only one adjuster bolt per wheel.

Some models incorporate a "click" arrangement with the bolt adjuster. The adjustment proceeds in clicks or notches. The wheel will often be locked temporarily as the adjuster passes over the center for each click. Thus, the adjuster is alternately hard and easy to turn. When the wheel is fully locked, back off 1–3 clicks.

TOOTHED ADJUSTING NUT

Remove the rubber cover from the backing plate. Align the hole in the brake backing plate with the adjusting nut. To spread the brake shoes, turn the toothed adjusting nut with a conventional screwdriver. Stop turning when a considerable drag is felt. Back off the nut a few notches so that the correct clearance is reached between the brake drum and the brake shoes. Make sure that the wheel rotates freely.

AUTOMATIC ADJUSTERS

No manual adjustment is necessary. The self adjuster operates whenever the hand or foot brake brakes (on some models) are used.

After Adjustment—All Models

After adjusting the brakes, reconnect the handbrake linkage. Make sure that there is no rear wheel drag with the handbrake released. Loosen the handbrake adjustment if necessary.

BRAKE PEDAL ADJUSTMENT

Before adjusting the pedal, make sure that the wheelbrakes are correctly adjusted. Adjust the pedal free play by means of the ad-

BRAKES   145

1. Push rod lock nut
2. Brake lamp switch
3. Brake lamp switch lock nut

Typical brake pedal adjustment

justable pushrod or by replacing shims between the master cylinder and the brake booster or firewall. Adjust the pedal height by means of the adjustable pedal arm stop pad in the driver's compartment. Free play should be approximately 0.04–0.20 in. on all models. Pedal height (floorboard to pedal pad) should be approximately 7 inches for the F10 and 301, and 6 inches for Stanza.

HYDRAULIC SYSTEM

Master Cylinder
Removal and Installation

Clean the outside of the cylinder thoroughly, particularly around the cap and fluid lines. Disconnect the fluid lines and cap them to exclude dirt. Remove the clevis pin connecting the pushrod to the brake pedal arm inside the vehicle. This pin need not be removed with the vacuum booster. Unbolt the master cylinder from the firewall and remove. The adjustable pushrod is used to adjust brake pedal free-play. If the pushrod is not adjustable, there will be shims between the cylinder and the mount. These shims, or the adjustable pushrod, are used to adjust brake pedal free play.

NOTE: *Ordinary brake fluid will boil and cause brake failure under the high temperatures developed in disc brake systems.*

DOT 3 or 4 brake fluid for disc brake systems must be used.

OVERHAUL

CAUTION: *Master cylinders are supplied to Datsun by two manufacturers: Nabco and Tokico. Parts between these manufacturers are not interchangeable. Be sure you obtain the correct rebuilding kit for your master cylinder.*

The master cylinder can be disassembled using the illustrations as a guide. Clean all parts in clean brake fluid. Replace the cylinder or piston as necessary if clearance between the two exceeds 0.006 in. Lubricate all parts with clean brake fluid on assembly. Master cylinder rebuilding kits, containing all the wearing parts, are available to simplify overhaul.

BRAKE PROPORTIONING VALVE

All Datsuns covered in this guide are equipped with brake proportioning valves of several different types. The valves all do the same job, which is to separate the front and rear brake lines, allowing them to function independently, and preventing the rear brakes from locking before the front brakes. Damage, such as brake line leakage, in either the front or rear brake system will not affect the normal operation of the unaffected system. If, in the event of a panic stop, the rear brakes lock up before the front brakes, it could mean the proportioning valve is defective. In that case, replace the entire proportioning valve.

Proportioning valve

Power Booster
REMOVAL AND INSTALLATION

1. Remove the master cylinder.
2. Detach the vacuum lines from the booster.

146 BRAKES

1. Reservoir cap
2. Filter
3. Reservoir tank assembly
4. Stopper ring
5. Stopper
6. Primary piston assembly
7. Primary return spring
8. Secondary piston assembly
9. Stopper screw
10. Secondary return spring
11. Plug
12. Check valve

F10 master cylinder

310 master cylinder

STOPPER BOLT
① 1.5-2.9 (0.15-0.30, 1.1-2.2)

PLUG
① 44-54 (4.5-5.5, 33-40)

①: N-M (KG-M, FI-LB)

BRAKES 147

Nabco Make

- RESERVOIR CAP
- FILTER
- RESERVOIR
- PISTON CUP (SECONDARY)
- PISTON CUP (PRIMARY)
- STOPPER RING
- PRIMARY PISTON ASSEMBLY
- SECONDARY PISTON
- SECONDARY PISTON RETURN SPRING
- CHECK VALVE (PRIMARY)
- CHECK VALVE (SECONDARY)
- PLUG
  ⓣ 44-54
  (4.5-5.5, 33-40)
- STOPPER SCREW
  ⓣ 1.5-2.9
  (0.15-0.3, 1.1-2.2)

Section: A-A

ⓣ: N-M (KG-M, FT-LB)

Tokico Make

- RESERVOIR CAP
- FILTER
- RESERVOIR
- SECONDARY PISTON RETURN SPRING
- PISTON CUP (SECONDARY)
- PISTON CUP (PRIMARY)
- SECTION: A-A
- STOPPER RING
- PRIMARY PISTON
- PRIMARY PISTON RETURN SPRING
- SECONDARY PISTON
- CHECK VALVE
- CHECK VALVE
- PLUG
  ⓣ 44-54 (4.5-5.5, 33-40)
- STOPPER SCREW
  ⓣ 2.0-3.4
  (0.20-0.35, 1.4-2.5)

SECTION A-A

ⓣ N-M (KG-M, FT-LB)

Stanza master cylinders

148 BRAKES

3. Detach the booster pushrod at the pedal clevis.

4. Unbolt the booster from the firewall and lift it out.

5. Installation is the reverse of removal. Adjust the length of the pushrod so that the distance between the pushrod clevis hole and the rear face of the booster is 5.12 inches. Torque the master cylinder to-booster nuts to 6–8 ft. lbs.; the booster-to-firewall nuts to 6–8 ft. lbs.

Power booster attaching points

System Bleeding

Bleeding is required whenever air in the hydraulic fluid causes a spongy feeling pedal and sluggish response. This is almost always the case after some part of the hydraulic system has been repaired or replaced.

1. Fill the master cylinder reservoir with the proper fluid. Special fluid is required for disc brakes.

2. The usual procedure is to bleed at the points farthest from the master cylinder first.

3. Fit a rubber hose over the bleeder screw. Submerge the other end of the hose in clean brake fluid in a clear glass container. Loosen the bleeder screw.

4. Slowly pump the brake pedal several times until fluid free of bubbles is discharged. An assistant is required to pump the pedal.

5. On the last pumping stroke, hold the pedal down and tighten the bleeder screw. Check the fluid level periodically during the bleeding operation.

6. Bleed the front brakes in the same way as the rear brakes. Note that some front drum brakes have two hydraulic cylinders and two bleeder screws. Both cylinders must be bled.

7. Check that the brake pedal is now firm. If not, repeat the bleeding operation.

FRONT DISC BRAKES

Disc Brake Pads
INSPECTION

You should be able to check the pad lining thickness without removing the pads. Check

1. Retaining ring
2. Boot
3. Bias ring
4. Piston A (inner piston)
5. Piston seal
6. Cylinder body
7. Piston B (outer piston)
8. Hanger spring
9. Spring
10. Pad
11. Clip
12. Clevis pin
13. Buffle plate
14. Yoke
15. Yoke spring

F10, 310 front brake

BRAKES 149

Stanza front brake

- PISTON SEAL RG
- PISTON
- DUST SEAL RG
- RETAINING RING
- CYLINDER BODY
- TORQUE MEMBER
- GUIDE PIN BOOT
- GUIDE PIN
  RG TO SLIDING PORTION
  Ⓣ 31-41 (3.2-4.2, 23-30)
- TORQUE MEMBER FIXING BOLT
  Ⓣ 72-97 (7.3-9.9, 53-72)
- PG TO PAD CONTACT AREA
- LOCK PIN BOOT
- LOCK PIN
  RG TO SLIDING PORTION
  Ⓣ 31-41 (3.2-4.2, 23-30)
- PAD SHIM
- PAD
- PAD RETAINER

Ⓣ: N-M (KG-M, FT-LB)
PG: PBC GREAT POINT
RG: RUBBER GREASE POINT

the Brake Specifications Chart at the end of this chapter to find the manufacturer's pad wear limit. However, this measurement may disagree with your state inspection laws. When replacing pads, always check the surface of the rotors for scoring or wear. The rotors should be removed for resurfacing if badly scored.

REMOVAL AND INSTALLATION

1. Raise and support the front of the car. Remove the wheels.
2. Remove the clip, pull out the pins, and remove the pad springs.
3. Remove the pads by pulling them out with pliers.
4. To install, first lightly coat the yoke groove and end surface of the piston with grease. Do not allow grease to contact the pads or rotor.
5. Open the bleeder screw slightly and push the outer piston into the cylinder until its end aligns with the end of the boot retaining ring. Do not push too far, which will require caliper disassembly to correct. Install the inner pad.
6. Pull the yoke toward the outside of the car to push the inner piston into place. Install the outer pad.
7. Apply the brakes a few times to seat the pads. Check the master cylinder and add fluid if necessary. Bleed the brakes if necessary.

Calipers and Brake Discs
OVERHAUL

1. Remove the pads.
2. Disconnect the brake tube.
3. Remove the two bottom strut assembly installation bolts to provide clearance.
4. Remove the caliper assembly mounting bolts.
5. Loosen the bleeder screw and press the pistons into their bores.
6. Clamp the yoke in a vise and tap the yoke head with a hammer to loosen the cylinder. Be careful that primary piston does not fall out.
7. Remove the bias ring from primary

150 BRAKES

piston. Remove the retaining rings and boots from both pistons. Depress and remove the pistons from the cylinder. Remove the piston seal from the cylinder carefully with the fingers so as not to mar the cylinder wall.

8. Remove the yoke springs from the yoke.
9. Wash all parts with clean brake fluid.
10. If the piston or cylinder is badly worn or scored, replace both. The piston surface is plated and must not be polished with emery paper. Replace all seals. The rotor can be removed and machined if scored, but final thickness must be at least 0.331 in. Runout must not exceed 0.001 in.
11. Lubricate the cylinder bore with clean brake fluid and install the piston seal.
12. Insert the bias ring into primary piston so that the rounded ring portion comes to the bottom of the piston. Primary piston has a small depression inside, while secondary does not.
13. Lubricate the pistons with clean brake fluid and insert into the cylinder. Install the boot and retaining ring. The yoke groove of the bias ring of primary piston must align with the yoke groove of the cylinder.
14. Install the yoke springs to the yoke so the projecting portion faces to the disc (rotor).
15. Lubricate the sliding portion of the cylinder and yoke. Assemble the cylinder and yoke by tapping the yoke lightly.
16. Replace the caliper assembly and pads. Torque the mounting bolts to 33–41 ft. lbs. Rotor bolt torque is 20–27 ft. lbs. Strut bolt torque is 33–44 ft. lbs. Bleed the system of air.

REAR DRUM BRAKES

Brake Drums

REMOVAL AND INSTALLATION

1. Raise the rear of the vehicle and support it on jack stands.
2. Remove the wheels.
3. Release the parking brake.
4. Remove the hub cap, cotter pin and wheel bearing locknut.
5. Pull off the drum, taking care not to drop the tapered bearing.
6. Installation is the reverse of removal. Adjust the wheel bearing. Torque the nut to 30 ft. lbs.

INSPECTION

After removing the brake drum, wipe out the accumulated dust with a damp cloth.

1. Dust cover
2. Shoe fixing pin
3. Lever assembly
4. Shoe
5. Return spring
6. Shoe fixing spring
7. Return spring
8. Wheel cylinder body
9. Piston cup
10. Piston
11. Dust cover
12. Adjust nut
13. Brake disc

F10 rear brake

BRAKES 151

1. Dust cover
2. Shoe fixing pin
3. Back plate
4. Adjuster assembly
5. Adjusting nut
6. Spring
7. Shoe
8. Return spring
9. Shoe fixing spring
10. Return spring
11. Wheel cylinder body
12. Piston cup
13. Piston
14. Dust cover
15. Wheel cylinder assembly

310 rear brake

ADJUSTER
WHEEL CYLINDER
ANTI-RATTLE PIN
BACK PLATE
SHOE, MINIMUM LINING THICKNESS
1.5 (0.059)
DIRECTION OF ROTATION
FRONT OF VEHICLE
RETURN SPRING
SPRING SEAT
ANTI-RATTLE SPRING
RETAINER
DRUM — MAXIMUM INNER DIAMETER
204.5 (8.05)

◄ : LUBRICATING POINT
UNIT: MM (IN)

Stanza rear brake

152 BRAKES

CAUTION: *Do not blow the brake dust out of the drums with compressed air or lung power. Brake linings contain asbestos, a known cancer causing substances. Dispose of the cloth after use.*

Inspect the drum for cracks, deep grooves, roughness, scoring, or out-of-roundness. Replace any brake drum which is cracked.

Smooth any slight scores by polishing the friction surface with the fine emery cloth. Heavy or extensive scoring will cause excessive brake lining wear and should be removed from the brake drum through resurfacing.

Brake Shoes

REMOVAL AND INSTALLATION

1. Raise the vehicle and remove the wheels.
2. Loosen the handbrake, cable, remove the clevis pin from the wheel cylinder lever, disconnect the handbrake cable, and remove the return pull spring.
3. Remove the brake drum, shoe retainers, return springs, and brake shoes. Loosen the brake adjusters if the drums are difficult to remove. Place a heavy rubber band around the cylinder to prevent the piston from coming out.
4. Clean the backing plate and check the wheel cylinder for leaks. To remove the wheel cylinder, remove the brake line, dust cover, securing nuts or plates and adjusting shims. Clearance between cylinder and piston should not exceed 0.006 in.

5. The drums must be machined if scored or out-of-round more than 0.008 in. The drum inside diameter must not be machined beyond 8.04 in.

Rear Wheel Bearings

ADJUSTMENT

1. Raise the rear of the vehicle and support it on jack stands.
2. Remove the wheel.
3. Remove the bearing dust cap. A pair of channel locks will usually do the trick.
4. Remove the cotter pin and nut cap if so equipped. Throw the cotter pin away.
5. Tighten the wheel bearing nut on the F10 to 18–22 ft. lbs, on the 310 to 29–33 ft. lbs. and on the Stanza 30–35 ft. lbs.
6. Rotate the drum back and forth a few revolutions to snug down the bearing.
7. On the F10, loosen the nut until it can be turned by hand, then tighten it with a hand held socket as far as it will go.
8. On the 310, and Stanza, after turning the wheel, recheck the torque of the nut, then loosen it 90° from its position.
9. Install the adjusting cap, if so equipped. Align the cotter pin holes in the nut or nut cap with the hole in the spindle by turning the nut clockwise on the F10. On the 310 and Stanza, tighten the nut no more than 15° to align the holes.
10. Install the cotter pin, bend up its ends, and install the dust cap.

Assemble the remaining parts.

1. Grease seal
2. Inner wheel bearing
3. Brake drum
4. Outer wheel bearing
5. Wheel bearing washer
6. Wheel bearing nut
7. Adjusting cap
8. O-ring
9. Hub cap
Tightening torque
Ⓐ: 39-44 N-m
  (4.0-4.5 kg-m, 29-33 ft-lb)

F10, 310 rear hub and bearing

BRAKES 153

Stanza rear hub and bearing

- GREAT SEAL MG
- INSIDE WHEEL BEARING MG
- WHEEL HUB (BRAKE DRUM)
- OUTSIDE WHEEL BEARING MG
- BEARING WASHER
- WHEEL BEARING NUT
  - ⓣ 39-44 (4.0-4.5, 29-33)
  - RETURN ANGLE: 90°
- ADJUSTING CAP
- O-RING MG
- COTTER PIN
- HUB CAP (MG INNER SIDE)

ADJUST WHEEL BEARING PRELOAD. REFER TO SECTION MA FOR ADJUSTING WHEEL BEARING PRELOAD.

MG: MULTI-PURPOSE GREASE POINT
ⓣ : N-M (KG-M, FT-LB)

PARKING BRAKE

ADJUSTMENT

Handbrake adjustments are generally not needed, unless the cables have stretched.

F10 and 310 Through 1980

There is an adjusting nut on the cable under the car, usually at the end of the front cable and near the point at which the two cables from the rear wheels come together (the

1. Warning lamp switch
2. Hand brake lever
3. Front cable
4. Cable supporter
5. Lock nut
6. Clevis
7. Adjuster
8. Return spring
9. Equalizer
10. Rear cable

F10 sedan and hatchback parking brake

154 BRAKES

1. Warning lamp switch
2. Hand brake lever
3. Front cable
4. Cable supporter
5. Counter lever
6. Return spring
7. Adjuster
8. Lock nut
9. Rear cable
10. Equalizer
11. Clevis
12. Wire bracket

F10 station wagon parking brake

equalizer). Some models also have a turnbuckle in the rear cable to compensate for cable stretching.

To adjust, proceed as follows:
1. Adjust the rear brakes with the parking brake fully released.
2. Apply the hand brake lever so that it is approximately 3–3¼ in. from its fully released position.
3. Adjust the parking brake turnbuckle, locknuts, or equalizer so that the rear brakes are locked.
4. Release the parking brake. The wheels should turn freely. If not, loosen the parking

1. Hand brake lever
2. Hand brake warning switch
3. Front cable
4. Adjuster
5. Rear cable

310 parking brake

BRAKES 155

Stanza parking brake

brake adjuster until the wheels turn with no drag.

Stanza and 1981–82 310

1. Make sure that the rear brakes are in good condition.
2. Carefully remove the dust boot from around the parking brake lever.
3. The adjustment is made by determining the amount of force needed to pull up on the lever. A force of 44 lbs. should be needed to raise the lever 7–8 notches or clicks.
4. To adjust the pull, raise and support the car on jackstands. There are two nuts on the handbrake clevis rod. Loosen the locknut and turn the adjusting nut to establish the correct pull.

Brake Specifications
All measurements given are in inches unless noted

Year	Model	Lug Nut Torque (ft. lbs.)	Master Cylinder Bore	Brake Disc Minimum Thickness	Brake Disc Maximum Run-Out	Drum Diameter	Drum Max. Wear Limit	Minimum Lining Thickness Front	Minimum Lining Thickness Rear
1977–78	F-10	58–65	0.750	0.339	0.0059	8.000	8.050	0.063	0.039
1979–82	310	58–72	0.8125	0.339	0.0047	8.000	8.050	0.079	0.059
1982	Stanza	58–72	0.8125	0.630	0.0059	8.000	8.050	0.080	0.059

NOTE: Minimum lining thickness is as recommended by the manufacturer. Due to variation in state inspection regulations, the minimum allowable thickness may be different than recommended by the manufacturer.

Body 9

You can repair most minor auto body damage yourself. Minor damage usually falls into one of several categories: (1) small scratches and dings in the paint that can be repaired without the use of body filler, (2) deep scratches and dents that require body filler, but do not require pulling, or hammering metal back into shape and (3) rust-out repairs. The repair sequences illustrated in this chapter are typical of these types of repairs. If you want to get involved in more complicated repairs including pulling or hammering sheet metal back into shape, you will probably need more detailed instructions. Chilton's *Minor Auto Body Repair, 2nd Edition* is a comprehensive guide to repairing auto body damage yourself.

TOOLS AND SUPPLIES

The list of tools and equipment you may need to fix minor body damage ranges from very basic hand tools to a wide assortment of specialized body tools. Most minor scratches, dings and rust holes can be fixed using an electric drill, wire wheel or grinder attachment, half-round plastic file, sanding block, various grades of sandpaper (#36, which is coarse through #600, which is fine) in both wet and dry types, auto body plastic, primer, touch-up paint, spreaders, newspaper and masking tape.

Most manufacturers of auto body repair products began supplying materials to professionals. Their knowledge of the best, most-used products has been translated into body repair kits for the do-it-yourselfer. Kits are available from a number of manufacturers and contain the necessary materials in the required amounts for the repair identified on the package.

Kits are available for a wide variety of uses, including:
- Rusted out metal
- All purpose kit for dents and holes
- Dents and deep scratches
- Fiberglass repair kit
- Epoxy kit for restyling.

Kits offer the advantage of buying what you need for the job. There is little waste and little chance of materials going bad from not being used. The same manufacturers also merchandise all of the individual products used—spreaders, dent pullers, fiberglass cloth, polyester resin, cream hardener, body filler, body files, sandpaper, sanding discs and holders, primer, spray paint, etc.

CAUTION: *Most of the products you will be using contain harmful chemicals, so be extremely careful. Always read the complete label before opening the containers. When*

BODY 157

you put them away for future use, be sure they are out of children's reach!

Most auto body repair kits contain all the materials you need to do the job right in the kit. So, if you have a small rust spot or dent you want to fix, check the contents of the kit before you run out and buy any additional tools.

ALIGNING BODY PANELS

Doors

There are several methods of adjusting doors. Your vehicle will probably use one of those illustrated.

Whenever a door is removed and is to be reinstalled, you should matchmark the position of the hinges on the door pillars. The holes of the hinges and/or the hinge attaching points are usually oversize to permit alignment of doors. The striker plate is also moveable, through oversize holes, permitting up-and-down, in-and-out and fore-and-aft movement. Fore-and-aft movement is made by adding or subtracting shims from behind the striker and pillar post. The striker should be adjusted so that the door closes fully and remains closed, yet enters the lock freely.

DOOR HINGES

Don't try to cover up poor door adjustment with a striker plate adjustment. The gap on each side of the door should be equal and uniform and there should be no metal-to-metal contact as the door is opened or closed.

1. Determine which hinge bolts must be loosened to move the door in the desired direction.
2. Loosen the hinge bolt(s) just enough to allow the door to be moved with a padded pry bar.
3. Move the door a small amount and check the fit, after tightening the bolts. Be sure that there is no bind or interference with adjacent panels.
4. Repeat this until the door is properly positioned, and tighten all the bolts securely.

Hood, Trunk or Tailgate

As with doors, the outline of hinges should be scribed before removal. The hood and trunk can be aligned by loosening the hinge bolts in their slotted mounting holes and moving the hood or trunk lid as necessary.

Door hinge adjustment

Move the door striker as indicated by arrows

Striker plate and lower block

158 BODY

Loosen the hinge boots to permit fore-and-aft and horizontal adjustment

The hood is adjusted vertically by stop-screws at the front and/or rear

The hood pin can be adjusted for proper lock engagement

The height of the hood at the rear is adjusted by loosening the bolts that attach the hinge to the body and moving the hood up or down

The base of the hood lock can also be repositioned slightly to give more positive lock engagement

The hood and trunk have adjustable catch locations to regulate lock engagement. Bumpers at the front and/or rear of the hood provide a vertical adjustment and the hood lockpin can be adjusted for proper engagement.

The tailgate on the station wagon can be adjusted by loosening the hinge bolts in their slotted mounting holes and moving the tailgate on its hinges. The latchplate and latch striker at the bottom of the tailgate opening can be adjusted to stop rattle. An adjustable bumper is located on each side.

RUST, UNDERCOATING, AND RUSTPROOFING

Rust

Rust is an electrochemical process. It works on ferrous metals (iron and steel) from the inside out due to exposure of unprotected surfaces to air and moisture. The possibility of rust exists practically nationwide—anywhere humidity, industrial pollution or chemical salts are present, rust can form. In coastal areas, the problem is high humidity and salt air; in snowy areas, the problem is chemical salt (de-icer) used to keep the roads clear, and in industrial areas, sulphur dioxide is present in the air from industrial pollution and is changed to sulphuric acid when it rains. The rusting process is accelerated by high temperatures, especially in snowy areas, when vehicles are driven over slushy roads and then left overnight in a heated garage.

Automotive styling also can be a contributor to rust formation. Spot welding of panels creates small pockets that trap moisture and form an environment for rust formation. Fortunately, auto manufacturers have been working hard to increase the corrosion protection of their products. Galvanized sheet metal enjoys much wider use, along with the increased use of plastic and various rust retardant coatings. Manufacturers are also designing out areas in the body where rust-forming moisture can collect.

To prevent rust, you must stop it before it gets started. On new vehicles, there are two ways to accomplish this.

First, the car or truck should be treated with a commercial rustproofing compound. There are many different brands of franchised rustproofers, but most processes involve spraying a waxy "self-healing" compound under the chassis, inside rocker panels, inside doors and fender liners and similar places where rust is likely to form. Prices for a quality rustproofing job range from $100–$250, depending on the area, the brand name and the size of the vehicle.

Ideally, the vehicle should be rustproofed as soon as possible following the purchase. The surfaces of the car or truck have begun to oxidize and deteriorate during shipping. In addition, the car may have sat on a dealer's lot or on a lot at the factory, and once the rust has progressed past the stage of light, powdery surface oxidation rustproofing is not likely to be worthwhile. Professional rustproofers feel that once rust has formed, rustproofing will simply seal in moisture already present. Most franchised rustproofing operations offer a 3–5 year warranty against rust-through, but will not support that warranty if the rustproofing is not applied within three months of the date of manufacture.

Undercoating should not be mistaken for rustproofing. Undercoating is a black, tar-like substance that is applied to the underside of a vehicle. Its basic function is to deaden noises that are transmitted from under the car. It simply cannot get into the crevices and seams where moisture tends to collect. In fact, it may clog up drainage holes and ventilation passages. Some undercoatings also tend to crack or peel with age and only create more moisture and corrosion attracting pockets.

The second thing you should do immediately after purchasing the car is apply a paint sealant. A sealant is a petroleum based product marketed under a wide variety of brand names. It has the same protective properties as a good wax, but bonds to the paint with a chemically inert layer that seals it from the air. If air can't get at the surface, oxidation cannot start.

The paint sealant kit consists of a base coat and a conditioning coat that should be applied every 6–8 months, depending on the manufacturer. The base coat must be applied before waxing, or the wax must first be removed.

Third, keep a garden hose handy for your car in winter. Use it a few times on nice days during the winter for underneath areas, and it will pay big dividends when spring arrives. Spraying under the fenders and other areas which even car washes don't reach will help remove road salt, dirt and other build-ups which help breed rust. Adjust the nozzle to a high-force spray. An old brush will help break up residue, permitting it to be washed away more easily.

It's a somewhat messy job, but worth it in the long run because rust often starts in those hidden areas.

At the same time, wash grime off the door sills and, more importantly, the under portions of the doors, plus the tailgate if you have a station wagon or truck. Applying a coat of wax to those areas at least once before and once during winter will help fend off rust.

When applying the wax to the under parts of the doors, you will note small drain holes. These holes often are plugged with undercoating or dirt. Make sure they are cleaned out to prevent water build-up inside the doors. A small punch or penknife will do the job.

Water from the high-pressure sprays in car washes sometimes can get into the housings for parking and taillights, so take a close look. If they contain water merely loosen the retaining screws and the water should run out.

160   BODY

Repairing Scratches and Small Dents

Step 1. This dent (arrow) is typical of a deep scratch or minor dent. If deep enough, the dent or scratch can be pulled out or hammered out from behind. In this case no straightening is necessary

Step 2. Using an 80-grit grinding disc on an electric drill grind the paint from the surrounding area down to bare metal. This will provide a rough surface for the body filler to grab

Step 3. The area should look like this when you're finished grinding

BODY 161

Step 4. Mix the body filler and cream hardener according to the directions

Step 5. Spread the body filler evenly over the entire area. Be sure to cover the area completely

Step 6. Let the body filler dry until the surface can just be scratched with your fingernail

162   BODY

Step 7. Knock the high spots from the body filler with a body file

Step 8. Check frequently with the palm of your hand for high and low spots. If you wind up with low spots, you may have to apply another layer of filler

Step 9. Block sand the entire area with 320 grit paper

BODY 163

Step 10. When you're finished, the repair should look like this. Note the sand marks extending 2—3 inches out from the repaired area

Step 11. Prime the entire area with automotive primer

Step 12. The finished repair ready for the final paint coat. Note that the primer has covered the sanding marks (see Step 10). A repair of this size should be able to be spotpainted with good results

REPAIRING RUST HOLES

One thing you have to remember about rust: even if you grind away all the rusted metal in a panel, and repair the area with any of the kits available, *eventually* the rust will return. There are two reasons for this. One, rust is a chemical reaction that causes pressure under the repair from the inside out. That's how the blisters form. Two, the back side of the panel (and the repair) is wide open to moisture, and unpainted body filler acts like a sponge. That's why the best solution to rust problems is to remove the rusted panel and install a new one or have the rusted area cut out and a new piece of sheet metal welded in its place. The trouble with welding is the expense; sometimes it will cost more than the car or truck is worth.

One of the better solutions to do-it-yourself rust repair is the process using a fiberglass cloth repair kit (shown here). This will give a strong repair that resists cracking and moisture and is relatively easy to use. It can be used on large or small holes and also can be applied over contoured surfaces.

Step 1. Rust areas such as this are common and are easily fixed

Step 2. Grind away all traces of rust with a 24-grit grinding disc. Be sure to grind back 3—4 inches from the edge of the hole down to bare metal and be sure all traces of rust are removed

BODY 165

Step 3. Be sure all rust is removed from the edges of the metal. The edges must be ground back to un-rusted metal

Step 4. If you are going to use release film, cut a piece about 2" larger than the area you have sanded. Place the film over the repair and mark the sanded area on the film. Avoid any unnecessary wrinkling of the film

Step 5. Cut 2 pieces of fiberglass matte. One piece should be about 1" smaller than the sanded area and the second piece should be 1" smaller than the first. Use sharp scissors to avoid loose ends

BODY

Step 6. Check the dimensions of the release film and cloth by holding them up to the repair area

Step 7. Mix enough repair jelly and cream hardener in the mixing tray to saturate the fiberglass material or fill the repair area. Follow the directions on the container

Step 8. Lay the release sheet on a flat surface and spread an even layer of filler, large enough to cover the repair. Lay the smaller piece of fiberglass cloth in the center of the sheet and spread another layer of repair jelly over the fiberglass cloth. Repeat the operation for the larger piece of cloth. If the fiberglass cloth is not used, spread the repair jelly on the release film, concentrated in the middle of the repair

BODY 167

Step 9. Place the repair material over the repair area, with the release film facing outward

Step 10. Use a spreader and work from the center outward to smooth the material, following the body contours. Be sure to remove all air bubbles

Step 11. Wait until the repair has dried tack-free and peel off the release sheet. The ideal working temperature is 65—90° F. Cooler or warmer temperatures or high humidity may require additional curing time

168 BODY

Step 12. Sand and feather-edge the entire area. The initial sanding can be done with a sanding disc on an electric drill if care is used. Finish the sanding with a block sander

Step 13. When the area is sanded smooth, mix some topcoat and hardener and apply it directly with a spreader. This will give a smooth finish and prevent the glass matte from showing through the paint

Step 14. Block sand the topcoat with finishing sandpaper

BODY 169

Step 15. To finish this repair, grind out the surface rust along the top edge of the rocker panel

Step 16. Mix some more repair jelly and cream hardener and apply it directly over the surface

Step 17. When it dries tack-free, block sand the surface smooth

Step 18. If necessary, mask off adjacent panels and spray the entire repair with primer. You are now ready for a color coat

AUTO BODY CARE

There are hundreds—maybe thousands—of products on the market, all designed to protect or aid your car's finish in some manner. There are as many different products as there are ways to use them, but they all have one thing in common—the surface must be clean.

Washing

The primary ingredient for washing your car is water, preferably "soft" water. In many areas of the country, the local water supply is "hard" containing many minerals. The little rings or film that is left on your car's surface after it has dried is the result of "hard" water.

Since you usually can't change the local water supply, the next best thing is to dry the surface before it has a chance to dry itself.

Into the water you usually add soap. Don't use detergents or common, coarse soaps. Your car's paint never truly dries out, but is always evaporating residual oils into the air. Harsh detergents will remove these oils, causing the paint to dry faster than normal. Instead use warm water and a non-detergent soap made especially for waxed surfaces or a liquid soap made for waxed surfaces or a liquid soap made for washing dishes by hand.

Other products that can be used on painted surfaces include baking soda or plain soda water for stubborn dirt.

Wash the car completely, starting at the top, and rinse it completely clean. Abrasive grit should be loaded off under water pressure; scrubbing grit off will scratch the finish. The best washing tool is a sponge, cleaning mitt or soft towel. Whichever you choose, replace it often as each tends to absorb grease and dirt.

Other ways to get a better wash include:

• Don't wash your car in the sun or when the finish is hot.

• Use water pressure to remove caked-on dirt.

• Remove tree-sap and bird effluence immediately. Such substances will eat through wax, polish and paint.

One of the best implements to dry your car is a turkish towel or an old, soft bath towel. Anything with a deep nap will hold any dirt in suspension and not grind it into the paint.

Harder cloths will only grind the grit into the paint making more scratches. Always start drying at the top, followed by the hood and trunk and sides. You'll find there's always more dirt near the rocker panels and wheelwells which will wind up on the rest of the car if you dry these areas first.

Cleaners, Waxes and Polishes

Before going any farther you should know the function of various products.

Cleaners—remove the top layer of dead pigment or paint.

Rubbing or polishing compounds—used to remove stubborn dirt, get rid of minor scratches, smooth away imperfections and partially restore badly weathered paint.

Polishes—contain no abrasives or waxes; they shine the paint by adding oils to the paint.

Waxes—are a protective coating for the polish.

CLEANERS AND COMPOUNDS

Before you apply any wax, you'll have to remove oxidation, road film and other types of pollutants that washing alone will not remove.

The paint on your car never dries completely. There are always residual oils evaporating from the paint into the air. When enough oils are present in the paint, it has a healthy shine (gloss). When too many oils evaporate the paint takes on a whitish cast known as oxidation. The idea of polishing and waxing is to keep enough oil present in the painted surface to prevent oxidation; but when it occurs, the only recourse is to remove the top layer of "dead" paint, exposing the healthy paint underneath.

Products to remove oxidation and road film are sold under a variety of generic names—polishes, cleaner, rubbing compound, cleaner/polish, polish/cleaner, self-polishing wax, pre-wax cleaner, finish restorer and many more. Regardless of name there are two types of cleaners—abrasive cleaners (sometimes called polishing or rubbing compounds) that remove oxidation by grinding away the top layer of "dead" paint, or chemical cleaners that dissolve the "dead" pigment, allowing it to be wiped away.

Abrasive cleaners, by their nature, leave thousands of minute scratches in the finish, which must be polished out later. These should only be used in extreme cases, but are usually the only thing to use on badly oxidized paint finishes. Chemical cleaners are much milder but are not strong enough for severe cases of oxidation or weathered paint.

The most popular cleaners are liquid or paste abrasive polishing and rubbing compounds. Polishing compounds have a finer abrasive grit for medium duty work. Rubbing compounds are a coarser abrasive and for heavy duty work. Unless you are familiar with how to use compounds, be very careful. Excessive rubbing with any type of compound or cleaner can grind right through the paint to primer or bare metal. Follow the directions on the container—depending on type, the cleaner may or may not be OK for your paint. For example, some cleaners are not formulated for acrylic lacquer finishes.

When a small area needs compounding or heavy polishing, it's best to do the job by hand. Some people prefer a powered buffer for large areas. Avoid cutting through the paint along styling edges on the body. Small, hand operations where the compound is applied and rubbed using cloth folded into a thick ball allow you to work in straight lines along such edges.

To avoid cutting through on the edges when using a power buffer, try masking tape. Just cover the edge with tape while using power. Then finish the job by hand with the tape removed. Even then work carefully. The paint tends to be a lot thinner along the sharp ridges stamped into the panels.

Whether compounding by machine or by hand, only work on a small area and apply the compound sparingly. If the materials are spread too thin, or allowed to sit too long, they dry out. Once dry they lose the ability to deliver a smooth, clean finish. Also, dried out polish tends to cause the buffer to stick in one spot. This in turn can burn or cut through the finish.

WAXES AND POLISHES

Your car's finish can be protected in a number of ways. A cleaner/wax or polish/cleaner followed by wax or variations of each all provide good results. The two-step approach (polish followed by wax) is probably slightly better but consumes more time and effort. Properly fed with oils, your paint should never need cleaning, but despite the best polishing job, it won't last unless it's protected with wax. Without wax, polish must be renewed at least once a month to prevent oxidation. Years ago (some still swear by it today), the best wax was made from the Brazilian palm, the Carnuba, favored for its vegetable base and high melting point. However, modern synthetic waxes are harder, which means they protect against moisture better, and chemically inert silicone is used for a long lasting protection. The only problem with silicone wax is that it penetrates all layers of paint. To repaint or touch up a panel or car protected by silicone wax, you have to completely strip the finish to avoid "fisheyes."

Under normal conditions, silicone waxes will last 4-6 months, but you have to be careful of wax build-up from too much waxing. Too thick a coat of wax is just as bad as no wax at all; it stops the paint from breathing.

Combination cleaners/waxes have become popular lately because they remove the old layer of wax plus light oxidation, while putting on a fresh coat of wax at the same time. Some cleaners/waxes contain abrasive cleaners which require caution, although many cleaner/waxes use a chemical cleaner.

Applying Wax or Polish

You may view polishing and waxing your car as a pleasant way to spend an afternoon, or as a boring chore, but it has to be done to keep the paint on your car. Caring for the paint doesn't require special tools, but you should follow a few rules.

1. Use a good quality wax.
2. Before applying any wax or polish, be sure the surface is completely clean. Just because the car looks clean, doesn't mean it's ready for polish or wax.
3. If the finish on your car is weathered, dull, or oxidized, it will probably have to be compounded to remove the old or oxidized paint. If the paint is simply dulled from lack of care, one of the non-abrasive cleaners known as polishing compounds will do the trick. If the paint is severely scratched or really dull, you'll probably have to use a rubbing compound to prepare the finish for waxing. If you're not sure which one to use, use the polishing compound, since you can easily ruin the finish by using too strong a compound.
4. Don't apply wax, polish or compound in direct sunlight, even if the directions on the can say you can. Most waxes will not cure properly in bright sunlight and you'll probably end up with a blotchy looking finish.
5. Don't rub the wax off too soon. The result will be a wet, dull looking finish. Let the wax dry thoroughly before buffing it off.
6. A constant debate among car enthusiasts is how wax should be applied. Some maintain pastes or liquids should be applied in a circular motion, but body shop experts have long thought that this approach results in barely detectable circular abrasions, especially on cars that are waxed frequently. They advise rubbing in straight lines, especially if any kind of cleaner is involved.
7. If an applicator is not supplied with the wax, use a piece of soft cheesecloth or very soft lint-free material. The same applies to buffing the surface.

SPECIAL SURFACES

One-step combination cleaner and wax formulas shouldn't be used on many of the special surfaces which abound on cars. The one-step materials contain abrasives to achieve a clean surface under the wax top coat. The abrasives are so mild that you could clean a car every week for a couple of years without fear of rubbing through the paint. But this same level of abrasiveness might, through repeated use, damage decals used for special trim effects. This includes wide stripes, wood-grain trim and other appliques.

Painted plastics must be cleaned with care. If a cleaner is too aggressive it will cut through the paint and expose the primer. If bright trim such as polished aluminum or chrome is painted, cleaning must be performed with even greater care. If rubbing compound is being used, it will cut faster than polish.

Abrasive cleaners will dull an acrylic finish. The best way to clean these newer finishes is with a non-abrasive liquid polish. Only dirt and oxidation, not paint, will be removed.

Taking a few minutes to read the instructions on the can of polish or wax will help prevent making serious mistakes. Not all preparations will work on all surfaces. And some are intended for power application while others will only work when applied by hand.

Don't get the idea that just pouring on some polish and then hitting it with a buffer will suffice. Power equipment speeds the operation. But it also adds a measure of risk. It's very easy to damage the finish if you use the wrong methods or materials.

Caring for Chrome

Read the label on the container. Many products are formulated specifically for chrome, but others contain abrasives that will scratch the chrome finish. If it isn't recommended for chrome, don't use it.

Never use steel wool or kitchen soap pads to clean chrome. Be careful not to get chrome cleaner on paint or interior vinyl surfaces. If you do, get it off immediately.

Troubleshooting 10

This section is designed to aid in the quick, accurate diagnosis of automotive problems. While automotive repairs can be made by many people, accurate troubleshooting is a rare skill for the amateur and professional alike.

In its simplest state, troubleshooting is an exercise in logic. It is essential to realize that an automobile is really composed of a series of systems. Some of these systems are interrelated; others are not. Automobiles operate within a framework of logical rules and physical laws, and the key to troubleshooting is a good understanding of all the automotive systems.

This section breaks the car or truck down into its component systems, allowing the problem to be isolated. The charts and diagnostic road maps list the most common problems and the most probable causes of trouble. Obviously it would be impossible to list every possible problem that could happen along with every possible cause, but it will locate MOST problems and eliminate a lot of unnecessary guesswork. The systematic format will locate problems within a given system, but, because many automotive systems are interrelated, the solution to your particular problem may be found in a number of systems on the car or truck.

USING THE TROUBLESHOOTING CHARTS

This book contains all of the specific information that the average do-it-yourself mechanic needs to repair and maintain his or her car or truck. The troubleshooting charts are designed to be used in conjunction with the specific procedures and information in the text. For instance, troubleshooting a point-type ignition system is fairly standard for all models, but you may be directed to the text to find procedures for troubleshooting an individual type of electronic ignition. You will also have to refer to the specification charts throughout the book for specifications applicable to your car or truck.

TOOLS AND EQUIPMENT

The tools illustrated in Chapter 1 (plus two more diagnostic pieces) will be adequate to troubleshoot most problems. The two other tools needed are a voltmeter and an ohmmeter. These can be purchased separately or in combination, known as a VOM meter.

In the event that other tools are required, they will be noted in the procedures.

TROUBLESHOOTING

Troubleshooting Engine Problems

See Chapters 2, 3, 4 for more information and service procedures.

Index to Systems

System	To Test	Group
Battery	Engine need not be running	1
Starting system	Engine need not be running	2
Primary electrical system	Engine need not be running	3
Secondary electrical system	Engine need not be running	4
Fuel system	Engine need not be running	5
Engine compression	Engine need not be running	6
Engine vacuum	Engine must be running	7
Secondary electrical system	Engine must be running	8
Valve train	Engine must be running	9
Exhaust system	Engine must be running	10
Cooling system	Engine must be running	11
Engine lubrication	Engine must be running	12

Index to Problems

Problem: Symptom	Begin at Specific Diagnosis, Number
Engine Won't Start:	
Starter doesn't turn	1.1, 2.1
Starter turns, engine doesn't	2.1
Starter turns engine very slowly	1.1, 2.4
Starter turns engine normally	3.1, 4.1
Starter turns engine very quickly	6.1
Engine fires intermittently	4.1
Engine fires consistently	5.1, 6.1
Engine Runs Poorly:	
Hard starting	3.1, 4.1, 5.1, 8.1
Rough idle	4.1, 5.1, 8.1
Stalling	3.1, 4.1, 5.1, 8.1
Engine dies at high speeds	4.1, 5.1
Hesitation (on acceleration from standing stop)	5.1, 8.1
Poor pickup	4.1, 5.1, 8.1
Lack of power	3.1, 4.1, 5.1, 8.1
Backfire through the carburetor	4.1, 8.1, 9.1
Backfire through the exhaust	4.1, 8.1, 9.1
Blue exhaust gases	6.1, 7.1
Black exhaust gases	5.1
Running on (after the ignition is shut off)	3.1, 8.1
Susceptible to moisture	4.1
Engine misfires under load	4.1, 7.1, 8.4, 9.1
Engine misfires at speed	4.1, 8.4
Engine misfires at idle	3.1, 4.1, 5.1, 7.1, 8.4

Sample Section

Test and Procedure	Results and Indications	Proceed to
4.1—Check for spark: Hold each spark plug wire approximately ¼" from ground with gloves or a heavy, dry rag. Crank the engine and observe the spark.	If no spark is evident:	4.2
	If spark is good in some cases:	4.3
	If spark is good in all cases:	4.6

TROUBLESHOOTING 175

Specific Diagnosis

This section is arranged so that following each test, instructions are given to proceed to another, until a problem is diagnosed.

Section 1—Battery

Test and Procedure	Results and Indications	Proceed to
1.1—Inspect the battery visually for case condition (corrosion, cracks) and water level.	If case is cracked, replace battery:	1.4
	If the case is intact, remove corrosion with a solution of baking soda and water (**CAUTION:** *do not get the solution into the battery*), and fill with water:	1.2

Inspect the battery case

1.2—Check the battery cable connections: Insert a screwdriver between the battery post and the cable clamp. Turn the headlights on high beam, and observe them as the screwdriver is gently twisted to ensure good metal to metal contact.	If the lights brighten, remove and clean the clamp and post; coat the post with petroleum jelly, install and tighten the clamp:	1.4
	If no improvement is noted:	1.3

TESTING BATTERY CABLE CONNECTIONS USING A SCREWDRIVER

1.3—Test the state of charge of the battery using an individual cell tester or hydrometer.	If indicated, charge the battery. **NOTE:** *If no obvious reason exists for the low state of charge (i.e., battery age, prolonged storage), proceed to:*	1.4

ADD THIS NUMBER TO THE HYDROMETER READING TO OBTAIN THE CORRECTED SPECIFIC GRAVITY

SUBTRACT THIS NUMBER FROM THE HYDROMETER READING TO OBTAIN THE CORRECTED SPECIFIC GRAVITY

Specific Gravity (@ 80° F.)

Minimum	Battery Charge
1.260	100% Charged
1.230	75% Charged
1.200	50% Charged
1.170	25% Charged
1.140	Very Little Power Left
1.110	Completely Discharged

The effects of temperature on battery specific gravity (left) and amount of battery charge in relation to specific gravity (right)

1.4—Visually inspect battery cables for cracking, bad connection to ground, or bad connection to starter.	If necessary, tighten connections or replace the cables:	2.1

176 TROUBLESHOOTING

Section 2—Starting System
See Chapter 3 for service procedures

Test and Procedure	Results and Indications	Proceed to
Note: Tests in Group 2 are performed with coil high tension lead disconnected to prevent accidental starting.		
2.1—Test the starter motor and solenoid: Connect a jumper from the battery post of the solenoid (or relay) to the starter post of the solenoid (or relay).	If starter turns the engine normally:	2.2
	If the starter buzzes, or turns the engine very slowly:	2.4
	If no response, replace the solenoid (or relay).	3.1
	If the starter turns, but the engine doesn't, ensure that the flywheel ring gear is intact. If the gear is undamaged, replace the starter drive.	3.1
2.2—Determine whether ignition override switches are functioning properly (clutch start switch, neutral safety switch), by connecting a jumper across the switch(es), and turning the ignition switch to "start".	If starter operates, adjust or replace switch:	3.1
	If the starter doesn't operate:	2.3
2.3—Check the ignition switch "start" position: Connect a 12V test lamp or voltmeter between the starter post of the solenoid (or relay) and ground. Turn the ignition switch to the "start" position, and jiggle the key.	If the lamp doesn't light or the meter needle doesn't move when the switch is turned, check the ignition switch for loose connections, cracked insulation, or broken wires. Repair or replace as necessary:	3.1
	If the lamp flickers or needle moves when the key is jiggled, replace the ignition switch.	3.3

Checking the ignition switch "start" position

STARTER RELAY (IF EQUIPPED)

2.4—Remove and bench test the starter, according to specifications in the engine electrical section.	If the starter does not meet specifications, repair or replace as needed:	3.1
	If the starter is operating properly:	2.5
2.5—Determine whether the engine can turn freely: Remove the spark plugs, and check for water in the cylinders. Check for water on the dipstick, or oil in the radiator. Attempt to turn the engine using an 18" flex drive and socket on the crankshaft pulley nut or bolt.	If the engine will turn freely only with the spark plugs out, and hydrostatic lock (water in the cylinders) is ruled out, check valve timing:	9.2
	If engine will not turn freely, and it is known that the clutch and transmission are free, the engine must be disassembled for further evaluation:	Chapter 3

TROUBLESHOOTING 177

Section 3—Primary Electrical System

Test and Procedure	Results and Indications	Proceed to
3.1—Check the ignition switch "on" position: Connect a jumper wire between the distributor side of the coil and ground, and a 12V test lamp between the switch side of the coil and ground. Remove the high tension lead from the coil. Turn the ignition switch on and jiggle the key.	If the lamp lights:	**3.2**
	If the lamp flickers when the key is jiggled, replace the ignition switch:	**3.3**
	If the lamp doesn't light, check for loose or open connections. If none are found, remove the ignition switch and check for continuity. If the switch is faulty, replace it:	**3.3**

Checking the ignition switch "on" position

3.2—Check the ballast resistor or resistance wire for an open circuit, using an ohmmeter. See Chapter 3 for specific tests.	Replace the resistor or resistance wire if the resistance is zero. **NOTE:** *Some ignition systems have no ballast resistor.*	**3.3**

Two types of resistors

3.3—On point-type ignition systems, visually inspect the breaker points for burning, pitting or excessive wear. Gray coloring of the point contact surfaces is normal. Rotate the crankshaft until the contact heel rests on a high point of the distributor cam and adjust the point gap to specifications. On electronic ignition models, remove the distributor cap and visually inspect the armature. Ensure that the armature pin is in place, and that the armature is on tight and rotates when the engine is cranked. Make sure there are no cracks, chips or rounded edges on the armature.	If the breaker points are intact, clean the contact surfaces with fine emery cloth, and adjust the point gap to specifications. If the points are worn, replace them. On electronic systems, replace any parts which appear defective. If condition persists:	**3.4**

178 TROUBLESHOOTING

Test and Procedure	Results and Indications	Proceed to
3.4—On point-type ignition systems, connect a dwell-meter between the distributor primary lead and ground. Crank the engine and observe the point dwell angle. On electronic ignition systems, conduct a stator (magnetic pickup assembly) test. See Chapter 3.	On point-type systems, adjust the dwell angle if necessary. **NOTE:** *Increasing the point gap decreases the dwell angle and vice-versa.*	**3.6**
	If the dwell meter shows little or no reading;	**3.5**
	On electronic ignition systems, if the stator is bad, replace the stator. If the stator is good, proceed to the other tests in Chapter 3.	

Dwell is a function of point gap

| **3.5**—On the point-type ignition systems, check the condenser for short: connect an ohmeter across the condenser body and the pigtail lead. | If any reading other than infinite is noted, replace the condenser | **3.6** |

Checking the condenser for short

| **3.6**—Test the coil primary resistance: On point-type ignition systems, connect an ohmmeter across the coil primary terminals, and read the resistance on the low scale. Note whether an external ballast resistor or resistance wire is used. On electronic ignition systems, test the coil primary resistance as in Chapter 3. | Point-type ignition coils utilizing ballast resistors or resistance wires should have approximately 1.0 ohms resistance. Coils with internal resistors should have approximately 4.0 ohms resistance. If values far from the above are noted, replace the coil. | **4.1** |

Check the coil primary resistance

TROUBLESHOOTING 179

Section 4—Secondary Electrical System
See Chapters 2–3 for service procedures

Test and Procedure	Results and Indications	Proceed to
4.1—Check for spark: Hold each spark plug wire approximately ¼" from ground with gloves or a heavy, dry rag. Crank the engine, and observe the spark.	If no spark is evident:	4.2
	If spark is good in some cylinders:	4.3
	If spark is good in all cylinders:	4.6

Check for spark at the plugs

4.2—Check for spark at the coil high tension lead: Remove the coil high tension lead from the distributor and position it approximately ¼" from ground. Crank the engine and observe spark. **CAUTION:** *This test should not be performed on engines equipped with electronic ignition.*	If the spark is good and consistent:	4.3
	If the spark is good but intermittent, test the primary electrical system starting at 3.3:	3.3
	If the spark is weak or non-existent, replace the coil high tension lead, clean and tighten all connections and retest. If no improvement is noted:	4.4
4.3—Visually inspect the distributor cap and rotor for burned or corroded contacts, cracks, carbon tracks, or moisture. Also check the fit of the rotor on the distributor shaft (where applicable).	If moisture is present, dry thoroughly, and retest per 4.1:	4.1
	If burned or excessively corroded contacts, cracks, or carbon tracks are noted, replace the defective part(s) and retest per 4.1:	4.1
	If the rotor and cap appear intact, or are only slightly corroded, clean the contacts thoroughly (including the cap towers and spark plug wire ends) and retest per 4.1:	
	If the spark is good in all cases:	4.6
	If the spark is poor in all cases:	4.5

Inspect the distributor cap and rotor

180 TROUBLESHOOTING

Test and Procedure	Results and Indications	Proceed to
4.4—Check the coil secondary resistance: On point-type systems connect an ohmmeter across the distributor side of the coil and the coil tower. Read the resistance on the high scale of the ohmmeter. On electronic ignition systems, see Chapter 3 for specific tests.	The resistance of a satisfactory coil should be between 4,000 and 10,000 ohms. If resistance is considerably higher (i.e., 40,000 ohms) replace the coil and retest per 4.1. **NOTE:** *This does not apply to high performance coils.*	

Testing the coil secondary resistance

4.5—Visually inspect the spark plug wires for cracking or brittleness. Ensure that no two wires are positioned so as to cause induction firing (adjacent and parallel). Remove each wire, one by one, and check resistance with an ohmmeter.	Replace any cracked or brittle wires. If any of the wires are defective, replace the entire set. Replace any wires with excessive resistance (over $8000\,\Omega$ per foot for suppression wire), and separate any wires that might cause induction firing.	4.6

Misfiring can be the result of spark plug leads to adjacent, consecutively firing cylinders running parallel and too close together

On point-type ignition systems, check the spark plug wires as shown. On electronic ignitions, do not remove the wire from the distributor cap terminal; instead, test through the cap

Spark plug wires can be checked visually by bending them in a loop over your finger. This will reveal any cracks, burned or broken insulation. Any wire with cracked insulation should be replaced

4.6—Remove the spark plugs, noting the cylinders from which they were removed, and evaluate according to the color photos in the middle of this book.	See following.	See following.

TROUBLESHOOTING

Test and Procedure	Results and Indications	Proceed to
4.7—Examine the location of all the plugs.	The following diagrams illustrate some of the conditions that the location of plugs will reveal.	4.8

Two adjacent plugs are fouled in a 6-cylinder engine, 4-cylinder engine or either bank of a V-8. This is probably due to a blown head gasket between the two cylinders

The two center plugs in a 6-cylinder engine are fouled. Raw fuel may be "boiled" out of the carburetor into the intake manifold after the engine is shut-off. Stop-start driving can also foul the center plugs, due to overly rich mixture. Proper float level, a new float needle and seat or use of an insulating spacer may help this problem

An unbalanced carburetor is indicated. Following the fuel flow on this particular design shows that the cylinders fed by the right-hand barrel are fouled from overly rich mixture, while the cylinders fed by the left-hand barrel are normal

If the four rear plugs are overheated, a cooling system problem is suggested. A thorough cleaning of the cooling system may restore coolant circulation and cure the problem

Finding one plug overheated may indicate an intake manifold leak near the affected cylinder. If the overheated plug is the second of two adjacent, consecutively firing plugs, it could be the result of ignition cross-firing. Separating the leads to these two plugs will eliminate cross-fire

Occasionally, the two rear plugs in large, lightly used V-8's will become oil fouled. High oil consumption and smoky exhaust may also be noticed. It is probably due to plugged oil drain holes in the rear of the cylinder head, causing oil to be sucked in around the valve stems. This usually occurs in the rear cylinders first, because the engine slants that way

TROUBLESHOOTING

Test and Procedure	Results and Indications	Proceed to
4.8—Determine the static ignition timing. Using the crankshaft pulley timing marks as a guide, locate top dead center on the compression stroke of the number one cylinder.	The rotor should be pointing toward the No. 1 tower in the distributor cap, and, on electronic ignitions, the armature spoke for that cylinder should be lined up with the stator.	4.8
4.9—Check coil polarity: Connect a voltmeter negative lead to the coil high tension lead, and the positive lead to ground (**NOTE:** *Reverse the hook-up for positive ground systems*). Crank the engine momentarily.	If the voltmeter reads up-scale, the polarity is correct:	5.1
	If the voltmeter reads down-scale, reverse the coil polarity (switch the primary leads):	5.1

Checking coil polarity

Section 5—Fuel System
See Chapter 4 for service procedures

Test and Procedure	Results and Indications	Proceed to
5.1—Determine that the air filter is functioning efficiently: Hold paper elements up to a strong light, and attempt to see light through the filter.	Clean permanent air filters in solvent (or manufacturer's recommendation), and allow to dry. Replace paper elements through which light cannot be seen:	5.2
5.2—Determine whether a flooding condition exists: Flooding is identified by a strong gasoline odor, and excessive gasoline present in the throttle bore(s) of the carburetor.	If flooding is not evident:	5.3
	If flooding is evident, permit the gasoline to dry for a few moments and restart.	
	If flooding doesn't recur:	5.7
	If flooding is persistent:	5.5

If the engine floods repeatedly, check the choke butterfly flap

5.3—Check that fuel is reaching the carburetor: Detach the fuel line at the carburetor inlet. Hold the end of the line in a cup (not styrofoam), and crank the engine.	If fuel flows smoothly:	5.7
	If fuel doesn't flow (**NOTE:** *Make sure that there is fuel in the tank*), or flows erratically:	5.4

Check the fuel pump by disconnecting the output line (fuel pump-to-carburetor) at the carburetor and operating the starter briefly

TROUBLESHOOTING

Test and Procedure	Results and Indications	Proceed to
5.4—Test the fuel pump: Disconnect all fuel lines from the fuel pump. Hold a finger over the input fitting, crank the engine (with electric pump, turn the ignition or pump on); and feel for suction.	If suction is evident, blow out the fuel line to the tank with low pressure compressed air until bubbling is heard from the fuel filler neck. Also blow out the carburetor fuel line (both ends disconnected):	5.7
	If no suction is evident, replace or repair the fuel pump: NOTE: *Repeated oil fouling of the spark plugs, or a no-start condition, could be the result of a ruptured vacuum booster pump diaphragm, through which oil or gasoline is being drawn into the intake manifold (where applicable).*	5.7
5.5—Occasionally, small specks of dirt will clog the small jets and orifices in the carburetor. With the engine cold, hold a flat piece of wood or similar material over the carburetor, where possible, and crank the engine.	If the engine starts, but runs roughly the engine is probably not run enough. If the engine won't start:	5.9
5.6—Check the needle and seat: Tap the carburetor in the area of the needle and seat.	If flooding stops, a gasoline additive (e.g., Gumout) will often cure the problem:	5.7
	If flooding continues, check the fuel pump for excessive pressure at the carburetor (according to specifications). If the pressure is normal, the needle and seat must be removed and checked, and/or the float level adjusted:	5.7
5.7—Test the accelerator pump by looking into the throttle bores while operating the throttle.	If the accelerator pump appears to be operating normally:	5.8
	If the accelerator pump is not operating, the pump must be reconditioned. Where possible, service the pump with the carburetor(s) installed on the engine. If necessary, remove the carburetor. Prior to removal:	5.8

Check for gas at the carburetor by looking down the carburetor throat while someone moves the accelerator

5.8—Determine whether the carburetor main fuel system is functioning: Spray a commercial starting fluid into the carburetor while attempting to start the engine.	If the engine starts, runs for a few seconds, and dies:	5.9
	If the engine doesn't start:	6.1

184 TROUBLESHOOTING

Test and Procedure	Results and Indications	Proceed to
5.9—Uncommon fuel system malfunctions: See below:	If the problem is solved: If the problem remains, remove and recondition the carburetor.	6.1

Condition	Indication	Test	Prevailing Weather Conditions	Remedy
Vapor lock	Engine will not restart shortly after running.	Cool the components of the fuel system until the engine starts. Vapor lock can be cured faster by draping a wet cloth over a mechanical fuel pump.	Hot to very hot	Ensure that the exhaust manifold heat control valve is operating. Check with the vehicle manufacturer for the recommended solution to vapor lock on the model in question.
Carburetor icing	Engine will not idle, stalls at low speeds.	Visually inspect the throttle plate area of the throttle bores for frost.	High humidity, 32–40° F.	Ensure that the exhaust manifold heat control valve is operating, and that the intake manifold heat riser is not blocked.
Water in the fuel	Engine sputters and stalls; may not start.	Pump a small amount of fuel into a glass jar. Allow to stand, and inspect for droplets or a layer of water.	High humidity, extreme temperature changes.	For droplets, use one or two cans of commercial gas line anti-freeze. For a layer of water, the tank must be drained, and the fuel lines blown out with compressed air.

Section 6—Engine Compression
See Chapter 3 for service procedures

6.1—Test engine compression: Remove all spark plugs. Block the throttle wide open. Insert a compression gauge into a spark plug port, crank the engine to obtain the maximum reading, and record.	If compression is within limits on all cylinders:	7.1
	If gauge reading is extremely low on all cylinders:	6.2
	If gauge reading is low on one or two cylinders: (If gauge readings are identical and low on two or more adjacent cylinders, the head gasket must be replaced.)	6.2

Checking compression

6.2—Test engine compression (wet): Squirt approximately 30 cc. of engine oil into each cylinder, and retest per 6.1.	If the readings improve, worn or cracked rings or broken pistons are indicated:	See Chapter 3
	If the readings do not improve, burned or excessively carboned valves or a jumped timing chain are indicated: NOTE: *A jumped timing chain is often indicated by difficult cranking.*	7.1

TROUBLESHOOTING 185

Section 7—Engine Vacuum
See Chapter 3 for service procedures

Test and Procedure	Results and Indications	Proceed to
7.1—Attach a vacuum gauge to the intake manifold beyond the throttle plate. Start the engine, and observe the action of the needle over the range of engine speeds.	See below.	See below

INDICATION: normal engine in good condition

Proceed to: 8.1

Normal engine
Gauge reading: steady, from 17–22 in./Hg.

INDICATION: sticking valves or ignition miss

Proceed to: 9.1, 8.3

Sticking valves
Gauge reading: intermittent fluctuation at idle

INDICATION: late ignition or valve timing, low compression, stuck throttle valve, leaking carburetor or manifold gasket

Proceed to: 6.1

Incorrect valve timing
Gauge reading: low (10–15 in./Hg) but steady

INDICATION: improper carburetor adjustment or minor intake leak.

Proceed to: 7.2

Carburetor requires adjustment
Gauge reading: drifting needle

INDICATION: ignition miss, blown cylinder head gasket, leaking valve or weak valve spring

Proceed to: 8.3, 6.1

Blown head gasket
Gauge reading: needle fluctuates as engine speed increases

INDICATION: burnt valve or faulty valve clearance. Needle will fall when defective valve operates

Proceed to: 9.1

Burnt or leaking valves
Gauge reading: steady needle, but drops regularly

INDICATION: choked muffler, excessive back pressure in system

Proceed to: 10.1

Clogged exhaust system
Gauge reading: gradual drop in reading at idle

INDICATION: worn valve guides

Proceed to: 9.1

Worn valve guides
Gauge reading: needle vibrates excessively at idle, but steadies as engine speed increases

White pointer = steady gauge hand

Black pointer = fluctuating gauge hand

Test and Procedure	Results and Indications	Proceed to
7.2—Attach a vacuum gauge per 7.1, and test for an intake manifold leak. Squirt a small amount of oil around the intake manifold gaskets, carburetor gaskets, plugs and fittings. Observe the action of the vacuum gauge.	If the reading improves, replace the indicated gasket, or seal the indicated fitting or plug: If the reading remains low:	8.1 7.3
7.3—Test all vacuum hoses and accessories for leaks as described in 7.2. Also check the carburetor body (dashpots, automatic choke mechanism, throttle shafts) for leaks in the same manner.	If the reading improves, service or replace the offending part(s): If the reading remains low:	8.1 6.1

Section 8—Secondary Electrical System
See Chapter 2 for service procedures

Test and Procedure	Results and Indications	Proceed to
8.1—Remove the distributor cap and check to make sure that the rotor turns when the engine is cranked. Visually inspect the distributor components.	Clean, tighten or replace any components which appear defective.	8.2
8.2—Connect a timing light (per manufacturer's recommendation) and check the dynamic ignition timing. Disconnect and plug the vacuum hose(s) to the distributor if specified, start the engine, and observe the timing marks at the specified engine speed.	If the timing is not correct, adjust to specifications by rotating the distributor in the engine: (Advance timing by rotating distributor opposite normal direction of rotor rotation, retard timing by rotating distributor in same direction as rotor rotation.)	8.3
8.3—Check the operation of the distributor advance mechanism(s): To test the mechanical advance, disconnect the vacuum lines from the distributor advance unit and observe the timing marks with a timing light as the engine speed is increased from idle. If the mark moves smoothly, without hesitation, it may be assumed that the mechanical advance is functioning properly. To test vacuum advance and/or retard systems, alternately crimp and release the vacuum line, and observe the timing mark for movement. If movement is noted, the system is operating.	If the systems are functioning: If the systems are not functioning, remove the distributor, and test on a distributor tester:	8.4 8.4
8.4—Locate an ignition miss: With the engine running, remove each spark plug wire, one at a time, until one is found that doesn't cause the engine to roughen and slow down.	When the missing cylinder is identified:	4.1

TROUBLESHOOTING

Section 9—Valve Train
See Chapter 3 for service procedures

Test and Procedure	Results and Indications	Proceed to
9.1—Evaluate the valve train: Remove the valve cover, and ensure that the valves are adjusted to specifications. A mechanic's stethoscope may be used to aid in the diagnosis of the valve train. By pushing the probe on or near push rods or rockers, valve noise often can be isolated. A timing light also may be used to diagnose valve problems. Connect the light according to manufacturer's recommendations, and start the engine. Vary the firing moment of the light by increasing the engine speed (and therefore the ignition advance), and moving the trigger from cylinder to cylinder. Observe the movement of each valve.	Sticking valves or erratic valve train motion can be observed with the timing light. The cylinder head must be disassembled for repairs.	See Chapter 3
9.2—Check the valve timing: Locate top dead center of the No. 1 piston, and install a degree wheel or tape on the crankshaft pulley or damper with zero corresponding to an index mark on the engine. Rotate the crankshaft in its direction of rotation, and observe the opening of the No. 1 cylinder intake valve. The opening should correspond with the correct mark on the degree wheel according to specifications.	If the timing is not correct, the timing cover must be removed for further investigation.	See Chapter 3

Section 10—Exhaust System

Test and Procedure	Results and Indications	Proceed to
10.1—Determine whether the exhaust manifold heat control valve is operating: Operate the valve by hand to determine whether it is free to move. If the valve is free, run the engine to operating temperature and observe the action of the valve, to ensure that it is opening.	If the valve sticks, spray it with a suitable solvent, open and close the valve to free it, and retest. If the valve functions properly: If the valve does not free, or does not operate, replace the valve:	 10.2 10.2
10.2—Ensure that there are no exhaust restrictions: Visually inspect the exhaust system for kinks, dents, or crushing. Also note that gases are flowing freely from the tailpipe at all engine speeds, indicating no restriction in the muffler or resonator.	Replace any damaged portion of the system:	11.1

TROUBLESHOOTING

Section 11—Cooling System
See Chapter 3 for service procedures

Test and Procedure	Results and Indications	Proceed to
11.1—Visually inspect the fan belt for glazing, cracks, and fraying, and replace if necessary. Tighten the belt so that the longest span has approximately ½" play at its midpoint under thumb pressure (see Chapter 1).	Replace or tighten the fan belt as necessary: *Checking belt tension*	11.2
11.2—Check the fluid level of the cooling system.	If full or slightly low, fill as necessary: If extremely low:	11.5 11.3
11.3—Visually inspect the external portions of the cooling system (radiator, radiator hoses, thermostat elbow, water pump seals, heater hoses, etc.) for leaks. If none are found, pressurize the cooling system to 14–15 psi.	If cooling system holds the pressure: If cooling system loses pressure rapidly, reinspect external parts of the system for leaks under pressure. If none are found, check dipstick for coolant in crankcase. If no coolant is present, but pressure loss continues: If coolant is evident in crankcase, remove cylinder head(s), and check gasket(s). If gaskets are intact, block and cylinder head(s) should be checked for cracks or holes. If the gasket(s) is blown, replace, and purge the crankcase of coolant: **NOTE:** *Occasionally, due to atmospheric and driving conditions, condensation of water can occur in the crankcase. This causes the oil to appear milky white. To remedy, run the engine until hot, and change the oil and oil filter.*	11.5 11.4 12.6
11.4—Check for combustion leaks into the cooling system: Pressurize the cooling system as above. Start the engine, and observe the pressure gauge. If the needle fluctuates, remove each spark plug wire, one at a time, noting which cylinder(s) reduce or eliminate the fluctuation.	Cylinders which reduce or eliminate the fluctuation, when the spark plug wire is removed, are leaking into the cooling system. Replace the head gasket on the affected cylinder bank(s). *Pressurizing the cooling system*	

TROUBLESHOOTING 189

Test and Procedure	Results and Indications	Proceed to
11.5—Check the radiator pressure cap: Attach a radiator pressure tester to the radiator cap (wet the seal prior to installation). Quickly pump up the pressure, noting the point at which the cap releases.	If the cap releases within ±1 psi of the specified rating, it is operating properly:	11.6
	If the cap releases at more than ±1 psi of the specified rating, it should be replaced:	11.6

Checking radiator pressure cap

11.6—Test the thermostat: Start the engine cold, remove the radiator cap, and insert a thermometer into the radiator. Allow the engine to idle. After a short while, there will be a sudden, rapid increase in coolant temperature. The temperature at which this sharp rise stops is the thermostat opening temperature.	If the thermostat opens at or about the specified temperature:	11.7
	If the temperature doesn't increase: (If the temperature increases slowly and gradually, replace the thermostat.)	11.7
11.7—Check the water pump: Remove the thermostat elbow and the thermostat, disconnect the coil high tension lead (to prevent starting), and crank the engine momentarily.	If coolant flows, replace the thermostat and retest per 11.6:	11.6
	If coolant doesn't flow, reverse flush the cooling system to alleviate any blockage that might exist. If system is not blocked, and coolant will not flow, replace the water pump.	

Section 12—Lubrication
See Chapter 3 for service procedures

Test and Procedure	Results and Indications	Proceed to
12.1—Check the oil pressure gauge or warning light: If the gauge shows low pressure, or the light is on for no obvious reason, remove the oil pressure sender. Install an accurate oil pressure gauge and run the engine momentarily.	If oil pressure builds normally, run engine for a few moments to determine that it is functioning normally, and replace the sender.	—
	If the pressure remains low:	12.2
	If the pressure surges:	12.3
	If the oil pressure is zero:	12.3
12.2—Visually inspect the oil: If the oil is watery or very thin, milky, or foamy, replace the oil and oil filter.	If the oil is normal:	12.3
	If after replacing oil the pressure remains low:	12.3
	If after replacing oil the pressure becomes normal:	—

190 TROUBLESHOOTING

Test and Procedure	Results and Indications	Proceed to
12.3—Inspect the oil pressure relief valve and spring, to ensure that it is not sticking or stuck. Remove and thoroughly clean the valve, spring, and the valve body.	If the oil pressure improves: If no improvement is noted:	— **12.4**
12.4—Check to ensure that the oil pump is not cavitating (sucking air instead of oil): See that the crankcase is neither over nor underfull, and that the pickup in the sump is in the proper position and free from sludge.	Fill or drain the crankcase to the proper capacity, and clean the pickup screen in solvent if necessary. If no improvement is noted:	**12.5**
12.5—Inspect the oil pump drive and the oil pump:	If the pump drive or the oil pump appear to be defective, service as necessary and retest per 12.1:	**12.1**
	If the pump drive and pump appear to be operating normally, the engine should be disassembled to determine where blockage exists:	**See Chapter 3**
12.6—Purge the engine of ethylene glycol coolant: Completely drain the crankcase and the oil filter. Obtain a commercial butyl cellosolve base solvent, designated for this purpose, and follow the instructions precisely. Following this, install a new oil filter and refill the crankcase with the proper weight oil. The next oil and filter change should follow shortly thereafter (1000 miles).		

TROUBLESHOOTING EMISSION CONTROL SYSTEMS

See Chapter 4 for procedures applicable to individual emission control systems used on specific combinations of engine/transmission/model.

TROUBLESHOOTING THE CARBURETOR

See Chapter 4 for service procedures

Carburetor problems cannot be effectively isolated unless all other engine systems (particularly ignition and emission) are functioning properly and the engine is properly tuned.

TROUBLESHOOTING

Condition	Possible Cause
Engine cranks, but does not start	1. Improper starting procedure 2. No fuel in tank 3. Clogged fuel line or filter 4. Defective fuel pump 5. Choke valve not closing properly 6. Engine flooded 7. Choke valve not unloading 8. Throttle linkage not making full travel 9. Stuck needle or float 10. Leaking float needle or seat 11. Improper float adjustment
Engine stalls	1. Improperly adjusted idle speed or mixture **Engine hot** 2. Improperly adjusted dashpot 3. Defective or improperly adjusted solenoid 4. Incorrect fuel level in fuel bowl 5. Fuel pump pressure too high 6. Leaking float needle seat 7. Secondary throttle valve stuck open 8. Air or fuel leaks 9. Idle air bleeds plugged or missing 10. Idle passages plugged **Engine Cold** 11. Incorrectly adjusted choke 12. Improperly adjusted fast idle speed 13. Air leaks 14. Plugged idle or idle air passages 15. Stuck choke valve or binding linkage 16. Stuck secondary throttle valves 17. Engine flooding—high fuel level 18. Leaking or misaligned float
Engine hesitates on acceleration	1. Clogged fuel filter 2. Leaking fuel pump diaphragm 3. Low fuel pump pressure 4. Secondary throttle valves stuck, bent or misadjusted 5. Sticking or binding air valve 6. Defective accelerator pump 7. Vacuum leaks 8. Clogged air filter 9. Incorrect choke adjustment (engine cold)
Engine feels sluggish or flat on acceleration	1. Improperly adjusted idle speed or mixture 2. Clogged fuel filter 3. Defective accelerator pump 4. Dirty, plugged or incorrect main metering jets 5. Bent or sticking main metering rods 6. Sticking throttle valves 7. Stuck heat riser 8. Binding or stuck air valve 9. Dirty, plugged or incorrect secondary jets 10. Bent or sticking secondary metering rods. 11. Throttle body or manifold heat passages plugged 12. Improperly adjusted choke or choke vacuum break.
Carburetor floods	1. Defective fuel pump. Pressure too high. 2. Stuck choke valve 3. Dirty, worn or damaged float or needle valve/seat 4. Incorrect float/fuel level 5. Leaking float bowl

TROUBLESHOOTING

Condition	Possible Cause
Engine idles roughly and stalls	1. Incorrect idle speed 2. Clogged fuel filter 3. Dirt in fuel system or carburetor 4. Loose carburetor screws or attaching bolts 5. Broken carburetor gaskets 6. Air leaks 7. Dirty carburetor 8. Worn idle mixture needles 9. Throttle valves stuck open 10. Incorrectly adjusted float or fuel level 11. Clogged air filter
Engine runs unevenly or surges	1. Defective fuel pump 2. Dirty or clogged fuel filter 3. Plugged, loose or incorrect main metering jets or rods 4. Air leaks 5. Bent or sticking main metering rods 6. Stuck power piston 7. Incorrect float adjustment 8. Incorrect idle speed or mixture 9. Dirty or plugged idle system passages 10. Hard, brittle or broken gaskets 11. Loose attaching or mounting screws 12. Stuck or misaligned secondary throttle valves
Poor fuel economy	1. Poor driving habits 2. Stuck choke valve 3. Binding choke linkage 4. Stuck heat riser 5. Incorrect idle mixture 6. Defective accelerator pump 7. Air leaks 8. Plugged, loose or incorrect main metering jets 9. Improperly adjusted float or fuel level 10. Bent, misaligned or fuel-clogged float 11. Leaking float needle seat 12. Fuel leak 13. Accelerator pump discharge ball not seating properly 14. Incorrect main jets
Engine lacks high speed performance or power	1. Incorrect throttle linkage adjustment 2. Stuck or binding power piston 3. Defective accelerator pump 4. Air leaks 5. Incorrect float setting or fuel level 6. Dirty, plugged, worn or incorrect main metering jets or rods 7. Binding or sticking air valve 8. Brittle or cracked gaskets 9. Bent, incorrect or improperly adjusted secondary metering rods 10. Clogged fuel filter 11. Clogged air filter 12. Defective fuel pump

TROUBLESHOOTING FUEL INJECTION PROBLEMS

Each fuel injection system has its own unique components and test procedures, for which it is impossible to generalize. Refer to Chapter 4 of this Repair & Tune-Up Guide for specific test and repair procedures, if the vehicle is equipped with fuel injection.

TROUBLESHOOTING ELECTRICAL PROBLEMS

See Chapter 5 for service procedures

For any electrical system to operate, it must make a complete circuit. This simply means that the power flow from the battery must make a complete circle. When an electrical component is operating, power flows from the battery to the component, passes through the component causing it to perform its function (lighting a light bulb), and then returns to the battery through the ground of the circuit. This ground is usually (but not always) the metal part of the car or truck on which the electrical component is mounted.

Perhaps the easiest way to visualize this is to think of connecting a light bulb with two wires attached to it to the battery. If one of the two wires attached to the light bulb were attached to the negative post of the battery and the other were attached to the positive post of the battery, you would have a complete circuit. Current from the battery would flow to the light bulb, causing it to light, and return to the negative post of the battery.

The normal automotive circuit differs from this simple example in two ways. First, instead of having a return wire from the bulb to the battery, the light bulb returns the current to the battery through the chassis of the vehicle. Since the negative battery cable is attached to the chassis and the chassis is made of electrically conductive metal, the chassis of the vehicle can serve as a ground wire to complete the circuit. Secondly, most automotive circuits contain switches to turn components on and off as required.

Every complete circuit from a power source must include a component which is using the power from the power source. If you were to disconnect the light bulb from the wires and touch the two wires together (don't do this) the power supply wire to the component would be grounded before the normal ground connection for the circuit.

Because grounding a wire from a power source makes a complete circuit—less the required component to use the power—this phenomenon is called a short circuit. Common causes are: broken insulation (exposing the metal wire to a metal part of the car or truck), or a shorted switch.

Some electrical components which require a large amount of current to operate also have a relay in their circuit. Since these circuits carry a large amount of current, the thickness of the wire in the circuit (gauge size) is also greater. If this large wire were connected from the component to the control switch on the instrument panel, and then back to the component, a voltage drop would occur in the circuit. To prevent this potential drop in voltage, an electromagnetic switch (relay) is used. The large wires in the circuit are connected from the battery to one side of the relay, and from the opposite side of the relay to the component. The relay is normally open, preventing current from passing through the circuit. An additional, smaller, wire is connected from the relay to the control switch for the circuit. When the control switch is turned on, it grounds the smaller wire from the relay and completes the circuit. This closes the relay and allows current to flow from the battery to the component. The horn, headlight, and starter circuits are three which use relays.

It is possible for larger surges of current to pass through the electrical system of your car or truck. If this surge of current were to reach an electrical component, it could burn it out. To prevent this, fuses, circuit breakers or fusible links are connected into the current supply wires of most of the major electrical systems. When an electrical current of excessive power passes through the component's fuse, the fuse blows out and breaks the circuit, saving the component from destruction.

Typical automotive fuse

A circuit breaker is basically a self-repairing fuse. The circuit breaker opens the circuit the same way a fuse does. However, when either the short is removed from the circuit or the surge subsides, the circuit breaker resets itself and does not have to be replaced as a fuse does.

A fuse link is a wire that acts as a fuse. It is normally connected between the starter relay and the main wiring harness. This connection is usually under the hood. The fuse link (if installed) protects all the

TROUBLESHOOTING

Most fusible links show a charred, melted insulation when they burn out

The test light will show the presence of current when touched to a hot wire and grounded at the other end

chassis electrical components, and is the probable cause of trouble when none of the electrical components function, unless the battery is disconnected or dead.

Electrical problems generally fall into one of three areas:

1. The component that is not functioning is not receiving current.
2. The component itself is not functioning.
3. The component is not properly grounded.

The electrical system can be checked with a test light and a jumper wire. A test light is a device that looks like a pointed screwdriver with a wire attached to it and has a light bulb in its handle. A jumper wire is a piece of insulated wire with an alligator clip attached to each end.

If a component is not working, you must follow a systematic plan to determine which of the three causes is the villain.

1. Turn on the switch that controls the inoperable component.
2. Disconnect the power supply wire from the component.
3. Attach the ground wire on the test light to a good metal ground.
4. Touch the probe end of the test light to the end of the power supply wire that was disconnected from the component. If the component is receiving current, the test light will go on.

NOTE: *Some components work only when the ignition switch is turned on.*

If the test light does not go on, then the problem is in the circuit between the battery and the component. This includes all the switches, fuses, and relays in the system. Follow the wire that runs back to the battery. The problem is an open circuit between the battery and the component. If the fuse is blown and, when replaced, immediately blows again, there is a short circuit in the system which must be located and repaired. If there is a switch in the system, bypass it with a jumper wire. This is done by connecting one end of the jumper wire to the power supply wire into the switch and the other end of the jumper wire to the wire coming out of the switch. If the test light lights with the jumper wire installed, the switch or whatever was bypassed is defective.

NOTE: *Never substitute the jumper wire for the component, since it is required to use the power from the power source.*

5. If the bulb in the test light goes on, then the current is getting to the component that is not working. This eliminates the first of the three possible causes. Connect the power supply wire and connect a jumper wire from the component to a good metal ground. Do this with the switch which controls the component turned on, and also the ignition switch turned on if it is required for the component to work. If the component works with the jumper wire installed, then it has a bad ground. This is usually caused by the metal area on which the component mounts to the chassis being coated with some type of foreign matter.

6. If neither test located the source of the trouble, then the component itself is defective. Remember that for any electrical system to work, all connections must be clean and tight.

TROUBLESHOOTING

Troubleshooting Basic Turn Signal and Flasher Problems
See Chapter 5 for service procedures

Most problems in the turn signals or flasher system can be reduced to defective flashers or bulbs, which are easily replaced. Occasionally, the turn signal switch will prove defective.

F = Front   R = Rear   ● = Lights off   ○ = Lights on

Condition		Possible Cause
Turn signals light, but do not flash		Defective flasher
No turn signals light on either side		Blown fuse. Replace if defective. Defective flasher. Check by substitution. Open circuit, short circuit or poor ground.
Both turn signals on one side don't work		Bad bulbs. Bad ground in both (or either) housings.
One turn signal light on one side doesn't work		Defective bulb. Corrosion in socket. Clean contacts. Poor ground at socket.
Turn signal flashes too fast or too slowly		Check any bulb on the side flashing too fast. A heavy-duty bulb is probably installed in place of a regular bulb. Check the bulb flashing too slowly. A standard bulb was probably installed in place of a heavy-duty bulb. Loose connections or corrosion at the bulb socket.
Indicator lights don't work in either direction		Check if the turn signals are working. Check the dash indicator lights. Check the flasher by substitution.
One indicator light doesn't light		On systems with one dash indicator: See if the lights work on the same side. Often the filaments have been reversed in systems combining stoplights with taillights and turn signals. Check the flasher by substitution. On systems with two indicators: Check the bulbs on the same side. Check the indicator light bulb. Check the flasher by substitution.

Troubleshooting Lighting Problems
See Chapter 5 for service procedures

Condition	Possible Cause
One or more lights don't work, but others do	1. Defective bulb(s) 2. Blown fuse(s) 3. Dirty fuse clips or light sockets 4. Poor ground circuit
Lights burn out quickly	1. Incorrect voltage regulator setting or defective regulator 2. Poor battery/alternator connections
Lights go dim	1. Low/discharged battery 2. Alternator not charging 3. Corroded sockets or connections 4. Low voltage output
Lights flicker	1. Loose connection 2. Poor ground. (Run ground wire from light housing to frame) 3. Circuit breaker operating (short circuit)
Lights "flare"—Some flare is normal on acceleration—If excessive, see "Lights Burn Out Quickly"	High voltage setting
Lights glare—approaching drivers are blinded	1. Lights adjusted too high 2. Rear springs or shocks sagging 3. Rear tires soft

Troubleshooting Dash Gauge Problems

Most problems can be traced to a defective sending unit or faulty wiring. Occasionally, the gauge itself is at fault. See Chapter 5 for service procedures.

Condition	Possible Cause
COOLANT TEMPERATURE GAUGE	
Gauge reads erratically or not at all	1. Loose or dirty connections 2. Defective sending unit. 3. Defective gauge. To test a bi-metal gauge, remove the wire from the sending unit. Ground the wire for an instant. If the gauge registers, replace the sending unit. To test a magnetic gauge, disconnect the wire at the sending unit. With ignition ON gauge should register COLD. Ground the wire; gauge should register HOT.
AMMETER GAUGE—TURN HEADLIGHTS ON (DO NOT START ENGINE). NOTE REACTION	
Ammeter shows charge Ammeter shows discharge Ammeter does not move	1. Connections reversed on gauge 2. Ammeter is OK 3. Loose connections or faulty wiring 4. Defective gauge

TROUBLESHOOTING

Condition	Possible Cause

OIL PRESSURE GAUGE

Gauge does not register or is inaccurate	1. On mechanical gauge, Bourdon tube may be bent or kinked. 2. Low oil pressure. Remove sending unit. Idle the engine briefly. If no oil flows from sending unit hole, problem is in engine. 3. Defective gauge. Remove the wire from the sending unit and ground it for an instant with the ignition ON. A good gauge will go to the top of the scale. 4. Defective wiring. Check the wiring to the gauge. If it's OK and the gauge doesn't register when grounded, replace the gauge. 5. Defective sending unit.

ALL GAUGES

All gauges do not operate All gauges read low or erratically All gauges pegged	1. Blown fuse 2. Defective instrument regulator 3. Defective or dirty instrument voltage regulator 4. Loss of ground between instrument voltage regulator and frame 5. Defective instrument regulator

WARNING LIGHTS

Light(s) do not come on when ignition is ON, but engine is not started Light comes on with engine running	1. Defective bulb 2. Defective wire 3. Defective sending unit. Disconnect the wire from the sending unit and ground it. Replace the sending unit if the light comes on with the ignition ON. 4. Problem in individual system 5. Defective sending unit

Troubleshooting Clutch Problems

It is false economy to replace individual clutch components. The pressure plate, clutch plate and throwout bearing should be replaced as a set, and the flywheel face inspected, whenever the clutch is overhauled. See Chapter 6 for service procedures.

Condition	Possible Cause
Clutch chatter	1. Grease on driven plate (disc) facing 2. Binding clutch linkage or cable 3. Loose, damaged facings on driven plate (disc) 4. Engine mounts loose 5. Incorrect height adjustment of pressure plate release levers 6. Clutch housing or housing to transmission adapter misalignment 7. Loose driven plate hub
Clutch grabbing	1. Oil, grease on driven plate (disc) facing 2. Broken pressure plate 3. Warped or binding driven plate. Driven plate binding on clutch shaft
Clutch slips	1. Lack of lubrication in clutch linkage or cable (linkage or cable binds, causes incomplete engagement) 2. Incorrect pedal, or linkage adjustment 3. Broken pressure plate springs 4. Weak pressure plate springs 5. Grease on driven plate facings (disc)

Troubleshooting Clutch Problems (cont.)

Condition	Possible Cause
Incomplete clutch release	1. Incorrect pedal or linkage adjustment or linkage or cable binding 2. Incorrect height adjustment on pressure plate release levers 3. Loose, broken facings on driven plate (disc) 4. Bent, dished, warped driven plate caused by overheating
Grinding, whirring grating noise when pedal is depressed	1. Worn or defective throwout bearing 2. Starter drive teeth contacting flywheel ring gear teeth. Look for milled or polished teeth on ring gear.
Squeal, howl, trumpeting noise when pedal is being released (occurs during first inch to inch and one-half of pedal travel)	Pilot bushing worn or lack of lubricant. If bushing appears OK, polish bushing with emery cloth, soak lube wick in oil, lube bushing with oil, apply film of chassis grease to clutch shaft pilot hub, reassemble. NOTE: Bushing wear may be due to misalignment of clutch housing or housing to transmission adapter
Vibration or clutch pedal pulsation with clutch disengaged (pedal fully depressed)	1. Worn or defective engine transmission mounts 2. Flywheel run out. (Flywheel run out at face not to exceed 0.005") 3. Damaged or defective clutch components

Troubleshooting Manual Transmission Problems
See Chapter 6 for service procedures

Condition	Possible Cause
Transmission jumps out of gear	1. Misalignment of transmission case or clutch housing. 2. Worn pilot bearing in crankshaft. 3. Bent transmission shaft. 4. Worn high speed sliding gear. 5. Worn teeth or end-play in clutch shaft. 6. Insufficient spring tension on shifter rail plunger. 7. Bent or loose shifter fork. 8. Gears not engaging completely. 9. Loose or worn bearings on clutch shaft or mainshaft. 10. Worn gear teeth. 11. Worn or damaged detent balls.
Transmission sticks in gear	1. Clutch not releasing fully. 2. Burred or battered teeth on clutch shaft, or sliding sleeve. 3. Burred or battered transmission mainshaft. 4. Frozen synchronizing clutch. 5. Stuck shifter rail plunger. 6. Gearshift lever twisting and binding shifter rail. 7. Battered teeth on high speed sliding gear or on sleeve. 8. Improper lubrication, or lack of lubrication. 9. Corroded transmission parts. 10. Defective mainshaft pilot bearing. 11. Locked gear bearings will give same effect as stuck in gear.
Transmission gears will not synchronize	1. Binding pilot bearing on mainshaft, will synchronize in high gear only. 2. Clutch not releasing fully. 3. Detent spring weak or broken. 4. Weak or broken springs under balls in sliding gear sleeve. 5. Binding bearing on clutch shaft, or binding countershaft. 6. Binding pilot bearing in crankshaft. 7. Badly worn gear teeth. 8. Improper lubrication. 9. Constant mesh gear not turning freely on transmission mainshaft. Will synchronize in that gear only.

TROUBLESHOOTING

Condition	Possible Cause
Gears spinning when shifting into gear from neutral	1. Clutch not releasing fully. 2. In some cases an extremely light lubricant in transmission will cause gears to continue to spin for a short time after clutch is released. 3. Binding pilot bearing in crankshaft.
Transmission noisy in all gears	1. Insufficient lubricant, or improper lubricant. 2. Worn countergear bearings. 3. Worn or damaged main drive gear or countergear. 4. Damaged main drive gear or mainshaft bearings. 5. Worn or damaged countergear anti-lash plate.
Transmission noisy in neutral only	1. Damaged main drive gear bearing. 2. Damaged or loose mainshaft pilot bearing. 3. Worn or damaged countergear anti-lash plate. 4. Worn countergear bearings.
Transmission noisy in one gear only	1. Damaged or worn constant mesh gears. 2. Worn or damaged countergear bearings. 3. Damaged or worn synchronizer.
Transmission noisy in reverse only	1. Worn or damaged reverse idler gear or idler bushing. 2. Worn or damaged mainshaft reverse gear. 3. Worn or damaged reverse countergear. 4. Damaged shift mechanism.

TROUBLESHOOTING AUTOMATIC TRANSMISSION PROBLEMS

Keeping alert to changes in the operating characteristics of the transmission (changing shift points, noises, etc.) can prevent small problems from becoming large ones. If the problem cannot be traced to loose bolts, fluid level, misadjusted linkage, clogged filters or similar problems, you should probably seek professional service.

Transmission Fluid Indications

The appearance and odor of the transmission fluid can give valuable clues to the overall condition of the transmission. Always note the appearance of the fluid when you check the fluid level or change the fluid. Rub a small amount of fluid between your fingers to feel for grit and smell the fluid on the dipstick.

If the fluid appears:	It indicates:
Clear and red colored	Normal operation
Discolored (extremely dark red or brownish) or smells burned	Band or clutch pack failure, usually caused by an overheated transmission. Hauling very heavy loads with insufficient power or failure to change the fluid often result in overheating. Do not confuse this appearance with newer fluids that have a darker red color and a strong odor (though not a burned odor).
Foamy or aerated (light in color and full of bubbles)	1. The level is too high (gear train is churning oil) 2. An internal air leak (air is mixing with the fluid). Have the transmission checked professionally.
Solid residue in the fluid	Defective bands, clutch pack or bearings. Bits of band material or metal abrasives are clinging to the dipstick. Have the transmission checked professionally.
Varnish coating on the dipstick	The transmission fluid is overheating

TROUBLESHOOTING DRIVE AXLE PROBLEMS

First, determine when the noise is most noticeable.

Drive Noise: Produced under vehicle acceleration.

Coast Noise: Produced while coasting with a closed throttle.

Float Noise: Occurs while maintaining constant speed (just enough to keep speed constant) on a level road.

External Noise Elimination

It is advisable to make a thorough road test to determine whether the noise originates in the rear axle or whether it originates from the tires, engine, transmission, wheel bearings or road surface. Noise originating from other places cannot be corrected by servicing the rear axle.

ROAD NOISE

Brick or rough surfaced concrete roads produce noises that seem to come from the rear axle. Road noise is usually identical in Drive or Coast and driving on a different type of road will tell whether the road is the problem.

TIRE NOISE

Tire noise can be mistaken as rear axle noise, even though the tires on the front are at fault. Snow tread and mud tread tires or tires worn unevenly will frequently cause vibrations which seem to originate elsewhere; *temporarily, and for test purposes only,* inflate the tires to 40–50 lbs. This will significantly alter the noise produced by the tires, but will not alter noise from the rear axle. Noises from the rear axle will normally cease at speeds below 30 mph on coast, while tire noise will continue at lower tone as speed is decreased. The rear axle noise will usually change from drive conditions to coast conditions, while tire noise will not. Do not forget to lower the tire pressure to normal after the test is complete.

ENGINE/TRANSMISSION NOISE

Determine at what speed the noise is most pronounced, then stop in a quiet place. With the transmission in Neutral, run the engine through speeds corresponding to road speeds where the noise was noticed. Noises produced with the vehicle standing still are coming from the engine or transmission.

FRONT WHEEL BEARINGS

Front wheel bearing noises, sometimes confused with rear axle noises, will not change when comparing drive and coast conditions. While holding the speed steady, lightly apply the footbrake. This will often cause wheel bearing noise to lessen, as some of the weight is taken off the bearing. Front wheel bearings are easily checked by jacking up the wheels and spinning the wheels. Shaking the wheels will also determine if the wheel bearings are excessively loose.

REAR AXLE NOISES

Eliminating other possible sources can narrow the cause to the rear axle, which normally produces noise from worn gears or bearings. Gear noises tend to peak in a narrow speed range, while bearing noises will usually vary in pitch with engine speeds.

Noise Diagnosis

The Noise Is:	Most Probably Produced By:
1. Identical under Drive or Coast	Road surface, tires or front wheel bearings
2. Different depending on road surface	Road surface or tires
3. Lower as speed is lowered	Tires
4. Similar when standing or moving	Engine or transmission
5. A vibration	Unbalanced tires, rear wheel bearing, unbalanced driveshaft or worn U-joint
6. A knock or click about every two tire revolutions	Rear wheel bearing
7. Most pronounced on turns	Damaged differential gears
8. A steady low-pitched whirring or scraping, starting at low speeds	Damaged or worn pinion bearing
9. A chattering vibration on turns	Wrong differential lubricant or worn clutch plates (limited slip rear axle)
10. Noticed only in Drive, Coast or Float conditions	Worn ring gear and/or pinion gear

TROUBLESHOOTING

Troubleshooting Steering & Suspension Problems

Condition	Possible Cause
Hard steering (wheel is hard to turn)	1. Improper tire pressure 2. Loose or glazed pump drive belt 3. Low or incorrect fluid 4. Loose, bent or poorly lubricated front end parts 5. Improper front end alignment (excessive caster) 6. Bind in steering column or linkage 7. Kinked hydraulic hose 8. Air in hydraulic system 9. Low pump output or leaks in system 10. Obstruction in lines 11. Pump valves sticking or out of adjustment 12. Incorrect wheel alignment
Loose steering (too much play in steering wheel)	1. Loose wheel bearings 2. Faulty shocks 3. Worn linkage or suspension components 4. Loose steering gear mounting or linkage points 5. Steering mechanism worn or improperly adjusted 6. Valve spool improperly adjusted 7. Worn ball joints, tie-rod ends, etc.
Veers or wanders (pulls to one side with hands off steering wheel)	1. Improper tire pressure 2. Improper front end alignment 3. Dragging or improperly adjusted brakes 4. Bent frame 5. Improper rear end alignment 6. Faulty shocks or springs 7. Loose or bent front end components 8. Play in Pitman arm 9. Steering gear mountings loose 10. Loose wheel bearings 11. Binding Pitman arm 12. Spool valve sticking or improperly adjusted 13. Worn ball joints
Wheel oscillation or vibration transmitted through steering wheel	1. Low or uneven tire pressure 2. Loose wheel bearings 3. Improper front end alignment 4. Bent spindle 5. Worn, bent or broken front end components 6. Tires out of round or out of balance 7. Excessive lateral runout in disc brake rotor 8. Loose or bent shock absorber or strut
Noises (see also "Troubleshooting Drive Axle Problems")	1. Loose belts 2. Low fluid, air in system 3. Foreign matter in system 4. Improper lubrication 5. Interference or chafing in linkage 6. Steering gear mountings loose 7. Incorrect adjustment or wear in gear box 8. Faulty valves or wear in pump 9. Kinked hydraulic lines 10. Worn wheel bearings
Poor return of steering	1. Over-inflated tires 2. Improperly aligned front end (excessive caster) 3. Binding in steering column 4. No lubrication in front end 5. Steering gear adjusted too tight
Uneven tire wear (see "How To Read Tire Wear")	1. Incorrect tire pressure 2. Improperly aligned front end 3. Tires out-of-balance 4. Bent or worn suspension parts

202 TROUBLESHOOTING

HOW TO READ TIRE WEAR

The way your tires wear is a good indicator of other parts of the suspension. Abnormal wear patterns are often caused by the need for simple tire maintenance, or for front end alignment.

Excessive wear at the center of the tread indicates that the air pressure in the tire is consistently too high. The tire is riding on the center of the tread and wearing it prematurely. Occasionally, this wear pattern can result from outrageously wide tires on narrow rims. The cure for this is to replace either the tires or the wheels.

Over-inflation

This type of wear usually results from consistent under-inflation. When a tire is under-inflated, there is too much contact with the road by the outer treads, which wear prematurely. When this type of wear occurs, and the tire pressure is known to be consistently correct, a bent or worn steering component or the need for wheel alignment could be indicated.

Under-inflation

Feathering is a condition when the edge of each tread rib develops a slightly rounded edge on one side and a sharp edge on the other. By running your hand over the tire, you can usually feel the sharper edges before you'll be able to see them. The most common causes of feathering are incorrect toe-in setting or deteriorated bushings in the front suspension.

Feathering

When an inner or outer rib wears faster than the rest of the tire, the need for wheel alignment is indicated. There is excessive camber in the front suspension, causing the wheel to lean too much putting excessive load on one side of the tire. Misalignment could also be due to sagging springs, worn ball joints, or worn control arm bushings. Be sure the vehicle is loaded the way it's normally driven when you have the wheels aligned.

One side wear

Cups or scalloped dips appearing around the edge of the tread almost always indicate worn (sometimes bent) suspension parts. Adjustment of wheel alignment alone will seldom cure the problem. Any worn component that connects the wheel to the suspension can cause this type of wear. Occasionally, wheels that are out of balance will wear like this, but wheel imbalance usually shows up as bald spots between the outside edges and center of the tread.

Cupping

Second-rib wear is usually found only in radial tires, and appears where the steel belts end in relation to the tread. It can be kept to a minimum by paying careful attention to tire pressure and frequently rotating the tires. This is often considered normal wear but excessive amounts indicate that the tires are too wide for the wheels.

Second-rib wear

Troubleshooting Disc Brake Problems

Condition	Possible Cause
Noise—groan—brake noise emanating when slowly releasing brakes (creep-groan)	Not detrimental to function of disc brakes—no corrective action required. (This noise may be eliminated by slightly increasing or decreasing brake pedal efforts.)
Rattle—brake noise or rattle emanating at low speeds on rough roads, (front wheels only).	1. Shoe anti-rattle spring missing or not properly positioned. 2. Excessive clearance between shoe and caliper. 3. Soft or broken caliper seals. 4. Deformed or misaligned disc. 5. Loose caliper.
Scraping	1. Mounting bolts too long. 2. Loose wheel bearings. 3. Bent, loose, or misaligned splash shield.
Front brakes heat up during driving and fail to release	1. Operator riding brake pedal. 2. Stop light switch improperly adjusted. 3. Sticking pedal linkage. 4. Frozen or seized piston. 5. Residual pressure valve in master cylinder. 6. Power brake malfunction. 7. Proportioning valve malfunction.
Leaky brake caliper	1. Damaged or worn caliper piston seal. 2. Scores or corrosion on surface of cylinder bore.
Grabbing or uneven brake action—Brakes pull to one side	1. Causes listed under "Brakes Pull". 2. Power brake malfunction. 3. Low fluid level in master cylinder. 4. Air in hydraulic system. 5. Brake fluid, oil or grease on linings. 6. Unmatched linings. 7. Distorted brake pads. 8. Frozen or seized pistons. 9. Incorrect tire pressure. 10. Front end out of alignment. 11. Broken rear spring. 12. Brake caliper pistons sticking. 13. Restricted hose or line. 14. Caliper not in proper alignment to braking disc. 15. Stuck or malfunctioning metering valve. 16. Soft or broken caliper seals. 17. Loose caliper.
Brake pedal can be depressed without braking effect	1. Air in hydraulic system or improper bleeding procedure. 2. Leak past primary cup in master cylinder. 3. Leak in system. 4. Rear brakes out of adjustment. 5. Bleeder screw open.
Excessive pedal travel	1. Air, leak, or insufficient fluid in system or caliper. 2. Warped or excessively tapered shoe and lining assembly. 3. Excessive disc runout. 4. Rear brake adjustment required. 5. Loose wheel bearing adjustment. 6. Damaged caliper piston seal. 7. Improper brake fluid (boil). 8. Power brake malfunction. 9. Weak or soft hoses.

TROUBLESHOOTING

Troubleshooting Disc Brake Problems (cont.)

Condition	Possible Cause
Brake roughness or chatter (pedal pumping)	1. Excessive thickness variation of braking disc. 2. Excessive lateral runout of braking disc. 3. Rear brake drums out-of-round. 4. Excessive front bearing clearance.
Excessive pedal effort	1. Brake fluid, oil or grease on linings. 2. Incorrect lining. 3. Frozen or seized pistons. 4. Power brake malfunction. 5. Kinked or collapsed hose or line. 6. Stuck metering valve. 7. Scored caliper or master cylinder bore. 8. Seized caliper pistons.
Brake pedal fades (pedal travel increases with foot on brake)	1. Rough master cylinder or caliper bore. 2. Loose or broken hydraulic lines/connections. 3. Air in hydraulic system. 4. Fluid level low. 5. Weak or soft hoses. 6. Inferior quality brake shoes or fluid. 7. Worn master cylinder piston cups or seals.

Troubleshooting Drum Brakes

Condition	Possible Cause
Pedal goes to floor	1. Fluid low in reservoir. 2. Air in hydraulic system. 3. Improperly adjusted brake. 4. Leaking wheel cylinders. 5. Loose or broken brake lines. 6. Leaking or worn master cylinder. 7. Excessively worn brake lining.
Spongy brake pedal	1. Air in hydraulic system. 2. Improper brake fluid (low boiling point). 3. Excessively worn or cracked brake drums. 4. Broken pedal pivot bushing.
Brakes pulling	1. Contaminated lining. 2. Front end out of alignment. 3. Incorrect brake adjustment. 4. Unmatched brake lining. 5. Brake drums out of round. 6. Brake shoes distorted. 7. Restricted brake hose or line. 8. Broken rear spring. 9. Worn brake linings. 10. Uneven lining wear. 11. Glazed brake lining. 12. Excessive brake lining dust. 13. Heat spotted brake drums. 14. Weak brake return springs. 15. Faulty automatic adjusters. 16. Low or incorrect tire pressure.

TROUBLESHOOTING

Condition	Possible Cause
Squealing brakes	1. Glazed brake lining. 2. Saturated brake lining. 3. Weak or broken brake shoe retaining spring. 4. Broken or weak brake shoe return spring. 5. Incorrect brake lining. 6. Distorted brake shoes. 7. Bent support plate. 8. Dust in brakes or scored brake drums. 9. Linings worn below limit. 10. Uneven brake lining wear. 11. Heat spotted brake drums.
Chirping brakes	1. Out of round drum or eccentric axle flange pilot.
Dragging brakes	1. Incorrect wheel or parking brake adjustment. 2. Parking brakes engaged or improperly adjusted. 3. Weak or broken brake shoe return spring. 4. Brake pedal binding. 5. Master cylinder cup sticking. 6. Obstructed master cylinder relief port. 7. Saturated brake lining. 8. Bent or out of round brake drum. 9. Contaminated or improper brake fluid. 10. Sticking wheel cylinder pistons. 11. Driver riding brake pedal. 12. Defective proportioning valve. 13. Insufficient brake shoe lubricant.
Hard pedal	1. Brake booster inoperative. 2. Incorrect brake lining. 3. Restricted brake line or hose. 4. Frozen brake pedal linkage. 5. Stuck wheel cylinder. 6. Binding pedal linkage. 7. Faulty proportioning valve.
Wheel locks	1. Contaminated brake lining. 2. Loose or torn brake lining. 3. Wheel cylinder cups sticking. 4. Incorrect wheel bearing adjustment. 5. Faulty proportioning valve.
Brakes fade (high speed)	1. Incorrect lining. 2. Overheated brake drums. 3. Incorrect brake fluid (low boiling temperature). 4. Saturated brake lining. 5. Leak in hydraulic system. 6. Faulty automatic adjusters.
Pedal pulsates	1. Bent or out of round brake drum.
Brake chatter and shoe knock	1. Out of round brake drum. 2. Loose support plate. 3. Bent support plate. 4. Distorted brake shoes. 5. Machine grooves in contact face of brake drum (Shoe Knock). 6. Contaminated brake lining. 7. Missing or loose components. 8. Incorrect lining material. 9. Out-of-round brake drums. 10. Heat spotted or scored brake drums. 11. Out-of-balance wheels.

Troubleshooting Drum Brakes (cont.)

Condition	Possible Cause
Brakes do not self adjust	1. Adjuster screw frozen in thread. 2. Adjuster screw corroded at thrust washer. 3. Adjuster lever does not engage star wheel. 4. Adjuster installed on wrong wheel.
Brake light glows	1. Leak in the hydraulic system. 2. Air in the system. 3. Improperly adjusted master cylinder pushrod. 4. Uneven lining wear. 5. Failure to center combination valve or proportioning valve.

Appendix

General Conversion Table

Multiply by	To convert	To	
2.54	Inches	Centimeters	.3937
30.48	Feet	Centimeters	.0328
.914	Yards	Meters	1.094
1.609	Miles	Kilometers	.621
6.45	Square inches	Square cm.	.155
.836	Square yards	Square meters	1.196
16.39	Cubic inches	Cubic cm.	.061
28.3	Cubic feet	Liters	.0353
.4536	Pounds	Kilograms	2.2045
3.785	Gallons	Liters	.264
.068	Lbs./sq. in. (psi)	Atmospheres	14.7
.138	Foot pounds	Kg. m.	7.23
1.014	H.P. (DIN)	H.P. (SAE)	.9861
—	To obtain	From	Multiply by

Note: 1 cm. equals 10 mm.; 1 mm. equals .0394".

Conversion—Common Fractions to Decimals and Millimeters

Common Fractions	Decimal Fractions	Millimeters (approx.)	Common Fractions	Decimal Fractions	Millimeters (approx.)	Common Fractions	Decimal Fractions	Millimeters (approx.)
1/128	.008	0.20	11/32	.344	8.73	43/64	.672	17.07
1/64	.016	0.40	23/64	.359	9.13	11/16	.688	17.46
1/32	.031	0.79	3/8	.375	9.53	45/64	.703	17.86
3/64	.047	1.19	25/64	.391	9.92	23/32	.719	18.26
1/16	.063	1.59	13/32	.406	10.32	47/64	.734	18.65
5/64	.078	1.98	27/64	.422	10.72	3/4	.750	19.05
3/32	.094	2.38	7/16	.438	11.11	49/64	.766	19.45
7/64	.109	2.78	29/64	.453	11.51	25/32	.781	19.84
1/8	.125	3.18	15/32	.469	11.91	51/64	.797	20.24
9/64	.141	3.57	31/64	.484	12.30	13/16	.813	20.64
5/32	.156	3.97	1/2	.500	12.70	53/64	.828	21.03
11/64	.172	4.37	33/64	.516	13.10	27/32	.844	21.43
3/16	.188	4.76	17/32	.531	13.49	55/64	.859	21.83
13/64	.203	5.16	35/64	.547	13.89	7/8	.875	22.23
7/32	.219	5.56	9/16	.563	14.29	57/64	.891	22.62
15/64	.234	5.95	37/64	.578	14.68	29/32	.906	23.02
1/4	.250	6.35	19/32	.594	15.08	59/64	.922	23.42
17/64	.266	6.75	39/64	.609	15.48	15/16	.938	23.81
9/32	.281	7.14	5/8	.625	15.88	61/64	.953	24.21
19/64	.297	7.54	41/64	.641	16.27	31/32	.969	24.61
5/16	.313	7.94	21/32	.656	16.67	63/64	.984	25.00
21/64	.328	8.33						

Conversion—Millimeters to Decimal Inches

mm	inches	mm	inches	mm	inches	mm	inches	mm	inches
1	.039 370	31	1.220 470	61	2.401 570	91	3.582 670	210	8.267 700
2	.078 740	32	1.259 840	62	2.440 940	92	3.622 040	220	8.661 400
3	.118 110	33	1.299 210	63	2.480 310	93	3.661 410	230	9.055 100
4	.157 480	34	1.338 580	64	2.519 680	94	3.700 780	240	9.448 800
5	.196 850	35	1.377 949	65	2.559 050	95	3.740 150	250	9.842 500
6	.236 220	36	1.417 319	66	2.598 420	96	3.779 520	260	10.236 200
7	.275 590	37	1.456 689	67	2.637 790	97	3.818 890	270	10.629 900
8	.314 960	38	1.496 050	68	2.677 160	98	3.858 260	280	11.032 600
9	.354 330	39	1.535 430	69	2.716 530	99	3.897 630	290	11.417 300
10	.393 700	40	1.574 800	70	2.755 900	100	3.937 000	300	11.811 000
11	.433 070	41	1.614 170	71	2.795 270	105	4.133 848	310	12.204 700
12	.472 440	42	1.653 540	72	2.834 640	110	4.330 700	320	12.598 400
13	.511 810	43	1.692 910	73	2.874 010	115	4.527 550	330	12.992 100
14	.551 180	44	1.732 280	74	2.913 380	120	4.724 400	340	13.385 800
15	.590 550	45	1.771 650	75	2.952 750	125	4.921 250	350	13.779 500
16	.629 920	46	1.811 020	76	2.992 120	130	5.118 100	360	14.173 200
17	.669 290	47	1.850 390	77	3.031 490	135	5.314 950	370	14.566 900
18	.708 660	48	1.889 760	78	3.070 860	140	5.511 800	380	14.960 600
19	.748 030	49	1.929 130	79	3.110 230	145	5.708 650	390	15.354 300
20	.787 400	50	1.968 500	80	3.149 600	150	5.905 500	400	15.748 000
21	.826 770	51	2.007 870	81	3.188 970	155	6.102 350	500	19.685 000
22	.866 140	52	2.047 240	82	3.228 340	160	6.299 200	600	23.622 000
23	.905 510	53	2.086 610	83	3.267 710	165	6.496 050	700	27.559 000
24	.944 880	54	2.125 980	84	3.307 080	170	6.692 900	800	31.496 000
25	.984 250	55	2.165 350	85	3.346 450	175	6.889 750	900	35.433 000
26	1.023 620	56	2.204 720	86	3.385 820	180	7.086 600	1000	39.370 000
27	1.062 990	57	2.244 090	87	3.425 190	185	7.283 450	2000	78.740 000
28	1.102 360	58	2.283 460	88	3.464 560	190	7.480 300	3000	118.110 000
29	1.141 730	59	2.322 830	89	3.503 903	195	7.677 150	4000	157.480 000
30	1.181 100	60	2.362 200	90	3.543 300	200	7.874 000	5000	196.850 000

To change decimal millimeters to decimal inches, position the decimal point where desired on either side of the millimeter measurement shown and reset the inches decimal by the same number of digits in the same direction. For example, to convert 0.001 mm to decimal inches, reset the decimal behind the 1 mm (shown on the chart) to 0.001; change the decimal inch equivalent (0.039″ shown) to 0.000039″.

Tap Drill Sizes

National Fine or S.A.E.

Screw & Tap Size	Threads Per Inch	Use Drill Number
No. 5	44	37
No. 6	40	33
No. 8	36	29
No. 10	32	21
No. 12	28	15
1/4	28	3
5/16	24	1
3/8	24	Q
7/16	20	W
1/2	20	29/64
9/16	18	33/64
5/8	18	37/64
3/4	16	11/16
7/8	14	13/16
1 1/8	12	1 3/64
1 1/4	12	1 11/64
1 1/2	12	1 27/64

Tap Drill Sizes

National Coarse or U.S.S.

Screw & Tap Size	Threads Per Inch	Use Drill Number
No. 5	40	39
No. 6	32	36
No. 8	32	29
No. 10	24	25
No. 12	24	17
1/4	20	8
5/16	18	F
3/8	16	5/16
7/16	14	U
1/2	13	27/64
9/16	12	31/64
5/8	11	17/32
3/4	10	21/32
7/8	9	49/64
1	8	7/8
1 1/8	7	63/64
1 1/4	7	1 7/64
1 1/2	6	1 11/32

APPENDIX

Decimal Equivalent Size of the Number Drills

Drill No.	Decimal Equivalent	Drill No.	Decimal Equivalent	Drill No.	Decimal Equivalent
80	.0135	53	.0595	26	.1470
79	.0145	52	.0635	25	.1495
78	.0160	51	.0670	24	.1520
77	.0180	50	.0700	23	.1540
76	.0200	49	.0730	22	.1570
75	.0210	48	.0760	21	.1590
74	.0225	47	.0785	20	.1610
73	.0240	46	.0810	19	.1660
72	.0250	45	.0820	18	.1695
71	.0260	44	.0860	17	.1730
70	.0280	43	.0890	16	.1770
69	.0292	42	.0935	15	.1800
68	.0310	41	.0960	14	.1820
67	.0320	40	.0980	13	.1850
66	.0330	39	.0995	12	.1890
65	.0350	38	.1015	11	.1910
64	.0360	37	.1040	10	.1935
63	.0370	36	.1065	9	.1960
62	.0380	35	.1100	8	.1990
61	.0390	34	.1110	7	.2010
60	.0400	33	.1130	6	.2040
59	.0410	32	.1160	5	.2055
58	.0420	31	.1200	4	.2090
57	.0430	30	.1285	3	.2130
56	.0465	29	.1360	2	.2210
55	.0520	28	.1405	1	.2280
54	.0550	27	.1440		

Decimal Equivalent Size of the Letter Drills

Letter Drill	Decimal Equivalent	Letter Drill	Decimal Equivalent	Letter Drill	Decimal Equivalent
A	.234	J	.277	S	.348
B	.238	K	.281	T	.358
C	.242	L	.290	U	.368
D	.246	M	.295	V	.377
E	.250	N	.302	W	.386
F	.257	O	.316	X	.397
G	.261	P	.323	Y	.404
H	.266	Q	.332	Z	.413
I	.272	R	.339		

Anti-Freeze Chart

Temperatures Shown in Degrees Fahrenheit +32 is Freezing

Cooling System Capacity Quarts	\multicolumn{14}{c}{Quarts of ETHYLENE GLYCOL Needed for Protection to Temperatures Shown Below}													
	1	2	3	4	5	6	7	8	9	10	11	12	13	14
10	+24°	+16°	+4°	−12°	−34°	−62°								
11	+25	+18	+8	−6	−23	−47								
12	+26	+19	+10	0	−15	−34	−57°							
13	+27	+21	+13	+3	−9	−25	−45							
14			+15	+6	−5	−18	−34							
15			+16	+8	0	−12	−26							
16			+17	+10	+2	−8	−19	−34	−52°					
17			+18	+12	+5	−4	−14	−27	−42					
18			+19	+14	+7	0	−10	−21	−34	−50°				
19			+20	+15	+9	+2	−7	−16	−28	−42				
20				+16	+10	+4	−3	−12	−22	−34	−48°			
21				+17	+12	+6	0	−9	−17	−28	−41			
22				+18	+13	+8	+2	−6	−14	−23	−34	−47°		
23				+19	+14	+9	+4	−3	−10	−19	−29	−40		
24				+19	+15	+10	+5	0	−8	−15	−23	−34	−46°	
25				+20	+16	+12	+7	+1	−5	−12	−20	−29	−40	−50°
26					+17	+13	+8	+3	−3	−9	−16	−25	−34	−44
27					+18	+14	+9	+5	−1	−7	−13	−21	−29	−39
28					+18	+15	+10	+6	+1	−5	−11	−18	−25	−34
29					+19	+16	+12	+7	+2	−3	−8	−15	−22	−29
30					+20	+17	+13	+8	+4	−1	−6	−12	−18	−25

For capacities over 30 quarts divide true capacity by 3. Find quarts Anti-Freeze for the ⅓ and multiply by 3 for quarts to add.

For capacities under 10 quarts multiply true capacity by 3. Find quarts Anti-Freeze for the tripled volume and divide by 3 for quarts to add.

To Increase the Freezing Protection of Anti-Freeze Solutions Already Installed

Cooling System Capacity Quarts	\multicolumn{5}{c}{From +20° F. to}					\multicolumn{5}{c}{From +10° F. to}					\multicolumn{4}{c}{From 0° F. to}			
	0°	−10°	−20°	−30°	−40°	0°	−10°	−20°	−30°	−40°	−10°	−20°	−30°	−40°
10	1¾	2¼	3	3½	3¾	¾	1½	2¼	2¾	3¼	¾	1½	2	2½
12	2	2¾	3½	4	4½	1	1¾	2½	3¼	3¾	1	1¾	2½	3¼
14	2¼	3¼	4	4¾	5½	1¼	2	3	3¾	4½	1	2	3	3½
16	2½	3½	4½	5¼	6	1¼	2½	3½	4¼	5¼	1¼	2¼	3¼	4
18	3	4	5	6	7	1½	2¾	4	5	5¾	1½	2½	3¾	4¾
20	3¼	4½	5¾	6¾	7½	1¾	3	4¼	5½	6½	1½	2¾	4¼	5¼
22	3½	5	6¼	7¼	8¼	1¾	3¼	4¾	6	7¼	1¾	3¼	4½	5½
24	4	5½	7	8	9	2	3½	5	6½	7½	1¾	3½	5	6
26	4¼	6	7½	8¾	10	2	4	5½	7	8¼	2	3¾	5½	6¾
28	4½	6¼	8	9½	10½	2¼	4¼	6	7½	9	2	4	5¾	7¼
30	5	6¾	8½	10	11½	2½	4½	6½	8	9½	2¼	4¼	6¼	7¾

Test radiator solution with proper hydrometer. Determine from the table the number of quarts of solution to be drawn off from a full cooling system and replace with undiluted anti-freeze, to give the desired increased protection. For example, to increase protection of a 22-quart cooling system containing Ethylene Glycol (permanent type) anti-freeze, from +20° F. to −20° F. will require the replacement of 6¼ quarts of solution with undiluted anti-freeze.

Index

A

Air cleaner, 3, 90
Air conditioning
    Sight glass inspection, 8
Alternator, 33
Antifreeze, 210
Automatic transmission
    Adjustment, 126
    Filter change, 16
    Removal and installation, 127
Axle
    Fluid recommendations, 11
    Lubricant level, 11

B

Ball joints, 131
Battery
    Jump starting, 16-17
    Maintenance, 38
Belt tension adjustment, 6
Body, 156
Brakes
    Adjustment, 144
    Bleeding, 144
    Caliper, 149
    Fluid level, 10
    Fluid recommendations, 10
    Front brakes, 148
    Master cylinder, 145
    Parking brake, 153
    Power booster, 145
    Proportioning valve, 145
    Rear brakes, 150
    Rear wheel bearings, 152

C

Camber, 133
Camshaft and bearings, 49, 53, 58-79
Capacities, 13
Carburetor
    Adjustment, 30, 96-100
    Overhaul, 100
    Replacement, 95
Carburetor cooling fan, 105
Caster, 133
Catalytic converter, 94
Charging system, 33
Chassis lubrication, 16
Choke, 98
Clutch
    Adjustment, 121
    Master cylinder, 124
    Replacement, 122
    Slave cylinder, 125
Condenser, 22
Connecting rod and bearings, 53, 58-79
Control arm, 133
Cooling system, 8, 56

Crankcase ventilation (PCV), 5, 80
Crankshaft, 58-79
Cylinder head
    Rebuilding, 58-79
    Removal and installation, 44
    Torque sequence, 44-45

D

Dents and scratches, 156-172
Distributor
    Removal and installation, 32
    Breaker points, 22
Driveshaft, 125
Dwell angle, 23
Dwell meter, 23

E

Electrical
    Chassis, 109
    Engine, 32
Electronic ignition, 24
Emission controls, 80
Engine
    Camshaft, 49, 53
    Cylinder head torque sequence, 44-45
    Exhaust manifold, 46
    Front cover, 47
    Identification, 3
    Intake manifold, 46
    Pistons and rings, 53
    Rebuilding, 58
    Removal and installation, 38
    Rocker arm (or shaft), 45
    Specifications, 40
    Timing belt, 53
    Timing chain (or gears), 49
    Tune-up, 18
Evaporative canister, 5, 85
Exhaust manifold, 46

F

Fan belt adjustment, 6
Firing order, 33
Fluid level checks
    Battery, 11
    Coolant, 11
    Engine oil, 10
    Master cylinder, 10
    Power steering pump, 11
    Front axle, 11
    Steering gear, 11
    Transmission, 10
Fluid recommendations, 13
Front suspension
    Ball joints, 131
    Lower control arm, 133
    Shock absorber, 129
    Spring, 129

INDEX

Front suspension (*continued*)
    Strut, 128
    Wheel alignment, 133
Fuel filter, 13
Fuel pump, 95
Fuel system, 95
Fuel tank, 105
Fuses and flashers, 117
Fusible links, 116

G

Gearshift linkage adjustment
    Automatic, 126
    Manual, 118

H

Hand brake, 153
Headlights, 116
Heater, 109
Heat riser, 6
Hoses, 9

I

Identification
    Vehicle, 3
    Engine, 3
    Transmission, 3
Idle speed and mixture, 30
Ignition switch, 139
Ignition timing, 28
Instrument cluster, 113
Intake manifold, 46

J

Jacking points, 16
Jump starting, 16, 17

L

Lower control arm, 133
Lubrication
    Chassis, 16
    Differential, 11
    Engine, 55
    Transmission, 16

M

Manifolds
    Intake, 46
    Exhaust, 46
Manual transmission, 118
Master cylinder, 145
Model identification, 3

O

Oil and fuel recommendations, 13
Oil change, 14

Oil filter (engine), 15
Oil pan, 55
Oil pump, 55

P

Parking brake, 153
Pistons and rings
    Installation, 53, 58-79
    Positioning, 53
PCV valve, 5, 80
Points, 22
Power steering pump, 140
Pushing, 16

R

Radiator, 56
Radio, 112
Rear suspension, 135
Regulator, 35
Rear main oil seal, 55
Rings, 53, 58-79
Rocker arm (or shaft), 45
Rust spots, 156-172

S

Safety notice, ii
Scratches and dents, 156-172
Serial number location, 3
Shock absorbers
    Front, 129
    Rear, 138
Spark plugs, 18
Specifications
    Alternator and regulator, 33
    Battery and starter, 39
    Brakes, 155
    Capacities, 13
    Carburetor, 102
    Crankshaft and connecting rod, 41
    Fuses, 117
    General engine, 40
    Piston and ring, 42
    Torque, 43
    Tune-up, 19
    Valve, 43
    Wheel alignment, 134
Speedometer cable, 113
Springs
    Front, 129
    Rear, 135
Starter, 36
Steering
    Gear, 140
    Lock, 139
    Wheel, 138
Stripped threads, 59
Struts, 128

INDEX

T

Thermostat, 57
Tie-rod, 139
Timing (ignition), 28
Tires, 12
Tools, 1
Towing, 16
Transmission
   Automatic, 126
   Manual, 118
   Fluid change, 15
Troubleshooting, 173
Tune-up
   Procedures, 18
   Specifications, 19
Turn signal switch, 139

V

Valves
   Adjustment, 29
   Specifications, 43
Vehicle identification, 3

W

Water pump, 56
Wheel alignment, 133
Wheel bearings, 152
Windshield wipers
   Linkage, 112
   Motor, 112

Chilton's Repair & Tune-Up Guides

The complete line covers domestic cars, imports, trucks, vans, RV's and 4-wheel drive vehicles.

BOOK CODE	TITLE	BOOK CODE	TITLE
# 7163	Aries 81-82	# 5821	GTX 68-73
# 7032	Arrow Pick-Up 79-81	# 6980	Honda 73-80
# 6637	Aspen 76-78	# 6845	Horizon 78-80
# 5902	Audi 70-73	# 5912	International Scout 67-73
# 7028	Audi 4000/5000 77-81	# 5998	Jaguar 69-74
# 6337	Audi Fox 73-75	# 7136	Jeep CJ 1945-81
# 5807	Barracuda 65-72	# 6739	Jeep Wagoneer, Commando, Cherokee 66-79
# 6931	Blazer 69-80	# 6962	Jetta 1980
# 5576	BMW 59-70	# 6931	Jimmy 69-81
# 6844	BMW 70-79	# 7059	J-2000 1982
# 5821	Belvedere 68-73	# 5905	Le Mans 68-73
# 7027	Bobcat	# 7055	Lynx 81-82 inc. EXP & LN-7
# 7045	Camaro 67-81	# 6634	Maverick 70-77
# 6695	Capri 70-77	# 6981	Mazda 71-80
# 6963	Capri 79-80	# 7031	Mazda RX-7 79-81
# 7059	Cavalier 1982	# 6065	Mercedes-Benz 59-70
# 5807	Challenger 65-72	# 5907	Mercedes-Benz 68-73
# 7037	Challenger (Import) 71-81	# 6809	Mercedes-Benz 74-79
# 7041	Champ 78-81	# 7128	Mercury 68-71 all full sized models
# 6316	Charger 71-75	# 6696	Mercury Mid-Size 71-78 inc. T-Bird, Montego & Cougar
# 7162	Chevette 76-82 inc. diesel		
# 7135	Chevrolet 68-81 all full size models	# 6780	MG 61-81
# 6936	Chevrolet/GMC Pick-Ups 70-80	# 6973	Monarch 75-80
# 6930	Chevrolet/GMC Vans 67-80	# 6542	Mustang 65-73
# 7051	Chevy Luv 72-81 inc. 4wd	# 6812	Mustang II 74-78
# 7056	Chevy Mid-Size 64-82 inc. El Camino, Chevelle, Laguna, Malibu & Monte Carlo	# 6963	Mustang 79-80
		# 6841	Nova 69-79
# 6841	Chevy II 62-68	# 7049	Omega 81-82
# 7059	Cimarron 1982	# 6845	Omni 78-80
# 7049	Citation 80-81	# 5792	Opel 64-70
# 7037	Colt 71-81	# 6575	Opel 71-75
# 6634	Comet 70-77	# 6473	Pacer 75-76
# 6316	Coronet 71-75	# 5982	Peugeot 70-74
# 6691	Corvair 60-69 inc. Turbo	# 7049	Phoenix 81-82
# 6576	Corvette 53-62	# 7027	Pinto 71-80
# 6843	Corvette 63-79	# 6552	Plymouth 68-76 all full sized models
# 6933	Cutlass 70-80	# 6934	Plymouth Vans 67-80
# 6324	Dart 68-76	# 5822	Porche 69-73
# 6962	Dasher 74-80	# 7048	Porche 924 & 928 76-81 inc. Turbo
# 5790	Datsun 61-72	# 6962	Rabbit 75-80
# 6960	Datsun 73-80	# 6331	Ramcharger/Trail Duster 74-75
# 6932	Datsun Z & ZX 70-80	# 7163	Reliant 81-82
# 7050	Datsun Pick-Ups 70-81 inc. 4wd	# 5821	Roadrunner 68-73
# 6324	Demon 68-76	# 5988	Saab 69-75
# 6554	Dodge 68-77 all full sized models	# 7041	Sapporo 78-81
# 6486	Dodge Charger 67-70	# 5821	Satellite 68-73
# 6934	Dodge Vans 67-80	# 6962	Scirocco 75-80
# 6326	Duster 68-76	# 7049	Skylark 80-81
# 7055	Escort 81-82 inc. EXP & LN-7	# 6982	Subaru 70-80
# 6320	Fairlane 62-75	# 5905	Tempest 68-73
# 6965	Fairmont 78-80	# 6320	Torino 62-75
# 6485	Fiat 64-70	# 5795	Toyota 66-70
# 7042	Fiat 69-81	# 7043	Toyota Celica & Supra 71-81
# 6846	Fiesta 78-80	# 7036	Toyota Corolla, Carina, Tercel, Starlet 67-81
# 7046	Firebird 67-81		
# 7128	Ford 68-81 all full sized models	# 7044	Toyota Corona, Cressida, Crown, Mark II 70-81
# 7140	Ford Bronco 66-81	# 7035	Toyota Pick-Ups 70-81
# 6983	Ford Courier 72-80	# 5910	Triumph 69-73
# 6696	Ford Mid-Size 71-78 inc. Torino, Gran Torino, Ranchero, Elite & LTD II	# 7162	T-1000 1982
		# 6326	Valiant 68-76
# 6913	Ford Pick-Ups 65-80 inc. 4wd	# 5796	Volkwagen 49-71
# 6849	Ford Vans 61-82	# 6837	Volkswagen 70-81
# 6935	GM Sub-compact 71-81 inc. Vega, Monza, Astre, Sunbird, Starfire & Skyhawk	# 6637	Volare 76-78
		# 6529	Volvo 56-69
# 6937	Granada 75-80	# 7040	Volvo 70-80
# 5905	GTO 68-73	# 6965	Zephyr 78-80

Chilton's Repair & Tune-Up Guides are available at your local retailer or by mailing a check or money order for **$9.95** plus **$1.00** to cover postage and handling to:

**Chilton Book Company
Dept. DM
Radnor, PA 19089**

NOTE: When ordering be sure to include your name & address, book code & title.